What's for Dinner?
MEAL-PLANNING COOKBOOK

by Grace White / Family Circle Food Editor

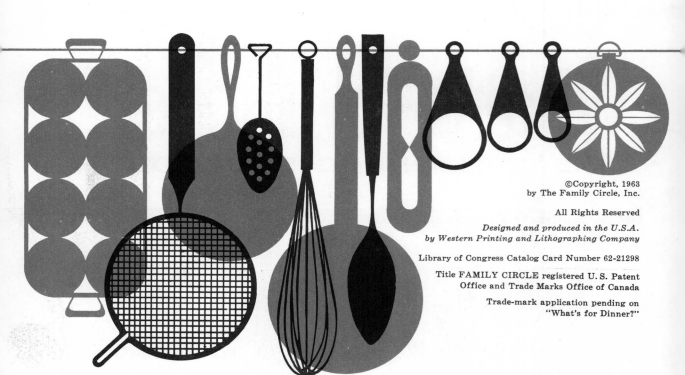

Contents

DEAR HOMEMAKER:

Proudly we present this cookbook—and a very special one, too—filled with practical helps to answer the day-by-day question "What shall I fix for dinner?" Since FAMILY CIRCLE first introduced its "What's for Dinner?" feature, many of you have thoughtfully written and told us what a mainstay of ideas it has become in your meal-planning. Now here is the best of our collection for your cooking inspiration.

Between the covers of this book you'll find family-meal ideas for all occasions. We've included favorite dinner roasts and how to turn them into new and different second-day treats; there are casserole meals, quick meals, no-meat meals, and salad meals. There's a big section on pocket-book-pampering meals, for don't we all constantly look for ways to make our food dollars buy more? Also there are fun meals for outdoor chefs, simple dinners for entertaining, ideas for party days and holidays—and even diet-happy dinners your whole family can enjoy.

Each of the menus—90 in all—stars recipes rated best by you and the staff of our Test Kitchens. And splashed throughout the book are color photographs that suggest ways to arrange and garnish your dinner choices.

We hope you'll keep this book in a handy nook in your kitchen and use it every day. May its ideas always help to make dinnertime easy for you and a happy time for the whole family!

Sincerely,

Grace White

Food Editor

HERE they are—the big six roasts: Beef, pork, chicken, ham, lamb, and veal. For company? Of course, choose a roast. For family? Even better, for most cuts are meaty enough to make some extra-special second-day treats. We call them planned-overs.

For Sunday, Monday, any day, beef heads the list. It's ready for the oven with little fuss, roasts just the way

America's favorite meal-makers

you like it best with little watching. Pork's plentiful all year round—and what succulent eating it makes! And chicken, baked plump and golden; ham asparkle with a tempting glaze; lamb or veal seasoned just right—each can turn any dinner into a feast.

Whatever your choice, be a smart shopper and buy a roast big enough for a second-meal treat. It will save you shopping time, cooking time, and many a penny. Ideas for favorite planned-over dishes follow in the next chapter.

◄ Budget-best chuck makes this handsome **Delmonico Beef Roast** *(recipe on page 12)* to carve in thick slices and serve with rich gravy. Recipe tells how to bake popping-high popovers in same oven

Best-loved family dinners

	MAIN DISH	VEGETABLE • SALAD	DESSERT	NICE TO ADD
PRIME RIB FAVORITE *(pictured on page 12)*	★Beef Rib Roast	Pan-browned Potatoes ★Savory Green Beans ★Three Greens Salad	★Party Pink Torte *(pictured on page 21)*	★Jellied Consomme Parfait ★Feather-puff Rolls
	For company or family get-togethers, you couldn't serve a more popular meat than this choice rib cut of tender lean beef with just enough bone to make good pickings or		to turn into soup. Meringue shell for the delectable dessert has a special cooking secret. It "bakes" while you sleep, gets its rosy strawberry crown just before serving	
BEEF MEAL-MAKER STAR *(pictured on cover and on page 8)*	★Delmonico Beef Roast ★Yorkshire Puffs ★Beef Pan Gravy	Buttered Limas Avocado-grapefruit Salad	Caramel-frosted Spice Layer Cake	Tomato-rice Soup (canned variety)
	Here's a perfect roast for any size family —thrifty, too. Just watch for specials on beef chuck roast and you'll see why. When tenderized (recipe tells how), it cooks so		juicy-tender, carves beautifully. Splurge and bake the tempting high-hat puffs to eat with your prize. And if yours is a gravy-loving family, recipe is here, also	
PORK DINNER, COUNTRY STYLE	★Glazed Pork Rib Roast ★Spicy Plums	Mashed Potatoes ★Baked Squash Rings with Carrot Sticks	★Cranberry-pear Pie	Coleslaw Corn Bread Coffee
	Moistly tender and savory sweet, yet spicy with a glistening plum glaze—that's this handsome pork roast. Do try its easy roast-ing way. While meat cooks, take advantage		of oven heat to make the buttery golden squash-and-carrot platemate, and warm bread at the last minute. Tangy cran-berries and mild pears make the pie topoff	
OVEN-EASY PORK ROAST *(pictured on page 14)*	★Harvest Stuffed Pork ★Rich Pork Gravy	Baked Sweet Potatoes ★Oven-glazed Onions Romaine Salad Bowl	★Lemon Snow	Piccalilli Relish
	Savory pork shoulder—a real bargain in scrumptious eating—headlines this hearty dinner. Buy a meaty fresh shoulder and ask your meat man to bone, but not tie it.		A sweet corn-and-herb stuffing goes into the bone pocket, then roast is ready to oven-braise to perfection. Buttery onions and rosy apple slices dress the platter	
DOUBLE-TREAT CHICKEN *(pictured on page 14)*	★Twin Roast Chickens ★Golden Peaches	★Rice Pilaf Corn and Green Beans Garden Lettuce	★Strawberry Angel Ribbon Loaf	Cream of Shrimp Soup Hot Biscuits
	Chicken ranks right at the top of the hit parade of roasts, for it can be served so many ways. Here twin roasters, stuffed with a savory dressing, are baked and		glazed with a golden peach sauce. Partners include toasty rice, double vegetable bowls, and lettuce salad. Dessert is angel cake layered with a luscious strawberry filling	
CHICKEN— EASY HEARTY FARE	★Pot-roasted Chicken with Cream Gravy	Parsley Noodles Buttered Broccoli Perfection Salad	★Sunny Cream Tart	★Golden Sesame Loaf Coffee
	Here's a way with chicken that copies a French chef's simple cooking trick. Start with a whole stewing chicken—no need to cut up—and simmer in seasoned beef broth.		Serve with creamy gravy and parsley-flecked noodles for a best-ever dinner. Dessert will please both fruit- and cream-pie fans; vary fruit to suit your fancy	

	MAIN DISH	VEGETABLE ● SALAD	DESSERT	NICE TO ADD

HAM TREASURE
(pictured on page 16)

*Glazed Ham
*Cherry-almond Sauce

*Peas in Noodle Nests
*Garden Salad

*Chocolate Velvet Bavarian
(pictured on page 23)

Endive Spears
*Daisy Biscuits

For tops in flavor and popularity, you can always count on ham—and what a vast array of sizes and kinds to choose from. Be smart: Bake a big one, for ham's a good keeper, a perfect mixer. Glaze, following your own favorite recipe, or choose one of those on page 17. Team with a vegetable duet and a rich creamy chocolate mold

---

HAM—PARTY PERFECT

*Roast Stuffed Fresh Ham

Scalloped Potatoes
*Olive Bouquet Salad

*Pear Praline Cobbler
*Mint Sparkle Sauce

Buttered Brussels Sprouts

If you're having company, feature this big fresh ham roast, fairly bursting with a spicy mincemeat stuffing and tangy sweet topping. Simple to fix and carve (for it has no bone), it's scrumptious eating, hot or cold. With it goes make-ahead scalloped potatoes and a picture-pretty green salad. Dessert: A crunchy cobbler to cut like pie

---

LAMB TEMPTER

*Savory Lamb Roast
*Golden Lamb Gravy

*Double-corn Bake
*Skillet Squash

Rhubarb Pie

*Sweet-sour Mushrooms
Currant Jelly

While lamb stars invitingly as a springtime roast, it's a treat all year round. If your family is large, or to have meat left for another meal, buy a whole leg. For a small family, a halved leg, either shank or butt end, is a good buy. Roast either this herb-onion-seasoned way. Its go-with: A golden corn pudding in place of potatoes

---

LAMB— FAR-EAST INSPIRED

*Curried Mock Duck

*Coconut Rice
Buttered Peas

*Buttermilk Sherbet
Vanilla Wafers

Chutney, peanuts diced bananas (curry condiments)

This partylike Oriental dish starts with thrifty lamb shoulder. Meat is boned, rolled, and tied—carving's a cinch—then simmered with curry seasonings. To serve with it, there's mint-flecked rice, and condiment choices. To fancy up the platter, garnish with pineapple cubes and kumquats threaded on skewers, kebab-style

---

LOW-COST VEAL SPECIAL

*Crisscross Veal Roast
*Brown Gravy

Mashed Potatoes
Italian Beans
Citrus Fruit Salad

*Turnover Caramel Custards

Crab-apple Jelly

Mention veal and almost everyone thinks of chops or cutlets, but here's another choice, equally tempting, yet lower in cost. It's boned rump of veal—all solid meat— to roast slowly, then slice and top with a rich brown gravy. Creamy custards serve prettily if baked ahead and chilled; when unmolded, caramel sauce covers each top

---

GERMAN- STYLE VEAL ROAST

*Veal Roll Paprikash with Poppy-seed Noodles

Buttered Asparagus
Hearts of Lettuce
French Dressing

*Apple Crumble

Butterflake Rolls
Carrot Sticks
Stuffed Olives

If you skip over veal when planning a pot roast, you're missing a real treat, and here's proof. This showy dish starts with veal shoulder simmered slowly until tender, then teamed with a nippy sour-cream gravy and served with buttery noodles. Time pudding to come from the oven just before serving so it'll be fragrantly warm

11

Beef Rib Roast rates as the choicest of all beef cuts —and how easy it is to fix and cook. Serve with crusty brown potatoes (cook them alongside meat), zesty French-cut green beans, and a crisp salad

MAIN DISHES

■ BEEF RIB ROAST

Count on about ¾ pound of beef, including bone, for each serving; so for a dinner for eight, buy an oven-ready, heavy 2- or regular 3-rib cut weighing 6 to 8 pounds. Rub roast all over with a mixture of 2 tablespoons flour, 1 teaspoon dry mustard, 1 teaspoon salt, and ½ teaspoon pepper. Place roast, fat side up, in roasting pan. (Ribs form their own rack.) If using a meat thermometer, insert bulb so it reaches meaty center without touching bone. Do not add water or cover pan. Roast in slow oven (325°), allowing 18 to 23 minutes per pound for rare, 23 to 28 minutes per pound for medium. Thermometer should register 140° for rare, 160° for medium. For easier carving, let roast stand 10 to 15 minutes before taking to table.

■ DELMONICO BEEF ROAST

Buy a chuck roast about 3 inches thick and weighing about 5 pounds. Because ways of cutting beef vary in different parts of the country, you may find this special in your supermarket labeled round-bone-arm chuck, blade, or California roast—to name just a few. Moisten roast with water, then sprinkle with instant seasoned meat tenderizer, following label directions. Rub well with flour, then place on rack in roasting pan. If using meat thermometer, insert bulb through side into meaty center. Roast in slow oven (325°), allowing about 25 minutes per pound if you like beef pink to medium with lots of juice. Thermometer should register 150°.

If your range has only one oven, bake YORKSHIRE PUFFS (recipe follows) along with the roast this easy way. Thirty minutes before meat is done, remove it from oven; reset oven regulator to hot (400°). Spoon enough hot drippings from pan to grease cups generously.

(Drippings help to flavor puffs, too.) Have batter ready and divide among cups; place in a shallow pan for easy handling and slide into oven. Return beef to oven; bake 30 minutes. Take out beef; let puffs bake 20 minutes longer. During the last 20 minutes you will have time to make gravy, if you wish, and complete rest of meal. Roast will carve better when allowed to stand for this time. Transfer roast to carving board; slice with a sharp knife across grain. Makes enough for 2 meals, 4 servings each.

BEEF PAN GRAVY—Tip roasting pan and let fat rise in one corner; skim off all but 2 tablespoons. Blend in 2 tablespoons flour; stir in 1½ cups water. Cook, stirring and scraping baked-on juices from bottom and sides of pan, until gravy thickens slightly and boils 1 minute. Season to taste with salt and pepper; stir in a little gravy coloring, if you wish. Make 1½ cups.

YORKSHIRE PUFFS

3 eggs
1 cup milk
1 cup sifted flour
½ teaspoon salt

1. Beat eggs slightly with rotary beater in bowl or 4-cup measure; add milk, flour, and salt. Beat briskly ½ minute; scrape side of bowl; beat 1½ minutes longer. Batter will be smooth and thin.
2. Grease 8 small custard cups with beef drippings from roast, or butter cups well. (Deep straight-side cups let puffs pop higher.) Divide batter evenly among them, filling about ⅓ full. Place, evenly spaced, in pan and set on oven shelf in back of roast or on shelf above.
3. Bake in hot oven (400°) 30 minutes. (Popovers will have puffed enough to hold their shape when you open oven door.) Take out roast. Bake puffs 20 minutes longer, or until richly golden. (If baking puffs separately, there's no need to peek at them while they're baking.) Makes 8 popover puffs.

Note: To keep puffs crisp and hot if they must wait a few minutes before serving, take from cups, make a small slit in the side of each to let steam escape. Place in pan and put back into hot oven with heat turned off and door open.

■ GLAZED PORK RIB ROAST

5 pounds loin, center, or rib cut of pork
1 teaspoon salt
½ teaspoon cinnamon
¼ teaspoon ground allspice
¾ cup sauce from Spicy Plums *(recipe follows)*

1. Rub pork with mixture of salt, cinnamon, and allspice. Place, fat side up, on rack in roasting pan. If using a meat thermometer, insert bulb into meaty center without touching bone. Do not add water or cover pan.
2. Roast in slow oven (325°), allowing 35 to 45 minutes per pound.
3. When pork is about half done, brush with thickened sauce from SPICY PLUMS. Continue roasting, basting with sauce every 30 minutes, until pork is completely done. Thermometer should register 185°. (This is one meat that should be cooked well-done.) Makes 6 servings.

SPICY PLUMS

1 can (1 pound, 14 ounces) purple plums
2 tablespoons cornstarch
½ teaspoon salt
¼ teaspoon ground cinnamon
⅛ teaspoon ground allspice
2 tablespoons lemon juice
1 tablespoon butter or margarine

1. Drain syrup from plums into medium-size saucepan. Put plums in a small bowl for Step 3.
2. Combine cornstarch, salt, and spices in cup; blend in 2 tablespoons syrup, then stir back into saucepan. Cook, stirring constantly, until sauce thickens and boils 3 minutes; stir in lemon juice and butter or margarine until well-blended.
3. Measure out about ¾ cup sauce for glazing pork; pour remaining over plums in bowl to serve with roast. Makes 6 servings.

◄ Succulent pork shoulder is boned, filled with golden corn stuffing, then oven-braised to make this **Harvest Stuffed Pork.** Rosy spiced apple rings and big onions glazed in a buttery sauce make tempting go-withs

■ HARVEST STUFFED PORK

5 to 6 pounds fresh pork shoulder, boned
2 eggs
4 cups coarse bread crumbs (8 slices)
1 can (12 or 16 ounces) whole-kernel corn, drained
1 small onion, chopped (¼ cup)
2 teaspoons salt
½ teaspoon pepper
½ teaspoon ground sage
½ cup water
1 jar (15 ounces) spiced apple rings

1. Buy a whole pork shoulder and ask your meatman to bone it for you. (Use bones for making soup stock.) At home, trim skin and any extra fat from roast.
2. Beat eggs in medium-size bowl; stir in bread crumbs, corn, onion, salt, pepper, and sage.
3. Stuff pocket in meat with mixture, packing in well to fill and give meat a rounded shape. Tie with string at 1-inch intervals.
4. Brown meat, fat side first, in heavy kettle or Dutch oven; remove from heat. If using a meat thermometer, insert in roast so bulb reaches meaty center. Pour water over; cover tightly.
5. Bake in slow oven (325°) 3½ hours, or just until meat is tender. Remove pork from kettle; strain liquid into a 4-cup measure to save for making RICH PORK GRAVY *(recipe follows)*. Return meat to kettle; bake, uncovered, 30 minutes longer, or until richly browned. Thermometer should register 185°.
6. Remove pork to heated platter; pour off any additional fat; keep pork hot while making gravy.
7. Garnish pork platter with spiced apple rings; slice pork and serve with gravy to spoon over. Makes enough for 2 meals, 6 servings each.

RICH PORK GRAVY—Skim off fat from strained liquid; add water, if needed, to make 4 cups. Return 4 tablespoons fat to kettle; blend in 4 tablespoons flour; cook, stirring all the time, just until mixture bubbles. Stir in strained liquid slowly; continue cooking and stirring, scraping baked-on juices from bottom and sides of kettle, until gravy thickens and boils 1 minute. Season with salt and pepper, if needed. Makes 4 cups.

◄ Don't these plump **Twin Roast Chickens** look fancy with their plattermates of golden peaches and toasty rice! Two vegetables, lettuce salad, and a creamy soup starter complete the main part of the meal

■ TWIN ROAST CHICKENS

2 small roasting chickens
    (about 3½ pounds each)
1 teaspoon salt
    Saucepan Stuffing *(recipe follows)*
2 tablespoons melted butter or margarine
    Golden Glaze and Golden Peaches
    (recipe follows)

1. Wash and dry chickens; sprinkle inside with salt; stuff neck and body cavities lightly with SAUCEPAN STUFFING; skewer neck skin to body and tie legs to tail. Place chickens on rack in shallow roasting pan; brush with melted butter or margarine.
2. Roast in moderate oven (375°) 1½ to 2 hours. (Figure roasting time at 30 minutes per pound for one bird. Chicken is done when drumstick moves easily at joint.)
3. About 20 minutes before chickens are done, brush with GOLDEN GLAZE. Continue roasting and brushing with glaze until chickens are done.
4. Serve on a heated platter with RICE PILAF *(recipe on page 19)*; garnish platter with GOLDEN PEACHES. Makes 6 servings.

SAUCEPAN STUFFING—Saute ½ cup chopped celery leaves and 2 tablespoons chopped onion lightly in ¼ cup (½ stick) butter or margarine in medium-size saucepan. Pour in ½ cup water; heat to boiling; remove from heat. Stir in 1¾ cups ready-mix bread stuffing (from an 8-ounce package); toss with fork just until moistened. Makes 2 cups.

GOLDEN GLAZE AND GOLDEN PEACHES—Drain syrup from 1 can (about 1 pound) cling-peach halves into small bowl. Arrange peaches, cut side up, in shallow baking dish. Blend 2 tablespoons bottled steak sauce into syrup for GOLDEN GLAZE. Brush peach halves with part of syrup; use remaining for twin chickens. Bake peaches in moderate oven (375°) along with chickens during last 20 minutes' roasting time. Makes 6 servings.

■ POT-ROASTED CHICKEN WITH CREAM GRAVY

4 tablespoons (½ stick) butter or margarine
1 stewing chicken (4 to 5 pounds)
2 teaspoons leaf thyme
1 can condensed beef broth
3 tablespoons flour
1 small can evaporated milk (⅔ cup)

1. Melt butter or margarine in heavy kettle or Dutch oven; brush part on inside of chicken, then sprinkle with 1 teaspoon thyme. Brown chicken lightly on all sides in remaining butter or margarine.
2. Turn chicken, breast side up; pour beef broth over; sprinkle with remaining 1 teaspoon thyme; cover tightly.
3. Simmer, basting a few times with pan juices, 1½ hours, or until tender. Remove to heated serving platter; keep hot while making gravy.
4. Pour broth from kettle into 4-cup measure. Let fat rise to top, then skim off. Add water to broth, if needed, to make 2½ cups.
5. Return 2 tablespoons fat to kettle; blend in flour; stir in broth. Cook, stirring constantly, until gravy thickens and boils 1 minute. Blend in evaporated milk; heat just to boiling.
6. Serve chicken with buttered noodles sprinkled with chopped parsley, if you like; spoon gravy over all. Makes 4 to 6 servings.

■ GLAZED HAM

Choose a whole or half ham, picnic, or canned ham, for all bake and glaze beautifully. Because supermarkets carry several varieties and sizes, see our GUIDE TO HAM BUYING on the next page for the kind and weight to suit your family need. Baking directions usually are printed on ham wrappers or cans, or follow these simple steps: Place ham, fat side up, on a rack in shallow baking pan. If fat layer has a thick skin over it, do not remove until ham is baked and ready for glazing. If fat layer is exposed, leave plain or score into 1-inch squares or diamonds. Roasting with a meat thermometer is a good cooking practice. If you use one, insert bulb into the thickest part of the meat without touching bone. Do not add water or cover pan. Bake, following this timetable:

HAM BAKING TIMETABLE

Oven temperature: 325°

Kind and weight	Total hours	Thermometer
Cook-before-eating Ham		
6 to 8 pounds	3¼	160°
8 to 10	3¼ to 3½	160°
10 to 15	3½ to 4½	160°
Picnic		
4 to 6	2½ to 3	170°
6 to 8	3 to 4	170°
Fully Cooked Ham		
6 to 8	2¼	130°
8 to 10	2¼ to 2½	130°
10 to 15	2½ to 3½	130°
Picnic		
3 to 5	1½ to 2	130°
5 to 7	2 to 2½	130°
Boned Rolled Ham		
8 to 10	2½ to 3	130°
10 to 12	3 to 3½	130°

Start glazing ham one hour before it is ready to be taken from the oven. Several recipes for sim-

Thick slices of **Glazed Ham** topped with almond-cherry sauce headline this pretty-as-spring dinner.

Crinkly golden noodle nests filled with peas and spears of buttery endive are vegetable go-withs

ple glazes are given below. For our pictured ham on opposite page, we chose OLD-TIME BROWN SUGAR. Remember to remove the thick skin over fat layer, if needed. It will almost peel off as you pull and snip it away. Score fat, if you wish, then spread or pat on glaze. Continue baking, basting ham every 10 minutes with more glaze or syrupy drippings in pan, 1 hour longer, or until top is richly golden. Remove from oven and let stand for 20 to 30 minutes for easier carving. Slice and serve with CHERRY–ALMOND SAUCE.

■ CHERRY–ALMOND SAUCE

1½ cups water
½ cup cider vinegar
1 cup firmly packed brown sugar
2 teaspoons mixed pickling spices
⅛ teaspoon anise seeds
1 jar (1 pound) maraschino cherries
2 tablespoons cornstarch
2 tablespoons butter or margarine
1 can (about 5 ounces) whole blanched almonds

1. Combine water, vinegar, brown sugar, pickling spices, and anise seeds in medium-size saucepan. Heat to boiling, then boil rapidly 10 minutes, or until syrup measures about 1 cup. Set aside for next step.
2. Drain syrup from cherries into 1-cup measure; add water, if needed, to make 1 cup. Blend 1 to 2 tablespoons into cornstarch until smooth in medium-size saucepan; stir in remaining syrup, then pour in brown-sugar syrup through strainer to remove spices.
3. Cook, stirring constantly, until sauce thickens and boils 3 minutes. Stir in butter or margarine.
4. Stuff an almond into each cherry; stir into hot sauce; heat just to boiling. Makes about 2 cups.

Simple-to-fix ham glazes

Makes enough for a whole ham.
Halve amounts for a half ham.

OLD-TIME BROWN SUGAR—Combine 1 cup firmly packed brown sugar, 1 teaspoon dry mustard, ¼ teaspoon ground cloves, and 2 tablespoons vinegar in a bowl. Stud scored ham with whole cloves before spreading with glaze.

ORANGE-HONEY—Mix 1 can (6 ounces) thawed frozen concentrated orange juice with ¾ cup honey and 1 teaspoon Worcestershire sauce.
PINEAPPLE-CURRY—Mix 1 cup pineapple preserves, ¼ cup dill-pickle juice (from jar of pickles), and 1 teaspoon curry powder.
CURRANT JELLY—Soften 1 cup currant jelly with 2 tablespoons hot water; stir in 2 tablespoons prepared mustard and ¼ teaspoon ground cloves.

Guide to ham buying

Most familiar and popular are the bouncing big hams sold either whole or cut in half. When halved, the rounded chunky part is called "butt", and the meaty leg-bone piece, "shank". Each will be labeled COOK BEFORE EATING or FULLY COOKED. (These terms are explained below.) The thrifty-priced smoked pork shoulder cut called "picnic" also carries a choice of either label. In addition, you will find boneless ham rolls, weighing as much as 12 pounds, but cut and sold in almost any weight you wish. And there is a big selection of canned ham, also boneless, weighing from 2 to 12 pounds. Here is a guide to help you with your shopping:

• **Cook-before-eating ham**—This is the regular smoked variety that must be baked until fully done. You can buy this ham whole, both bone-in and boneless, weighing as little as 6 pounds or as much as 15 to 20 pounds.

• **Fully-cooked ham**—This looks like the cook-before-eating variety, but it can be eaten with no further cooking. However, baking it for a short time per pound (see our TIMETABLE) brings out all of its luscious full sweet flavor and juiciness. Like the cook-before-eating ham, it comes bone-in or boneless, and whole or cut. You'll find very little shrinkage with this ham (processing has taken care of that), so even if the price per pound is higher than for other types, it may still be your best buy.

• **Picnic**—This choice is a cut with a budget price tag and is clearly labeled cook-before-eating or fully-cooked PICNIC at the meat counter. It is cut from the forequarters of the animal, then cured and smoked the same as regular ham. When either baked or simmered, it tastes just like ham.

• **Boned rolled ham**—This is fully cooked ham with the bone removed, fat trimmed, and the sweet solid meat rolled and wrapped in a transparent covering. It weighs 8 to 12 pounds, but can be bought cut up. Bake following HAM BAKING TIMETABLE.

• **Canned ham**—This is the perfect choice for a special dinner or for easy party refreshments, for each ham is boneless, skinless, fully cooked, and slices beautifully—hot or cold. Directions for heating are on the can. Then, if you wish, you can glaze the top. Be sure to read the storing directions. If the can is marked PERISHABLE, it *must* be kept in the refrigerator until opened.

How much ham should you buy?

Count on a minimum of ¼ pound for each serving of boneless ham, and ½ pound for the bone-in type. This is usually a good rule of thumb. But when ham is on special, you'll want to buy a big enough cut for a dividend dish or two.

17

■ ROAST STUFFED FRESH HAM

1 small onion, chopped (¼ cup)
1 tablespoon butter or margarine
1 cup prepared mincemeat
1 apple, cored and diced
¼ teaspoon ground cloves
6- to 8-pound fresh ham, boned
1 cup apple jelly

1. Saute onion in butter or margarine until golden in small saucepan; stir in mincemeat, apple, and cloves. Stuff into pocket of boned ham; skewer or tie meat with string.
2. Place, fat side up, on rack in roasting pan. If using meat thermometer, insert so bulb reaches meaty center.
3. Roast in slow oven (325°), allowing 40 to 45 minutes per pound. Thermometer should register 185°.
4. One hour before ham is done, take from oven; if small band of shank skin is still on, cut off with knife; score fat into diamonds.
5. Brush top with some of the apple jelly. Continue to bake, brushing often with jelly, 1 hour longer, or until ham is tender and top is richly glazed. Makes 8 to 12 servings.

■ SAVORY LAMB ROAST

Buy a whole leg, weighing 6 to 7 pounds for 6 servings and some left for a second meal. Rub well with flour; sprinkle with seasoned salt and pepper. Place roast on rack, fat side up, in roasting pan. Scatter 1 onion, sliced, and ¼ teaspoon rosemary in bottom of pan. If using a meat thermometer, insert into meaty center without touching bone. Roast, uncovered, in slow oven (325°), allowing 30 minutes per pound or 180° for well-done. Remove to heated platter; keep hot while making GOLDEN LAMB GRAVY.
GOLDEN LAMB GRAVY—Remove rack; tip pan and let fat rise in one corner; skim off all fat. Return 4 tablespoons fat to pan; blend in 4 tablespoons flour; cook, stirring all the time, just until mixture bubbles. Stir in 2 cups water; continue cooking and stirring, scraping baked-on juices from bottom and sides of pan, until gravy thickens and boils 1 minute. Season, if needed. Makes 2 cups.

■ CURRIED MOCK DUCK

4 pounds lamb shoulder, boned and rolled
2 teaspoons curry powder
1 tablespoon salad oil
1 large onion, chopped (1 cup)
1 cup chopped celery
1 clove of garlic, sliced
1 apple, pared, cored, and diced
¼ cup catsup
1½ teaspoons salt

1. Rub lamb well with curry powder; brown in

salad oil in large heavy kettle or Dutch oven; remove and set aside for Step 3.
2. Saute onion, celery, and garlic in same kettle; stir in apple, ½ cup water, catsup, and salt.
3. Return browned meat to kettle; cover; simmer 2½ hours, or until meat is tender. Remove to heated serving platter; keep hot.
4. Skim all fat from liquid in kettle. Strain liquid into a bowl, pressing vegetables through; return to kettle and heat to boiling.
5. Slice meat; serve with heated sauce and curry condiments. Makes 6 servings.

■ CRISSCROSS VEAL ROAST

3 to 4 pounds rump of veal, boned
1 large onion, sliced
½ teaspoon salt
½ teaspoon paprika
⅛ teaspoon pepper
½ pound fat salt pork, cut into ½-inch-wide strips
Brown Gravy (recipe follows)

1. Fill pocket with onion slices; fold meat over; hold in shape with skewers or string. Rub all over with mixture of salt, paprika, and pepper.
2. Crisscross salt-pork strips over top, fastening with wooden picks to hold in place. Place meat on rack in small roasting pan. If using meat thermometer, insert so bulb reaches meaty center.
3. Roast in slow oven (325°), allowing 30 minutes per pound, or about 2 hours for a 4-pound cut. Thermometer should register 180°. Cut away strings on roast. Remove roast to heated serving platter; keep hot while making gravy. Makes 6 servings.
BROWN GRAVY — Strain drippings from pan into 1-cup measure; add enough water to make 1 cup. Stir 1 tablespoon flour into pan, then add drippings mixture. Cook over low heat, stirring constantly, until gravy thickens and boils 1 minute. Stir in ½ teaspoon grated lemon rind; season to taste with salt and pepper. Makes 1 cup.

■ VEAL ROLL PAPRIKASH

2 strips bacon
1 large onion, chopped (1 cup)
3 to 4 pounds boned and rolled veal shoulder
1 tablespoon paprika
1 teaspoon salt
½ cup water
1 green pepper, cut into rings
1 tablespoon flour
1 cup dairy sour cream
Buttered hot noodles
1 teaspoon poppy seeds

1. Fry bacon until crisp in heavy kettle or Dutch oven; remove and set aside for Step 4. Saute onion lightly in same kettle.
2. Rub veal well with mixture of paprika and

salt; brown lightly in kettle with onion. Add water; cover.

3. Simmer 2½ hours, or until meat is tender. Arrange pepper rings on top; cook 10 minutes longer. Remove meat, without disturbing rings, to heated serving platter; keep hot while making gravy.
4. Let fat rise to top of juices in kettle; skim well. Blend flour with 1 tablespoon cold water in a cup; stir into liquid in kettle. Cook, stirring constantly, until gravy thickens and boils 1 minute; remove from heat. Crumble in bacon, then slowly stir in sour cream. (Sour cream may curdle on standing, so add it just before serving time.)
5. Slice meat and serve with buttered hot noodles sprinkled with poppy seeds. Makes 6 to 8 servings.

VEGETABLES

■ SAVORY GREEN BEANS

3 packages frozen French-style green beans
6 tablespoons bottled thin French dressing
2 pimientos, chopped
½ teaspoon salt
   Dash of pepper

Cook beans, following label directions; drain. Add French dressing, pimientos, salt, and pepper; toss lightly to mix well. Serve hot. Makes 8 servings.

■ BAKED SQUASH RINGS WITH CARROT STICKS

3 small acorn squashes
4 medium-size carrots, scraped
½ cup (1 stick) butter or margarine, melted
2 tablespoons water
¼ teaspoon mixed Italian herbs

1. Cut squashes into ½-inch-thick rings; scoop out seeds but do not pare.
2. Place squash rings in single layer in large shallow baking pan; lay 4 or 5 carrot sticks on top of each.
3. Combine remaining ingredients in cup; drizzle over vegetables; cover pan tightly.
4. Bake in slow oven (325°) 1 hour, or until tender. Makes 6 servings.

■ OVEN-GLAZED ONIONS

6 large onions, peeled
4 tablespoons brown sugar
2 tablespoons water
½ teaspoon salt
4 tablespoons (½ stick) butter or margarine, melted

1. Parboil onions in boiling salted water in large saucepan 15 to 20 minutes, or until almost tender but still firm enough to hold their shape; drain.
2. Combine brown sugar, water, salt, and melted butter or margarine in 6-cup shallow baking dish. Roll each onion in mixture and arrange in single layer in same dish; cover.
3. Bake in slow oven (325°), turning 2 or 3 times, 30 minutes, or until tender and golden. Makes 6 servings.

■ RICE PILAF

1 cup uncooked rice
2 tablespoons salad oil or olive oil
¾ cup chopped green onions
½ cup chopped green pepper
¼ cup chopped parsley
1 can (about 14 ounces) chicken broth
1 teaspoon salt
¼ teaspoon pepper

1. Saute rice in salad oil or olive oil in large frying pan, stirring often, just until golden.
2. Stir in green onions, green pepper, parsley, chicken broth, salt, and pepper; pour into 6-cup baking dish; cover.
3. Bake in moderate oven (375°) 30 to 40 minutes, or until rice is tender and liquid is absorbed; toss lightly with a fork before serving. Makes 6 servings.

■ PEAS IN NOODLE NESTS

3 cups (half an 8-ounce package) regular noodles
Shortening for deep frying
2 packages (10 ounces each) frozen peas
½ cup light or table cream
4 tablespoons (½ stick) butter or margarine

1. Cook noodles in boiling salted water in large saucepan *just 5 minutes*. (They should be not quite tender.) Drain; rinse under running cold water; drain again, then spread out in a large flat pan.
2. Melt shortening to a depth of 2 inches in deep heavy saucepan; heat to 375°. (Or use an electric fryer, following manufacturer's directions.)
3. Divide noodles into 8 equal-size portions. Drop, one portion at a time, from slotted spoon into hot fat. (It will bubble up immediately.) As noodles come to the top (you can see them through bubbling fat), gather toward one side of pan with spoon and shape into a round. (If any bits tend to stick to spoon, push off with a fork.) Hold with spoon for a few seconds, or just until firm enough to keep its shape. When golden-brown underneath, turn; fry just long enough to brown other side. (Each noodle nest takes less than 2 minutes to cook.) Let fat reheat to 375° between each frying.
4. Drain on paper toweling; keep warm in heated oven while cooking remaining noodle nests and peas. (Or make nests several hours ahead and reheat in slow oven [325°] for about 10 minutes before serving.)
5. Cook peas, following label directions; drain. Pour cream over; season with butter or margarine; heat just until cream is bubbly.
6. Place a noodle ring on each serving plate; spoon creamy peas over. Makes 8 servings.

■ DOUBLE-CORN BAKE

4 cups milk
3 tablespoons butter or margarine
1½ teaspoons salt
1 cup white corn meal
4 eggs, separated
1 teaspoon baking powder
1 can (8 ounces) cream-style corn
Paprika

1. Scald 3 cups milk with butter or margarine and salt in top of large double boiler directly over low heat. Combine corn meal with remaining 1 cup milk; gradually stir into scalded milk. Cook, stirring constantly, just until thickened; place over boiling water; cover; cook 5 minutes longer.
2. Beat egg whites until they stand in firm peaks in large bowl. Beat egg yolks with baking powder in medium-size bowl; blend a little hot corn-meal mixture into yolks; stir in remaining hot corn meal, then corn. Fold into beaten egg whites.
3. Pour into buttered 8-cup baking dish; sprinkle with paprika.
4. Bake in slow oven (325°) 1 hour, or until puffy-golden and set in center. Serve at once. Makes 6 servings.

■ SKILLET SQUASH

6 small yellow squashes
3 tablespoons butter or margarine
Salt and pepper
2 tablespoons chopped parsley

1. Wash, trim ends, and halve squashes lengthwise, then crosswise to make 2-inch sticks.
2. Saute slowly in butter or margarine in medium-size saucepan, turning often, 10 minutes, or until tender.
3. Season with salt and pepper; sprinkle with parsley. Makes 6 servings.

■ COCONUT RICE

1 cup uncooked rice
3 tablespoons melted butter or margarine
2 tablespoons chopped fresh mint
OR: 2 teaspoons dried mint flakes
3 tablespoons flaked coconut

Cook rice, following label directions. Toss with butter or margarine and mint. Spoon into heated serving bowl; sprinkle with coconut. Makes 6 servings.

SALADS

■ THREE GREENS SALAD

8 cups broken mixed salad greens
(escarole, Chinese cabbage, water cress)
1 can (2 ounces) rolled anchovy fillets
Basil Dressing (recipe follows)
1 cup croutons

1. Fill a large salad bowl with mixed greens. Drain anchovies, saving oil for dressing; sprinkle fillets over greens. (This much can be done ahead if bowl is covered with foil or transparent wrap and kept chilled.)
2. Just before serving, sprinkle with BASIL DRESSING and croutons; toss lightly to coat greens well. Makes 8 servings.

BASIL DRESSING—Combine ¼ cup olive oil or salad oil, 2 tablespoons wine vinegar or cider vinegar, 1 teaspoon anchovy oil (from canned anchovies), ½ teaspoon basil, ½ teaspoon sugar, ¼ teaspoon salt, and ⅛ teaspoon pepper in small jar with tight-fitting cover; shake well to mix. Makes about ⅓ cup.

GARDEN SALAD

2 heads leaf or Boston lettuce
1 large ripe avocado, peeled, halved, and pitted
2 tablespoons lemon juice
2 teaspoons grated onion
1 teaspoon salt
¼ cup mayonnaise or salad dressing

1. Remove cores from lettuce; separate leaves. Wash well, then dry thoroughly. Tear into bite-size pieces in salad bowl.
2. Mash avocado in medium-size bowl. (There should be about 1⅓ cups.) Blend in remaining ingredients; cover tightly and chill. (Prepare dressing only an hour ahead, so it will keep its bright green color.)
3. Just before serving, spoon over lettuce in salad bowl; toss lightly to mix. Makes 8 servings.

OLIVE BOUQUET SALAD

1 head Boston lettuce
1 jar (10 ounces) large stuffed olives, drained
1 can (9 ounces) large ripe olives, drained
Oil-and-vinegar Dressing (recipe follows)

1. Remove core from lettuce; run cold water through head to loosen leaves; drain well.
2. Place on serving plate and gently pull leaves apart so head resembles a rose; tuck stuffed and ripe olives between leaves. Drizzle with OIL-AND-VINEGAR DRESSING; serve with additional dressing. Makes 8 servings.

OIL-AND-VINEGAR DRESSING—Combine ¾ cup salad oil, ¼ cup cider vinegar, ½ teaspoon salt, and ⅛ teaspoon pepper in small jar with tight-fitting cover; shake well to mix; chill. Shake again just before serving. Makes 1 cup.

DESSERTS

PARTY PINK TORTE

6 egg whites
½ teaspoon cream of tartar
¼ teapoon salt
1½ cups sugar
1 teaspoon vanilla
¼ cup slivered blanched almonds
2 cups (1 pint) strawberries, washed
OR: 1 package (10 ounces) frozen sliced strawberries, thawed
1 cup cream for whipping
Red food coloring

1. Turn on oven to hot (400°).
2. Beat egg whites, cream of tartar, and salt until foamy-white and double in volume in large bowl.
3. Beat in sugar, 1 tablespoon at a time, beating well after each, until meringue stands in firm peaks. (Sugar should be completely dissolved before adding more. Beating should take about 30 minutes.) Fold in vanilla.
4. Spoon meringue into buttered 8-inch spring-form pan. (Its straight sides open with a clamp and metal bottom comes out.) Make a slight hollow in center with a spoon; sprinkle slivered almonds over.
5. Place in hot oven (400°); close oven door and turn heat off immediately. Leave torte to slow-bake, *without peeking even once,* overnight, or at least 12 hours.
6. Remove torte from oven; leave in pan until ready to fill and decorate. To remove, loosen around edge with knife; release spring and carefully lift off side of pan. Carefully slide torte off pan onto serving plate.
7. About 1 hour before serving, hull and slice enough strawberries to make 1 cup; spoon over meringue. (If using frozen berries, drain well, saving a few for garnishing edge of plate.)
8. Beat cream until stiff in small bowl; blend in a few drops red food coloring to tint a delicate pink. Spoon over strawberries; chill. Garnish torte with remaining whole or sliced berries; slice in wedges with a sharp knife. Makes 1 eight-inch torte.

Note: To blanch and sliver almonds, buy shelled almonds in a 6-ounce bag or 5-ounce can. Place in small bowl; pour boiling water over. Let stand 5 minutes, or until skins wrinkle; drain; slip off skins. Split nuts; place, flat side down, on cutting board; cut lengthwise into slivers to make amount needed.

Try this very special **Party Pink Torte** for it's "baking" magic. Shell is an easy-make soft meringue to crown with lots of juicy strawberries, almond slivers, and billowy whipped cream tinted ever so delicately

CRANBERRY-PEAR PIE

    1 stick piecrust mix
    2 cups fresh cranberries
    ½ small orange, halved and seeded
    4 small ripe pears, halved, pared, and cored
    1 teaspoon grated lemon rind
    1¼ cups sugar
    ¼ teaspoon cinnamon
    2 tablespoons flour
    ⅛ teaspoon salt
    1 tablespoon melted butter or margarine

1. Prepare piecrust mix, following label directions, or make pastry from your own favorite one-crust recipe. Roll out to a 12-inch round on lightly floured pastry cloth or board; fit into a 9-inch pie plate. Trim overhang to ½ inch; turn under flush with rim; flute.
2. Put cranberries, orange, and 1 pear through food chopper, using coarse knife. (Save remaining 3 pears for Step 4.) Combine fruits with grated lemon rind in medium-size bowl.
3. Combine sugar and cinnamon in small bowl; save 2 tablespoons for topping; mix flour and salt into remaining, then stir into fruits. Spoon into prepared shell.
4. Arrange pear halves, rounded side up, spoke-fashion on top; brush with melted butter or margarine; sprinkle with saved 2 tablespoons sugar-cinnamon mix.
5. Bake in hot oven (400°) 50 minutes, or just until pears are soft but still firm enough to hold their shape. Cool completely on wire rack. Makes 1 nine-inch pie.

LEMON SNOW

    ¾ cup sugar
    1 envelope unflavored gelatin
    ¼ teaspoon salt
    1¼ cups boiling water
    1 teaspoon grated lemon rind
    ¼ cup lemon juice
    2 eggs, separated
    Custard Sauce (recipe follows)

1. Combine sugar, gelatin, and salt in large bowl. Add boiling water, stirring until gelatin is dissolved; stir in lemon rind and juice.
2. Place bowl in a pan of ice and water; chill, stirring often, 5 minutes, or until mixture is as thick as unbeaten egg white.
3. Stir in unbeaten egg whites, saving yolks for sauce. Beat vigorously with an electric or rotary beater until mixture triples in volume and begins to hold its shape. (Beating will take about 10 minutes.)
4. Pour into a 6-cup mold; chill 3 to 4 hours, or until firm.
5. To unmold, run a sharp-tip, thin-blade knife around top of mold, then dip *very quickly* in and out of a pan of hot water. Cover mold with serving plate; turn upside down, then gently lift off mold. Serve with CUSTARD SAUCE. Makes 6 to 8 servings.

CUSTARD SAUCE—Beat 2 egg yolks and 2 whole eggs slightly in top of double boiler; beat in ¼ cup sugar and 2 cups milk. Cook over simmering water, stirring constantly, 15 minutes, or until custard thickens slightly and coats a metal spoon. Remove from heat; strain into a small bowl; stir in 1 teaspoon vanilla. Chill. Just before serving, beat until fluffy light. Makes 3 cups.

STRAWBERRY ANGEL RIBBON LOAF

Cake

    1 package white angel-cake mix
    1 teaspoon vanilla
    ¼ teaspoon almond extract

Filling

    1 package (8 ounces) cream cheese
    ¼ cup 10X (confectioners' powdered) sugar
    ¼ cup milk
    2 teaspoons lemon juice
    6 drops red food coloring
    2 cups strawberries, washed, hulled, and sliced

Frosting

    1 cup cream for whipping
    2 tablespoons 10X (confectioners' powdered) sugar
    1 teaspoon vanilla
    3 drops red food coloring

1. Make cake: Prepare angel-cake mix, following label directions; blend in vanilla and almond extract. Spoon batter into 2 ungreased loaf pans, 9x5x3.
2. Bake in slow oven (325°) 45 minutes, or until tops spring back when lightly pressed with fingertips. Turn pans upside down and set on cans or glasses to cool completely.
3. Bake filling: Blend cream cheese with 10X sugar in small bowl; gradually blend in milk, lemon juice, and just enough food coloring to tint mixture a delicate pink.
4. Slice one angel-cake loaf lengthwise to make 4 layers. (Save second cake for another meal.) Place 1 layer on small cooky sheet or tray; spread with part of cheese mixture, then cover with part of strawberries. Repeat with remaining layers, filling, and strawberries to re-form loaf. Chill until 1 hour before serving.
5. Make frosting: Beat cream until stiff in medium-size bowl; fold in 10X sugar, vanilla, and just enough food coloring to tint cream a delicate pink. Frost sides and top of loaf; chill until serving time. Cut crosswise into about 1-inch slices. Makes 6 to 8 servings.

■ SUNNY CREAM TART

1 nine-inch Graham-cracker Crust
   (*recipe follows*)
1 package vanilla-flavor instant pudding mix
   Milk
1 cup dairy sour cream
2 tablespoons sugar
1½ teaspoons cornstarch
1 can (1 pound) apricot halves
1 tablespoon lemon juice
2 bananas, sliced

1. Make and chill GRAHAM-CRACKER CRUST.
2. Prepare pudding mix, following label directions and substituting 1 cup dairy sour cream for 1 cup of the milk called for on package. Pour into prepared crust; let stand 15 minutes to set.
3. Mix sugar and cornstarch in small saucepan. Drain apricots; stir ¼ cup syrup and lemon juice into saucepan. Cook, stirring constantly, until glaze boils 1 minute; cool slightly.
4. Arrange apricot halves and banana slices in rings on top of creamy layer; spoon glaze over fruits; chill.

GRAHAM-CRACKER CRUST—Mix 1¼ cups packaged graham-cracker crumbs, ¼ cup sugar, and 4 tablespoons (½ stick) melted butter or margarine in small bowl; press in bottom and around side of 9-inch pie plate. Chill about 15 minutes before filling. Makes 1 nine-inch pie.

■ CHOCOLATE VELVET BAVARIAN

1 envelope unflavored gelatin
¾ cup sugar
½ teaspoon salt
¼ teaspoon nutmeg
3 squares unsweetened chocolate
1 cup milk
½ cup cold coffee
1 teaspoon vanilla
4 eggs, separated
1 cup cream for whipping
   After-dinner peppermint patties

1. Mix gelatin, ½ cup sugar, salt, and nutmeg in top of double boiler. (Save remaining ¼ cup sugar for Step 3.) Add chocolate, milk, coffee, and vanilla; heat over simmering water until chocolate melts; beat until smooth with rotary or electric beater.
2. Beat egg yolks in medium-size bowl; stir in part of hot chocolate mixture; stir back into mixture in top of double boiler. Cook over simmering water, stirring constantly, 3 to 5 minutes, or until mixture thickens and coats a metal spoon; remove from heat. Pour into large bowl; chill until as thick as unbeaten egg white.
3. Beat egg whites until foamy-white and

Each spoonful of this **Chocolate Velvet Bavarian** tastes lusciously smooth and fudgy. Make it in your handsomest mold — it turns out perfectly. Snowy-white peppermint patties circle top for a pretty trim

double in volume in medium-size bowl; beat in saved ¼ cup sugar, 1 tablespoon at a time, beating well after each addition until meringue forms soft peaks. Beat cream until stiff in second bowl. Beat thickened gelatin until fluffy; fold in meringue, then whipped cream.
4. Pour into a 6-cup mold; chill overnight, or until firm.
5. To unmold, run a sharp-tip, thin-blade knife around top of mold, then dip mold *very quickly* in and out of a pan of hot water. Invert onto chilled serving plate; lift off mold. Garnish with peppermint patties as pictured above. Serve plain or with additional whipped cream, if you like. Makes 6 to 8 servings.

■ BUTTERMILK SHERBET

4 cups buttermilk
1 cup sugar
1½ cups light corn syrup
1 tablespoon grated lemon rind
½ cup lemon juice

1. Combine buttermilk and sugar in a large bowl; stir until sugar is completely dissolved. Blend in corn syrup, lemon rind and juice.
2. Pour into 2 dry ice-cube trays; freeze until firm about 1 inch around edges. Stir until smooth; freeze until firm. Makes 6 servings.

■ PEAR PRALINE COBBLER

1 can (about 20 ounces) minted pineapple chunks
1 can (1 pound, 13 ounces) pear halves
½ roll refrigerated oatmeal cookies
¼ cup firmly packed light brown sugar
1 tablespoon flour
Mint Sparkle Sauce (recipe follows)

1. Drain pineapple chunks and pears, keeping fruits separate. Combine syrups in small bowl and save for making sauce.
2. Split the half-roll of cooky dough lengthwise; slice half into 12 one-fourth-inch-thick half-moons; press, rounded side up, around sides of a 9-inch pie plate.
3. Toss pineapple with half the brown sugar and all the flour in small bowl; spoon into pie plate, mounding in center; arrange pear halves, narrow end toward center, on top. Crumble remaining half of cooky dough between pear halves; sprinkle pears with remaining brown sugar.
4. Bake in moderate oven (375°) 30 minutes, or until cookies are crisp and brown. Serve warm or cold with MINT SPARKLE SAUCE. Makes 8 servings.

MINT SPARKLE SAUCE—Measure syrups from pineapple chunks and pears. Add water, if needed, to make 2½ cups. Blend ½ cup sugar and 3 tablespoons cornstarch in small saucepan; stir in measured syrups. Cook, stirring constantly, until mixture thickens and boils 3 minutes. Remove from heat; stir in 2 tablespoons lemon juice. Serve warm or cold. Makes 2½ cups.

■ TURNOVER CARAMEL CUSTARDS

¾ cup sugar
½ cup hot water
4 eggs
¼ teaspoon salt
1 teaspoon vanilla
3 cups milk, scalded

1. Melt ½ cup sugar just until golden in small heavy saucepan over low heat. (Save remaining ¼ cup for next step.) Stir in hot water *very slowly.* (Watch it, for mixture will bubble up.) Heat until sugar is dissolved and turns syrupy. Spoon into 6 six-ounce custard cups, dividing evenly.
2. Beat eggs slightly with saved ¼ cup sugar, salt, and vanilla in 4-cup measure; slowly stir in scalded milk. Strain into custard cups.
3. Place cups, not touching, in baking pan on oven shelf; fill pan with boiling water as near as possible to level of custard in cups.
4. Bake in slow oven (325°) 40 minutes, or just until center is set but still soft. (Do not overbake, for custard will set as it cools.) Remove cups from water at once.
5. Serve warm or chilled, in cups, or unmold

by first loosening custards around edges with a thin-blade knife, then inverting onto serving dishes. Makes 6 servings.

■ APPLE CRUMBLE

6 medium-size tart cooking apples, pared, cored, and sliced
½ cup granulated sugar
2 tablespoons lemon juice
½ cup sifted flour
¼ cup firmly packed brown sugar
½ teaspoon nutmeg
4 tablespoons (½ stick) butter or margarine

1. Place apples in buttered 9-inch pie plate; sprinkle with granulated sugar and lemon juice.
2. Combine flour, brown sugar, and nutmeg in small bowl; cut in butter or margarine with pastry blender until mixture is crumbly. Sprinkle over apples; pat down lightly.
3. Bake in moderate oven (350°) 45 minutes, or until juices bubble up and topping is golden. Serve warm with cream or ice cream, if you wish. Makes 6 servings.

NICE TO ADD

■ JELLIED CONSOMME PARFAIT

2 cans condensed consomme
½ cup dairy sour cream
3 dashes bottled red-pepper seasoning

1. Chill consomme several hours, or overnight, to jell well.
2. When ready to serve, mash lightly with a fork; spoon into 8 parfait or juice glasses, dividing evenly.
3. Season sour cream with red-pepper seasoning; spoon on top. Garnish each with a thin slice of cucumber or radish, if you like. Makes 8 servings.

■ FEATHER-PUFF ROLLS

⅔ cup milk
½ cup shortening
¼ cup sugar
1½ teaspoons salt
2 packages active dry yeast
OR: 2 cakes compressed yeast, crumbled
½ cup very warm water
2 eggs, well beaten
4 cups sifted flour

1. Scald milk in small saucepan; stir in shortening, sugar, and salt; cool to lukewarm.
2. Sprinkle or crumble yeast into very warm water in large bowl. (Very warm water should feel comfortably warm when dropped

on wrist.) Stir until yeast dissolves, then stir in milk mixture and eggs.

3. Sift in half the flour; beat until smooth. Stir in remaining flour to make a soft dough; beat 100 times with a spoon, or about 1 minute with an electric beater. (This makes rolls feather-light.)
4. Coat top of dough lightly with soft shortening; cover; let rise in warm place, away from draft, 1 hour, or until double in bulk.
5. Punch dough down; beat well again, the same as in Step 3. Divide dough and shape into 24 small balls; place in buttered muffin-pan cups; cover. Let rise in warm place 30 minutes, or until double in bulk.
6. Bake in moderate oven (375°) 20 minutes, or until golden. Makes 2 dozen rolls.

■ GOLDEN SESAME LOAF

2 tablespoons butter or margarine
1 package refrigerated sesame dinner rolls

1. Melt butter or margarine in small loaf pan, 7x3x3. (Or make your own pan with double-thick foil.)
2. Open rolls; unroll, sesame-seed side down, on waxed paper. Fold each short end toward middle to form a double layer. (Ends should just meet.)
3. Place loaf in melted butter in pan, then turn over in pan so seam side will be down.
4. Bake in hot oven (400°) 25 minutes, or until golden. Remove from pan; cut into thick slices; serve hot. Makes 6 servings.

■ DAISY BISCUITS

2 cups sifted flour
3 teaspoons baking powder
1 teaspoon salt
½ cup shortening
¾ cup milk
Poppy seeds

1. Sift flour, baking powder, and salt into medium-size bowl. Cut in shortening with pastry blender until mixture is crumbly; add milk all at once; stir just until flour mixture is moistened.
2. Turn dough out onto lightly floured pastry cloth or board; knead lightly for half a minute. Roll out to ½-inch thickness; cut into rounds with floured 2-inch cutter; place on greased cooky sheet.
3. Shape each biscuit into petals by making 8 evenly spaced cuts around circle almost to center with sharp knife, then press down center with fingertip to make a well to hold poppy seeds. Brush tops of biscuits lightly with more milk; fill well of each with poppy seeds.

4. Bake in hot oven (425°) 12 minutes, or until lightly browned. Makes 12 biscuits. To reheat: Place in paper bag; sprinkle *very lightly* with water. Fold bag over to close tightly; heat in hot oven (400°) for 3 to 5 minutes.

■ SWEET-SOUR MUSHROOMS

1 pound fresh mushrooms
  OR: 2 cans (6 ounces each) whole mushrooms, drained*
2 tablespoons olive oil or salad oil
1 tablespoon lemon juice
3 tablespoons sugar
½ teaspoon salt
¼ cup white vinegar
2 tablespoons water

1. Rinse fresh mushrooms in cold water; trim stem ends; cut large ones in half or quarters; leave small ones whole.
2. Saute in olive oil or salad oil in large frying pan, stirring often and turning to coat with oil, 3 to 4 minutes. Sprinkle lemon juice over; spoon into medium-size bowl.
3. Heat sugar, salt, vinegar, and water to boiling in same frying pan; pour over mushrooms; cover; chill. Makes 2 cups.
* If using drained canned mushrooms, omit Steps 1 and 2. Just heat the vinegar-sugar mixture with 2 tablespoons mushroom juice instead of water in small saucepan; pour hot over mushrooms in small bowl.

*I*T'S Monday morning. And isn't it fun to start off with a dinner bounty in the refrigerator to help speed you on your way with a new week of meal planning.

The recipes that follow here take little fussing, for the main ingredient —meat from your big dinner roast— is ready and waiting. Among them

Planned-over treats from your dinner meats

you'll find temptingly different dishes using cooked beef, pork, chicken, ham, lamb, and veal. Some are planned specially for family; others are dolled up handsomely enough for a party.

Along with the main-dish suggestions are go-withs to complete each meal. Each takes advantage of simple-to-fix foods, and includes serving or garnishing tips to give it your own creative touch.

We hope you will like our planned-overs habit, for it does save time, effort, and money. But best—and most important—of all, it pays such big dividends in eating pleasure!

◄ Cubed roast lamb, bacon, molasses, and snappy seasonings go into this homey **Lamb and Lima Bake** *(recipe on page 32).* Crunchy apple slaw and corn bread, with a green vegetable, complete main course

Bonus meals from your dinner roasts

	MAIN DISH	VEGETABLE • SALAD	DESSERT	NICE TO ADD
SIMPLE BIT OF LUXURY	★Beef Strips in Sour Cream Parsley Noodles	Mixed Vegetables ★Grapefruit-carrot Salad	★Date-nut Pudding	Coffee
	Roast beef stages a popular repeat, Continental style, in this mealtime treat. Generous strips of meat simmer invitingly in a zippy tomato-mushroom sauce, then		team with sour cream in a rich gravy to spoon over parsley-flecked noodles. A good short-order special for busy days, it's ready as fast as you can cook vegetables	
ORIENTAL FANCY *(pictured on page 29)*	★Peking Pork	Hot Cooked Rice ★Chinese Vegetable Bowl	★Whirligig Cake	★Chicken-corn Soup ★Spiced Watermelon Pickle
	This exotic gourmet-looking dish starts with thin slices of roast pork brushed with a soy-rich sauce, then broiled invitingly brown and crisp around the edges. For		party serving, fan slices on top of a big bowlful of vegetables crisp-cooked, Oriental style. Serve with snowy hot rice, then finish off with a fruity cakelike dessert treat	
PARTY-TIME SPECIAL	★Chicken Jambalaya	★Hominy Squares ★Broccoli Saute ★Honey Pear Salad	Double-treat Gelatin Dessert Cookies	Mixed Olives ★Toasted Garlic Sticks
	You'll need just 2 cups diced cooked chicken plus a few shrimps or ham cubes for this party dish. And it cooks quickly in its creole sauce. Salad is a pear varia-		tion of popular Waldorf with a creamy honey-lemon dressing. For a sparkling dessert, serve two flavors of cubed fruit gelatin with big spoonfuls of whipped cream	
INDIAN FLAVOR FEAST	★Veal Curry	★Rice Mingle ★Soy Green Beans	Pineapple Cubes with Mint ★Lemon Snaps	Tomato Relish, Sliced Radishes, Coconut (curry condiments)
	Fragrant, spicy-hot curry turns leftover veal into a real prize-winning main dish. Serve with plenty of fluffy hot rice and condiments—both sweet and sour—to		sprinkle over. To top off this Indian–style dinner, plan a dessert that's cool and refreshing. Pineapple chunks, still partly frozen, and cookies make a perfect choice	
FLASHY TEASER *(pictured on page 31)*	★French Ham-and-cheese Fondue	★Vegetable Bouquet Salad Tray	★Cinnamon Baked Apples with Lemon Sherbet	Chilled Tomato Juice Buttered Hard Rolls
	With only 3 cups of ham chunks on hand, you're set to make this puffy tempter—and what a joy of a make-ahead. Put it together *hours* ahead, or even the night before, then		chill, for this is the secret to making it puff so handsomely. Just before mealtime, bake along with dessert apples to serve oven-warm topped with a dip of frosty sherbet	
EVERYDAY FAVORITE *(pictured on page 26)*	★Lamb and Lima Bake	★Mexican Spinach ★Confetti Cabbage Salad	Plum Compote (canned fruit) Ginger Cookies	★Corn-bread loaf
	A treasure of hearty eating for any day —that's this oven combo of limas and lamb dashed with peppy seasonings and dark molasses. Long, slow cooking is the		secret to its wonderfully homespun flavor. Make hot bread ahead, then reheat just before dinnertime. Add a few orange sections to plums, if you like, for easy dessert	

MAIN DISHES

■ BEEF STRIPS IN SOUR CREAM

1 large onion, chopped (1 cup)
2 tablespoons butter or margarine
2 to 3 cups julienne strips roast beef
1 can (about 11 ounces) spaghetti sauce with
    mushrooms
1 cup dairy sour cream
    Parsley noodles

1. Saute onion in butter or margarine in large
frying pan; add beef and brown lightly.
2. Stir in spaghetti sauce; simmer 5 minutes.
Stir in sour cream *very slowly;* heat *just to
boiling.*
3. Serve over hot noodles sprinkled with parsley, if you wish. Makes 4 to 6 servings.

Peking Pork starts with roast pork, sliced ever so
thin, then brushed with a soy-sparked sauce and

■ PEKING PORK

1 clove of garlic, peeled
1 chicken-bouillon cube
2 tablespoons sugar
½ cup water
¼ cup soy sauce
12 thin slices roast pork
    Hot cooked rice

1. Combine garlic (leave whole), bouillon cube,
sugar, water, and soy sauce in small saucepan; heat to boiling; simmer 5 minutes to
blend flavors; remove garlic.
2. Place pork slices in single layer on broiler
rack; brush with sauce.
3. Broil 4 inches from heat, brushing several
times with sauce, 5 minutes on each side, or
until crisp and brown. Serve with rice.
Makes 4 servings.

broiled crispy brown. Serve with a big bowlful of
vegetables, Oriental style, and plenty of hot rice

■ CHICKEN JAMBALAYA

1 cup sliced celery
1 medium-size onion, chopped (½ cup)
½ clove of garlic, minced
2 tablespoons butter or margarine
2 cans (about 1 pound each) stewed tomatoes
1 tablespoon sugar
1 bay leaf
½ teaspoon salt
⅛ teaspoon pepper
2 cups diced cooked chicken
1 pound fresh or frozen shrimps, cooked, shelled, and deveined*
OR: 1 can (about 5 ounces) deveined shrimps, drained and rinsed

1. Saute celery, onion, and garlic in butter or margarine until soft in large frying pan. Stir in tomatoes, sugar, bay leaf, salt, and pepper; heat just to boiling.
2. Stir in chicken and shrimps; heat just until bubbly-hot. Remove bay leaf before serving. Makes 6 servings.
   *Or use 1 cup diced cooked ham.

Note: To cook fresh or frozen shrimps, place in colander and wash under running cold water. (If frozen, they will separate easily and start to thaw.) Remove shell this way: Hold each shrimp rounded-shell-side down; break off feelers. Run thumb under shell, bending it back, then ease out shrimp. Make a shallow cut down curve of back and lift out black sand vein with tip of knife. Drop shrimps into simmering water seasoned with salt, a slice of lemon and onion, and a few pickling spices in large frying pan. Simmer about 5 minutes for fresh shrimps, 15 to 20 minutes for frozen, or just until tender. Lift out at once with tongs or slotted spoon.

■ VEAL CURRY

1 large onion, chopped (1 cup)
¼ teaspoon ground ginger
3 tablespoons butter or margarine
1 tablespoon flour
1 tablespoon curry powder
1 teaspoon salt
1 cup boiling water
1 beef-bouillon cube
1 can (8 ounces) sliced peaches, drained
2 cups cubed roast veal
3 whole cloves
2 tablespoons seedless raisins

1. Saute onion with ginger in butter or margarine until soft in medium-size frying pan; remove from heat. Blend in flour, curry powder, and salt.
2. Add water and bouillon cube; cook slowly, stirring constantly, until sauce thickens and boils 1 minute. Stir in remaining ingredients; cover; cook slowly 30 minutes to blend flavors.
3. Serve with Rice Mingle (*recipe on page 33*) and a variety of condiments of your choice. Makes 4 servings.

■ FRENCH HAM-AND-CHEESE FONDUE

3 cups cubed French bread (about ½ loaf)
3 cups cubed cooked ham
½ pound Cheddar cheese, cut in 1-inch cubes
3 tablespoons flour
1 tablespoon dry mustard
3 tablespoons melted butter or margarine
4 eggs
3 cups milk
Few drops bottled red-pepper seasoning

1. Make a layer of one third of the bread, ham, and cheese cubes in a buttered, straight-side 8-cup baking dish.
2. Mix flour and mustard in a cup; sprinkle about 1 tablespoonful over layer; drizzle 1 tablespoonful melted butter or margarine over. Repeat with remaining bread, ham, cheese, flour mixture, and butter or margarine to make 2 more layers.
3. Beat eggs with milk and red-pepper seasoning until foamy in medium-size bowl; pour over layers in baking dish. Cover; chill at least 4 hours, or even overnight.
4. Bake, uncovered, in moderate oven (350°) 1 hour, or until puffed and golden. Serve at once. Makes 6 servings.

French Ham-and-cheese Fondue—an easy-fix dish— ▶ turns day-after ham into a showy company teaser, and it's a perfect make-ahead *(see recipe)*. Colorful vegetable tray doubles as salad and vegetable

■ **CHINESE VEGETABLE BOWL**

¼ cup peanut oil or salad oil
1 Bermuda onion, sliced thin
2 cups thinly sliced celery
1 can (6 ounces) sliced mushrooms
1 package frozen Chinese pea pods
    OR: 1 package frozen Italian green beans
2 cups coarsely chopped Chinese cabbage
1 cup coarsely chopped escarole
1 can (5 ounces) water chestnuts, drained and
    sliced
Soy sauce

1. Heat peanut oil or salad oil in large frying pan; saute onion lightly 2 to 3 minutes. Add celery and liquid from mushrooms; cover; steam 5 minutes.
2. Lay Chinese pea pods or green beans, Chinese cabbage, escarole, water chestnuts, and mushrooms in layers on top. Cover; steam 5 minutes longer, or just until crisply cooked.
3. Toss together, salad-bowl style; serve plain, or pass soy sauce separately to sprinkle over. Makes 4 servings.

■ **HOMINY SQUARES**

2 cups water
½ cup milk
1 teaspoon salt
½ cup hominy grits
¼ cup chopped celery
2 tablespoons chopped onion
⅛ teaspoon powdered sage
4 tablespoons (½ stick) butter or margarine
¼ cup chopped parsley
    Dash of pepper
¼ cup flour
    Butter, margarine, shortening, or bacon
    drippings

1. Heat water, milk, and salt to boiling in medium-size saucepan; stir in grits. Cook over low heat, stirring often, 30 minutes, or until very thick.
2. While hominy cooks, saute celery and onion with sage in butter or margarine until golden in small frying pan.
3. Stir celery mixture, parsley, and pepper into cooked hominy; pour into shallow pan. Cool, then chill 1 hour, or until mixture holds its shape when cut.
4. Cut either into serving-size squares or oblongs. Dip each into flour in a pie plate to coat both sides lightly.
5. Saute slowly, turning once, in butter, margarine, shortening, or bacon drippings in large frying pan, 10 minutes on each side, or until golden and heated through. Makes 6 servings.

■ **LAMB AND LIMA BAKE**

1 pound (2 cups) large dried lima beans
4 cups water
2 teaspoons salt
1 cup grated raw carrots
4 slices bacon
2 cups cubed roast lamb
2 tablespoons salad oil
1 large onion, chopped (1 cup)
1 clove of garlic, minced
1 can (about 1 pound) tomatoes
¼ cup molasses

1. Cover lima beans with water in large kettle; heat to boiling; cover; cook 2 minutes. Remove from heat; let stand 30 minutes.
2. Reheat beans to boiling; add salt, grated carrot, and bacon. (Do not cut slices.) Cover; cook 45 minutes, or until skins of beans burst when you blow on a few in a spoon.
3. While beans cook, brown lamb lightly in salad oil in large frying pan. Push to one side of pan and saute onion and garlic lightly; stir in tomatoes and molasses; cover; simmer 15 minutes.
4. Remove bacon from beans and save for next step. Stir lamb mixture into beans; pour into a 12-cup baking dish; cover tightly.
5. Bake in slow oven (325°) 2 hours; remove cover; crisscross saved strips of bacon on top of casserole. Bake 1 hour longer, or until beans are tender. Makes 6 servings.

■ BROCCOLI SAUTE

6 stalks of celery, sliced
4 tablespoons (½ stick) butter or margarine
1 package (10 ounces) frozen chopped broccoli
¼ cup water
½ teaspoon salt
⅛ teaspoon pepper
   Juice of half a lemon

1. Saute celery lightly in butter or margarine in medium-size saucepan; add frozen broccoli, water, salt, and pepper; cover.
2. Heat to boiling; cook 5 minutes. Break up broccoli with a fork; cover again; cook 5 to 8 minutes longer, or just until crisply tender.
3. Spoon into serving bowl; squeeze lemon juice over. Makes 6 servings.

■ MEXICAN SPINACH

2 packages (10 ounces each) frozen leaf spinach
1 tablespoon olive oil or salad oil
1 tablespoon minced onion
1 hard-cooked egg, sliced

1. Cook spinach, following label directions. Drain thoroughly; chop coarsely with two knives.
2. Heat olive oil or salad oil and onion in medium-size saucepan. Add chopped spinach; toss lightly.
3. Spoon into heated serving dish; garnish with egg slices. Makes 6 servings.

■ SOY GREEN BEANS

1 pound green beans
2 tablespoons salad oil
2 tablespoons butter or margarine
½ cup water
2 tablespoons soy sauce
½ teaspoon sugar

1. Tip, split, and halve green beans. Cook quickly, stirring constantly, in salad oil and butter or margarine in large frying pan, 3 to 4 minutes, or just until shiny-moist.
2. Stir in remaining ingredients. Cover; steam 8 to 10 minutes, or just until beans are crisply tender. Makes 4 servings.

■ RICE MINGLE

½ cup brown rice
1 teaspoon salt
3 cups boiling water
½ cup uncooked white rice
1 pimiento, diced
¼ cup chopped pecans or pistachio nuts

1. Stir brown rice and salt into boiling water in large heavy saucepan; cover; simmer 20 minutes.

2. Stir in white rice; cover again; simmer, stirring once or twice with a fork, 15 to 20 minutes longer, or until rices are tender and water is absorbed.
3. Stir in pimiento and nuts. Heat, shaking pan gently, 1 to 2 minutes to dry and fluff rice. Makes 4 servings.

SALADS

■ HONEY PEAR SALAD

3 large ripe pears, quartered, cored, pared, and diced
1½ cups diced celery
½ cup seedless raisins
1 tablespoon honey
1 tablespoon lemon juice
⅓ cup mayonnaise or salad dressing
   Lettuce

Combine pears, celery, and raisins in medium-size bowl. Stir honey and lemon juice into mayonnaise or salad dressing in 1-cup measure; pour over fruits and toss lightly to mix; chill. Spoon into lettuce cups. Makes 6 servings.

■ VEGETABLE BOUQUET SALAD TRAY

2 small yellow squashes, sliced, cooked, and drained
1 package (10 ounces) frozen cut green beans, cooked and drained
2 carrots, scraped, sliced, cooked, and drained
6 tablespoons bottled French dressing
1 pimiento, chopped
1 tablespoon pickled tiny white onions
1 tablespoon chopped parsley

1. Place vegetables in separate small bowls; drizzle each with 2 tablespoons dressing; toss lightly to mix. Cover and chill for at least an hour to blend flavors.
2. Just before serving, spoon each vegetable into a small serving bowl. Sprinkle pimiento over squashes, onions over green beans, and parsley over carrots. Makes 6 servings.

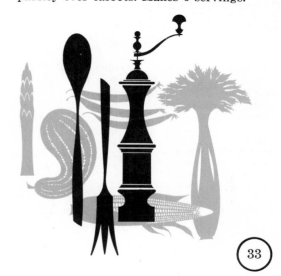

■ CONFETTI CABBAGE SALAD

6 cups finely shredded cabbage
1 medium-size red eating apple, cored and chopped
⅓ cup mayonnaise or salad dressing
¼ cup apple cider or apple juice
1 teaspoon salt
1 teaspoon sugar
⅛ teaspoon pepper
½ cup chopped walnuts
Paprika

1. Combine cabbage and apple in large bowl.
2. Blend mayonnaise or salad dressing, apple cider or apple juice, salt, sugar, and pepper in 1-cup measure. Stir into cabbage mixture; toss to mix well. Chill.
3. When ready to serve, pile into a shallow serving bowl; place walnuts in a ring on top; sprinkle with paprika. Makes 6 servings.

■ GRAPEFRUIT-CARROT SALAD

2 large grapefruits
OR: 1 can (1 pound) grapefruit sections
1 bunch of water cress
2 cups grated raw carrots
¼ cup French dressing

1. Pare and section grapefruits, or drain canned grapefruit well. (Save juice to add to fruit cup or fruit-juice beverage for another meal.)
2. Arrange water cress on individual salad plates. Place grapefruit sections in a ring on top, dividing evenly; fill with grated carrots. Spoon French dressing over. Makes 6 servings.

DESSERTS

■ WHIRLIGIG CAKE

1 can (about 1 pound) pear halves
¾ cup pear syrup from can
2 tablespoons lemon juice
2 tablespoons brown sugar
1 tablespoon cornstarch
1 sponge layer (2 to a package)

1. Drain and measure syrup from pears; add water, if needed, to make ¾ cup. Add lemon juice.
2. Mix brown sugar and cornstarch in small saucepan; stir in syrup mixture. Cook, stirring constantly, until sauce thickens and boils 3 minutes.
3. Place a sponge layer on deep serving plate. (Use second layer for lunchbox dessert.) Arrange drained pears, rounded side up, in wheel design on top. Spoon hot sauce over and let soak into cake. Serve warm, cut in wedges. Makes 4 to 6 servings.

■ DATE-NUT PUDDING

½ cup granulated sugar
3 tablespoons butter or margarine
1½ cups sifted flour
1½ teaspoons baking powder
½ teaspoon cinnamon
⅛ teaspoon salt
¾ cup milk
1 cup pitted chopped dates
½ cup chopped walnuts
½ teaspoon vanilla
½ teaspoon grated orange rind
2 cups boiling water
1 cup firmly packed brown sugar

1. Mix granulated sugar and 1 tablespoon butter or margarine in medium-size bowl. (Save remaining butter or margarine for Step 3.)
2. Sift flour, baking powder, cinnamon, and salt onto waxed paper; blend, alternately with milk, into sugar mixture. Stir in dates, walnuts, vanilla, and orange rind; pour into buttered pan, 9x9x2.
3. Combine water, brown sugar, and remaining 2 tablespoons butter or margarine in small saucepan; heat to boiling; pour over batter.
4. Bake in moderate oven (350°) 45 minutes, or until top is sticky-firm. Serve warm, with ice cream, if desired. Makes 9 servings.

■ CINNAMON BAKED APPLES

6 medium-size baking apples
1 cup sugar
½ cup water
1 two-inch stick cinnamon

1. Wash and core apples; pare halfway to bottom. Stand in deep baking dish.
2. Combine sugar and water in 2-cup measure; pour over apples. Drop in cinnamon stick.
3. Bake in moderate oven (350°), basting often with syrup in dish, 50 minutes, or until apples are tender, but still firm enough to hold their shape. Makes 6 servings.

■ LEMON SNAPS

¾ cup (1½ sticks) butter or margarine
1¼ cups sugar
1 egg
½ teaspoon vanilla
½ teaspoon lemon extract
¼ cup milk
2 cups sifted flour
1 teaspoon baking powder
½ teaspoon salt
¼ teaspoon baking soda
1 tablespoon grated lemon rind

1. Cream butter or margarine with ¾ cup sugar until light in medium-size bowl. (Save remaining ½ cup for Step 3.) Beat in egg, vanilla, lemon extract, and milk.
2. Sift in flour, baking powder, salt, and baking soda, a little at a time, blending well after each addition. Chill an hour, or until firm.
3. Form into marble-size balls (about 1 teaspoonful for each) by rolling lightly between palms of hands. Roll each in mixture of saved ½ cup sugar and lemon rind to coat well. Place 2 inches apart on ungreased cooky sheets.
4. Bake in moderate oven (350°) 8 to 10 minutes, or until tops are crackled and edges are brown. Cool on wire racks. Makes 5 dozen.

NICE TO ADD

■ CHICKEN-CORN SOUP

2 cans condensed chicken-vegetable soup
1 can (about 1 pound) cream-style corn
2½ cups water
2 tablespoons chopped parsley

1. Combine all ingredients in medium-size saucepan; heat slowly, stirring often, just to boiling.
2. Pour into heated soup bowls; serve with chowder crackers or saltines, if you wish. Makes 6 servings.

■ CORN-BREAD LOAF

1 package corn-muffin mix
1 cup sifted flour
1 egg
Milk or water

1. Combine corn-muffin mix and flour in medium-size bowl.
2. Beat egg slightly in small bowl; add milk or water called for in recipe on package for corn muffins plus ¼ cup more. Stir into flour mixture, following label directions. Pour into greased loaf pan, 9x5x3.
3. Bake in hot oven (400°) 35 minutes, or until golden. Makes 1 loaf. (Bake ahead, if you like, then wrap in foil, and reheat in slow oven [325°] 15 minutes just before serving.)

■ TOASTED GARLIC STICKS

1 long thin loaf French bread
½ cup bottled garlic spread
½ cup (1 stick) butter, margarine, or salad oil
½ cup grated Parmesan cheese

1. Cut bread into 4 equal-size pieces; split, then halve each to make 16 sticklike chunks.
2. Heat garlic spread with butter, margarine or salad oil until melted in medium-size saucepan; stir to blend.
3. Dip bread, cut-sides down, in hot mixture; sprinkle lightly with cheese. Place, without touching, on cooky sheet.
4. Toast in very hot oven (450°) 5 minutes, or until golden. Makes 16 sticks.

■ SPICED WATERMELON PICKLE

Rind from half of a large watermelon (about 2 pounds)
8 cups water (for brine)
½ cup salt
4 cups sugar
1 lemon, thinly sliced
1 tablespoon whole cloves
1 tablespoon whole allspice
6 one-inch sticks of cinnamon
2 cups vinegar
2 cups water (for syrup)

1. Pare green skin from watermelon; cut rind into 1-inch cubes. (There should be about 8 cups.) Soak overnight in brine of 8 cups water and salt in large bowl.
2. Drain; place in kettle; cover with fresh water. Heat to boiling, then simmer 10 minutes, or just until cubes are tender but still firm; drain.
3. While rind drains, combine sugar, lemon, cloves, allspice, cinnamon, vinegar, and 2 cups water in same kettle; heat to boiling; stir in drained rind. Simmer, stirring often from bottom of pan, 1 hour, or until rind is clear and syrup is thick.
4. Ladle rind and spice evenly into hot sterilized jars; fill to brim with remaining hot syrup. Seal, following manufacturer's directions. Label and store in a cool dry place. Makes 6 eight-ounce jars.

Note: To sterilize jars: Place in large kettle with water to cover; heat to boiling; cover; boil 15 minutes. Turn off heat; leave in hot water until ready to fill.

GLORY be to meat loaves! They're the mainstay of many a family—even company—meal, and what a smart choice to favor the food budget. Other plusses: They go together fast, hold happily if dinner's delayed, and taste equally scrumptious as a cold sandwich filling.

Most meat loaves start with ground beef or a mixture of beef and pork or veal. But consider, too, meat choices such as corned beef mixed with potatoes and seasonings, then wrapped and baked in a flaky pastry blanket. (It's pictured at the left.) Or save some of your big ham roast to grind, then make into a loaf and bake with a sparkling fruit glaze. Veal stands high

Meat loaves you can bank on

in gourmet appeal, and our favorite recipe here combines it with grated carrots and sour cream. Even liver-snubbers are likely to change their minds when so-good-for-you liver shows up on the table in a handsome loaf capped with a tart-sweet topper.

Recipes for all these loaves are here, with suggestions to round out each meal. Do keep them right up front on your list, for you're really on the right track when you bank on meat loaves.

◀ Biscuitlike crust bakes golden around a spicy meat-and-potato filling for the **Jumbo Corned-beef Roll** *(recipe on page 40).* Double vegetable bowl and tart jellied aspic salad round out the main course

Meat-loaf meals with a fancy touch

	MAIN DISH	VEGETABLE • SALAD	DESSERT	NICE TO ADD
CORNED-BEEF DIVIDEND *(pictured on page 36)*	★Jumbo Corned-beef Roll ★Mustard Sauce	Buttered Broccoli and Cauliflowerets with Croutons	Fruit Cocktail with Lime Ice	★Double Tomato Aspic Dill Pickles
	Here's a treat with corned beef from another day's dinner. Mixed with potatoes and seasonings, it bakes in a biscuitlike blanket. With it goes a tart mustard		sauce to spoon over each savory slice. For a vegetable, combine cooked broccoli and cauliflower with buttery croutons. Spicy salad mold uses tomatoes two ways	
DOUBLE TREAT WITH BEEF *(pictured on page 39)*	★Duchess Meat-loaf Pie	★Saucedish Tomatoes Relish Crisps	Chocolate Mint Pudding (from a mix)	★Buttermilk Foldovers
	This homey loaf "bakes" atop the range, looks pretty with its snowy potato crown. For easy cooking, onion-soup mix both seasons the meat and makes the gravy.		While meat cooks, mix and bake biscuits —recipe gives a quick shaping trick— heat tomatoes, and fix salad-relish tray of sliced sweet peppers and crisp carrots	
NEW WAY WITH BEEF *(pictured on page 40)*	★Surprise Meat Loaf	★Country Green Beans	Neapolitan Ice Cream Spongecake	Lettuce Bowl Blue-cheese Dressing
	Ground beef takes on a subtle smoky flavor in this loaf, for canned canape bacon spread is its key seasoner. To serve prettily, edge platter with mashed-potato puffs		broiled until golden, then top loaf with cherry tomatoes sauteed just until hot. Other vegetable mate is different, too, for savory liquid from beans goes into sauce	
HAM BOUNTY	★Ham and Cracker Round ★Glazed Peaches	★Panned Potatoes Buttered Cabbage	Hot Gingerbread Squares with Applesauce	Marinated Mixed Vegetables in Lettuce Cups
	When you bake ham, be sure there's enough left over for this mellow loaf. Grind chunks —it takes just 6 cups—season, shape, and bake. Peaches go into the oven during last		20 minutes. Potatoes are ready as quickly as you can slice and pan-fry them. Dessert starts with a mix, or bake your favorite homemade gingerbread; serve oven-warm	
FLAVOR PLUS WITH LIVER	★Country Liver Loaf	★Hungarian Potatoes Buttered Peas with Celery	★Upside-down Pineapple Cake *(pictured on page 44)*	Coleslaw with Green-pepper Rings
	Even though your family may claim it doesn't like liver, try this tempter just once, for it teams thrifty beef or lamb liver with a can of spicy chopped ham.		A tart-sweet sauce is spooned on after baking. Potatoes scallop mealy moist in bouillon, with tomatoes for a fresh flavor. Start them baking first, then fix meat	
VEAL IS THE STAR *(pictured on page 42)*	★Gourmet Veal Loaf with ★Salad Tomatoes	Mashed Potatoes ★Golden Corn Pudding	Cherry Pie	Cream of Pea Soup Raw Relishes
	Just 1½ pounds ground veal shoulder make this mildly seasoned moist loaf. Its gourmet touches? Shreds of golden carrots and tangy-rich sour cream. For		company, unmold onto a plank or broiler-proof platter, pipe or spoon mashed potatoes alongside with salad-dressing-topped tomatoes, and broil until potatoes are brown	

Duchess Meat-loaf Pie (*recipe on page 40*) goes together quickly, cooks almost as fast. Other main-course go-withs: Spoon-up tomatoes, crisp carrots and sweet pepper rings, and hot-from-oven biscuits

MAIN DISHES

■ JUMBO CORNED-BEEF ROLL

4 cups cut-up cooked corned beef (about 1
    pound)
1 medium-size onion, peeled
2 medium-size potatoes, cooked, peeled, and diced
2 eggs, slightly beaten
⅛ teaspoon pepper·
½ cup milk (for meat loaf)
2 cups sifted flour
1 teaspoon salt
⅓ cup shortening
⅔ cup milk (for crust)
    Mustard Sauce (recipe follows)

1. Put corned beef and onion through food
   chopper, using coarse blade. Mix with potatoes, eggs, pepper, and ½ cup milk in medium-size bowl; set aside for Step 4.
2. Sift flour and salt into medium-size bowl;
   cut in shortening with pastry blender until
   mixture is crumbly; blend in ⅔ cup milk
   with fork just until flour is completely
   moist—the same as for biscuits.
3. Turn dough out onto lightly floured pastry
   cloth or board; knead gently 5 or 6 times;
   roll out to a rectangle, 12x10.
4. Spoon meat mixture in loaf shape, 9x4, in

center of pastry; fold pastry up over loaf;
seal edges. Place, seam side down, on greased
cooky sheet; cut several slits in top of pastry
to allow steam to escape.
5. Bake in hot oven (425°) 30 minutes, or until
   pastry is golden-brown. Slice and serve with
   MUSTARD SAUCE. Makes 6 servings.
MUSTARD SAUCE — Blend ½ cup mayonnaise or
salad dressing, ¼ cup dairy sour cream, 1 tablespoon prepared mustard, and ¼ teaspoon
Worcestershire sauce in 1-cup measure. Makes
about ¾ cup.

■ DUCHESS MEAT-LOAF PIE

1 envelope onion-soup mix
1½ cups water
2 pounds ground beef
    Hot mashed potatoes

1. Stir soup mix into water in a 2-cup measure.
2. Measure out ½ cup and blend into ground
   beef in large bowl. Shape mixture into a
   thick 8-inch round patty in large frying pan;
   cut into 6 wedges.
3. Pour remaining soup over; cover. Cook over
   medium heat 25 minutes, or until done.
4. To serve, spoon hot mashed potatoes into a
   mound on top of meat; dip gravy from bottom of pan with a spoon and drizzle over.
   Makes 6 servings.

◀ **Surprise Meat Loaf** goes with puffs of golden-tipped potatoes and one-bite cherry tomatoes to make this colorful platter. Canned meat spread gives this loaf its deliciously rich secret flavor

■ SURPRISE MEAT LOAF

2 pounds ground beef
2 cans (3 ounces each) bacon spread
¾ cup chopped parsley
½ cup fine dry bread crumbs
1 egg
1 tablespoon instant minced onion
2 teaspoons salt
2 teaspoons basil
⅛ teaspoon pepper
1 cup tomato juice
  Potato Swirls (recipe follows)
  Butter-blistered Cherry Tomatoes
    (recipe follows)

1. Combine ground beef, bacon spread, parsley, bread crumbs, egg, instant onion, salt, basil, pepper and tomato juice in large bowl; mix lightly with a fork just until blended. Shape into a loaf about 9x5x3 in a greased shallow baking pan.
2. Bake in moderate oven (375°) 45 minutes, or until done as you like beef.
3. Place loaf on a heated serving platter; surround with POTATO SWIRLS; top with a few BUTTER-BLISTERED CHERRY TOMATOES. Serve any remaining vegetables separately. Makes 6 to 8 servings.

POTATO SWIRLS:—Prepare 2 envelopes instant mashed potatoes, following label directions; drop by tablespoonfuls onto buttered cooky sheet. Melt 2 tablespoons butter or margarine in small frying pan; brush on tops of potatoes. Broil 3 to 5 minutes, or until potatoes are lightly browned. Makes 6 to 8 servings.

BUTTER-BLISTERED CHERRY TOMATOES—Saute 2 cups (1 pint) washed and stemmed cherry tomatoes in any remaining butter or margarine in same frying pan, adding a little more butter if needed, 5 minutes, or just until skins blister. Sprinkle lightly with salt and pepper. Makes 6 to 8 servings.

■ HAM AND CRACKER ROUND

6 cups cut-up cooked ham (about 1½ pounds)
1 medium-size onion, peeled
15 unsalted soda crackers
1 egg
¼ cup water
½ teaspoon marjoram
⅛ teaspoon pepper
¼ cup pancake syrup
1 teaspoon prepared mustard
  Glazed Peaches (recipe follows)

1. Put ham, onion, and crackers through food chopper, using coarse blade. Mix with egg, water, marjoram, and pepper in large bowl.

2. Shape mixture into a round loaf in greased shallow baking pan; score top.
3. Bake in moderate oven (350°) 30 minutes; baste with mixture of pancake syrup and prepared mustard. Bake 30 minutes longer, or until richly browned. Serve in wedges with GLAZED PEACHES. Makes 6 servings.

GLAZED PEACHES — Arrange 1 can (about 1 pound) drained cling peach halves, cut side up, in pie plate. Dot with 2 tablespoons butter or margarine; sprinkle with 2 tablespoons brown sugar mixed with ¼ teaspoon ground ginger. Bake in moderate oven (350°), basting once with buttery syrup in dish, 20 minutes, or until richly glazed. Makes 6 servings.

■ COUNTRY LIVER LOAF

1 pound beef or lamb liver, sliced
1 can (12 ounces) chopped ham
1 small onion, peeled
1 cup soft bread crumbs (2 slices)
1 egg
¾ cup milk
1 tablespoon bottled steak sauce
¼ teaspoon thyme
½ cup apple jelly
2 teaspoons lemon juice

1. Snip out veiny parts and skin from liver. Simmer liver in salted, gently boiling water to cover in medium-size frying pan 5 minutes; drain.
2. Put liver, ham, and onion through food chopper, using coarse blade. Mix with bread crumbs, egg, milk, steak sauce, and thyme in large bowl. Pack firmly into greased loaf pan, 9x5x3.
3. Bake in moderate oven (350°) 45 minutes, or until brown. Unmold onto heated platter.
4. Heat jelly with lemon juice, stirring constantly, just to boiling in small saucepan. Spoon on top of hot loaf. Makes 6 servings.

■ GOURMET VEAL LOAF

1½ pounds ground veal shoulder meat
 2 cups grated raw carrots
 1 small onion, chopped (¼ cup)
 1 can (3 to 4 ounces) chopped mushrooms
½ cup fine dry bread crumbs
 1 teaspoon salt
¼ teaspoon pepper
 1 cup dairy sour cream
   Salad Tomatoes *(recipe follows)*
 3 cups seasoned hot mashed potatoes

1. Combine all ingredients, except SALAD
   TOMATOES and mashed potatoes, in large
   bowl; mix lightly with fork.
2. Spoon into loaf pan, 9x5x3; invert onto
   shallow baking pan; carefully remove loaf
   pan. Score top of loaf lightly.
3. Bake in moderate oven (350°) 1 hour and
   15 minutes, or until rich golden brown on top.
4. Place baked loaf on plank or broilerproof
   platter; edge with SALAD TOMATOES and
   ribbons of mashed potatoes. Broil 10 to 12
   minutes, or until tomatoes are bubbly-hot
   and potatoes are lightly tipped with brown.
   Sprinkle tomatoes with finely chopped parsley, if you wish. Makes 4 to 6 servings.

SALAD TOMATOES—Cut out stems from 4 large
ripe tomatoes, then halve each tomato crosswise.
Brush cut sides generously with melted butter
or margarine or bottled Italian salad dressing.

◀ This **Gourmet Veal Loaf** owes its special flavor to rich sour cream and flecks of grated carrots. For a party, serve on a plank with fluffy mashed potatoes and big rosy tomato moons with a buttery topping

VEGETABLES

■ PANNED POTATOES

6 tablespoons (¾ stick) butter or margarine
6 medium-size potatoes, cooked, peeled, and cut in
   ¼-inch-thick slices
¼ teaspoon seasoned salt
   Dash of pepper

1. Melt butter or margarine in large frying pan; stir in potato slices; sprinkle with seasoned salt and pepper.
2. Cook over low heat, turning several times carefully so as not to break slices, 10 minutes, or until golden. Makes 6 servings.

■ HUNGARIAN POTATOES

2 chicken-bouillon cubes
2 cups boiling water
2 tablespoons flour
1 teaspoon salt
1 teaspoon paprika
¼ teaspoon pepper
1 large onion, chopped (1 cup)
4 cups thinly sliced pared raw potatoes
   (about 6 medium-size)
2 medium-size tomatoes, cut into wedges
2 tablespoons butter or margarine

1. Dissolve bouillon cubes in boiling water in 2-cup measure.
2. Combine flour, salt, paprika, and pepper in a cup.
3. Spread onion over bottom of buttered 8-cup baking dish. Layer half the potatoes, flour mixture, and tomatoes over; repeat, ending with tomatoes. Dot with butter or margarine; slowly pour bouillon over; cover with lid or foil.
4. Bake in moderate oven (350°) 30 minutes; uncover. Bake, pressing potatoes down several times with spoon to keep moist, 1 to 1½ hours longer, or until tender. Let stand about 10 minutes before serving to let potatoes absorb some of the liquid. Makes 6 servings.

■ SAUCEDISH TOMATOES

2 tablespoons butter or margarine
6 medium-size tomatoes, quartered
1 teaspoon salt
½ teaspoon sugar

1. Melt butter or margarine in large saucepan; stir in tomatoes. Sprinkle with salt and sugar; cover.
2. Cook over low heat, 5 to 10 minutes, or just until skins blister. Serve in saucedishes. Makes 6 servings.

■ COUNTRY GREEN BEANS

2 cans (1 pound each) cut green beans
1 small onion, chopped (¼ cup)
4 tablespoons (½ stick) butter or margarine
4 tablespoons flour
1 teaspoon salt
⅛ teaspoon pepper
1 small can evaporated milk (⅔ cup)

1. Drain liquid from green beans; measure 1⅓ cups into a 2-cup measure and save for making sauce in next step.
2. Saute onion in butter or margarine just until soft in medium-size frying pan; remove from heat. Blend in flour, salt, and pepper; stir in measured liquid from beans and evaporated milk.
3. Cook, stirring constantly, until sauce thickens and boils 1 minute. Stir in green beans; heat slowly, stirring often, 10 minutes, or until bubbly-hot. Makes 6 servings.

■ GOLDEN CORN PUDDING

2 cups corn kernels (cut from 3 or 4
   ears uncooked corn)
   OR: 1 can (12 or 16 ounces) whole-kernel
   corn, drained
2 tablespoons chopped pimiento
1 tablespoon chopped parsley
1 tablespoon grated onion
1 tablespoon sugar
1 teaspoon salt
   Dash of pepper
2 eggs
1½ cups scalded milk
1 tablespoon butter or margarine

1. Combine corn, pimiento, parsley, onion, sugar, salt and pepper in buttered shallow 6-cup baking dish. Beat eggs slightly in 4-cup measure; slowly stir in scalded milk, then butter or margarine.
2. Pour over corn in baking dish; stir just to blend. Place dish in a shallow pan on oven shelf; pour boiling water into pan as near as possible to level of custard.
3. Bake in moderate oven (350°) 50 minutes, or until center is almost set but still soft; remove from water at once. Makes 6 servings.
Note: To cut kernels from fresh corn: Husk corn and remove silks. Holding ear upright on a cutting board covered with foil or waxed paper, or in a shallow dish, slice downward, 2 or 3 rows at a time with sharp knife. Try not to cut too deeply into hulls. Hold cob over measuring cup, press out remaining pulp and milk with back of knife. Spoon kernels into cup; repeat until you have enough for your recipe.

43

Golden pineapple and rosy cherries top feathery nut cake in this **Upside-down Pineapple Cake.** For top-ping design shown above, arrange pineapple spears in each quarter of pan at right angles to each other

DESSERTS

■ UPSIDE-DOWN PINEAPPLE CAKE

Topping

4 tablespoons (½ stick) butter or margarine
¾ cup firmly packed light brown sugar
⅛ teaspoon salt
1 can (about 1 pound, 4 ounces) pineapple spears, drained
12 maraschino cherries, quartered

Cake

2 eggs, separated
2 cups sifted cake flour
2½ teaspoons baking powder
½ teaspoon ground ginger
¼ teaspoon salt
½ cup (1 stick) butter or margarine
1 cup granulated sugar
½ teaspoon grated lemon rind
½ teaspoon vanilla
½ cup milk
½ cup finely chopped walnuts

1. Make topping: Melt butter or margarine in baking pan, 9x9x2; stir in brown sugar and salt. Cook, stirring constantly, over low heat, until bubbly; remove from heat. Arrange pineapple spears and cherries in rows on sugar mixture.
2. Make cake: Beat egg whites just until they stand in firm peaks in small bowl.
3. Sift flour, baking powder, ginger, and salt onto waxed paper.
4. Cream butter or margarine with sugar until fluffy in large bowl with spoon or electric mixer; beat in egg yolks, lemon rind, and vanilla. Blend in dry ingredients alternately with milk; fold in walnuts and beaten egg whites. Pour over fruits in pan.
5. Bake in moderate oven (350°) 1 hour, or until top springs back when lightly pressed with fingertip.
6. Cool on wire rack 5 minutes; cover pan with serving plate; quickly turn upside down, then carefully lift off baking pan. Serve warm or cold, topped with plain or whipped cream or vanilla ice cream. Makes 8 servings.

NICE TO ADD

■ DOUBLE TOMATO ASPIC

1 can (about 1 pound) tomatoes
1 envelope unflavored gelatin
1 tablespoon mixed pickling spices
1 teaspoon salt
⅛ teaspoon pepper
1 cup tomato juice
1 tablespoon lemon juice

1. Drain liquid from tomatoes into small sauce-pan. Spoon tomatoes into 6 six-ounce molds or pan, 8x8x2; set aside for Step 3.
2. Soften gelatin in tomato liquid; stir in mixed pickling spices, salt, and pepper. Heat to boiling; simmer 5 minutes to blend flavors. Stir in tomato and lemon juices.
3. Strain over tomatoes in molds or pan. Chill several hours, or until firm.
4. Unmold on crisp lettuce, or if molded in pan, divide in half, then cut each half in thirds. Serve plain or with mayonnaise or salad dressing, if you wish. Makes 6 servings.

■ BUTTERMILK FOLDOVERS

2¼ cups sifted flour
3 teaspoons baking powder
½ teaspoon salt
¼ teaspoon baking soda
⅓ cup shortening
1 cup buttermilk
1 tablespoon salad oil

1. Sift flour, baking powder, salt, and soda into large bowl. Cut in shortening with pastry blender until mixture is crumbly; stir in buttermilk just until mixture is moistened.
2. Turn dough out onto floured pastry cloth or board; knead gently for ½ minute. Roll out to a rectangle, 14x10; brush with salad oil; fold in half. (Biscuits bake in a double layer, pull apart easily for buttering.) Cut into rounds with a 2-inch cutter; reroll, fold, and cut out any trimmings. Place on ungreased cooky sheet.
3. Bake in very hot oven (450°) 12 minutes, or until crusty-golden. Makes about 1 dozen.

*P*LAN dinner around a casserole and you're far ahead in these ways: It's a perfect fix-early, bake-later choice. It's a budget booster, for how tastefully you can dress up plain food. It's easy to serve, and best of all—good hearty eating.

When entertaining, you can't beat a casserole, for it stands well until time to go into the oven, then bakes with little or no watching. And what hostess doesn't appreciate that? Still other bonuses: It takes perfectly to buffet serving, waits happily if someone is tardy, and, on a keep-hot tray,

Count on casseroles

it stays cozy-warm until guests are ready for seconds.

In this chapter we have included our most popular casseroles. Some are homey; others, partylike; and none calls for really expensive food or fancy fussing. For example, just a pound of ground beef goes into the spicy Mexican bake. In the cassoulet, it's thrifty stewing lamb that simmers long and lazily for its mellow flavor. Other dishes start with easy-cook chicken, heat-and-eat canned meat, and flavorful cheese.

If you're not already a casserole cook, do give these a try, for they're proof enough that casseroles are a cook's best friend.

◄ Thrifty broiler-fryers blend with rice and zesty seasonings in this tempting **Spanish Chicken** *(recipe on page 50).* Vegetable partners: Golden squash rings and hot broccoli salad dressed with a tart sauce

Easygoing casserole meals

	CASSEROLE	VEGETABLE • SALAD	DESSERT	NICE TO ADD
INSPIRATION FROM MEXICO *(pictured on page 49)*	★Tamale Bake	★Triple Melon Salad ★Golden Dressing	★Mocha Drink-a-dessert	Sesame-seed Crackers Buttered Green Beans
	Our neighbors to the south inspired this meal-in-a-dish with ground beef—just 1 pound for 6 servings—corn meal, tomatoes, cheese, and peppery seasonings. Fix ahead,		if you like, then bake while you make a fruit salad—so refreshing with chili. Dessert-beverage—to sip, then spoon—blends coffee with milk and chocolate ice cream	
CHICKEN'S ALWAYS TOPS *(pictured on page 46)*	★Spanish Chicken	★Golden Squash ★Hot Broccoli Salad	Purple Plums with Sour-cream Topping	★Celery Chip Rolls
	Husky pieces of chicken, browned first, bake atop rice in this hearty casserole. Spanish-rice–seasoning mix in an envelope gives it its zesty flavor. Broccoli salad—		served hot—doubles as a second vegetable to go with sauteed yellow squash. For dessert, chill canned plums, then top each serving with a spoonful of sour cream	
LAMB WITH A FRENCH FLAIR	★Lamb Cassoulet	Chopped Cabbage-cucumber Salad Coleslaw Dressing	Butter-pecan Ice-cream Sundae	French Bread and Butter
	Plan ahead with this casserole, for the secret to its homey old-fashioned flavor is long, slow cooking. First simmer thrifty lamb stewing meat (from a combination		package of meaty shank, chops, and chunks), then mix with beans, bacon, and salami, and bake. For salad, toss chopped vegetables with bottled coleslaw dressing	
HIGH STYLE "ON-HANDS" *(pictured on page 51)*	★Dixie Dandy	★Braised Endive ★Onion-radish-ring Salad	★Blueberry Turnovers	Tomato Juice ★Cheddar Puffs
	Pork luncheon meat, sweet potatoes, and applesauce from your cupboard go into this quick-fix casserole. Stud meat with cloves, then bake with potatoes atop applesauce.		Apricot sauce glazes meat as it heats. Vegetable choice cooks quickly, needs only a simple buttery topper. Cheese-rich hot bread and dessert can go in oven with casserole	
HOSTESSING DELIGHT	★Party Lasagna	Mixed Green Salad Italian Dressing	Orange-coconut Layer Cake	Crusty Rolls Parsley Butter Pickled Red Peppers
	Layers of peppery meat sauce, noodles, and cheese stack up to this bargain dish with an Italian accent. Recipe makes lots, so it's perfect for entertaining—and sauce		can be made ahead. For bread, mix chopped parsley with butter or margarine, then spread on hard rolls. Bake cake from a mix, frost, and drift with flaked coconut	
JUST FOR FAMILY *(pictured on page 53)*	★Macaroni Favorite	★Celery Peas Carrot and Green-onion Sticks	★Lemon Meringue Pie	Cold Cuts Italian Bread Sticks
	Macaroni-and-cheese rates with almost everybody, and here it's dressed up with mushrooms, pimientos, and rosy tomato wedges. Meat isn't really needed, but if you		like, arrange a platter of assorted cold cuts to go with casserole. While fixing salad nibbles, cut enough extra carrots to tuck into a plastic bag for snacktimes	

Tamale Bake (*recipe on page 50*) is hearty with ground beef, vegetables, and cheese in a golden corn-meal nest. To go along, plan a cool fruit salad and a tall creamy coffee-chocolate dessert-beverage

MAIN DISHES

■ TAMALE BAKE

1 cup corn meal
1 pound ground beef
1 medium-size onion, chopped (½ cup)
½ cup chopped green pepper
1 envelope spaghetti-sauce mix
1 tablespoon chili powder
1 can (about 1 pound) tomatoes
1 can (7 ounces) pitted ripe olives, halved
1 cup grated Cheddar cheese (¼ pound)

1. Cook corn meal, following label directions for corn-meal mush. Pour about half into an 8-cup shallow baking dish; spread evenly. Pour remaining into a greased pan, 9x5x3; chill.
2. Press ground beef into a large patty in large frying pan; brown 5 minutes on each side; break up into chunks; push to one side.
3. Add onion and green pepper; saute just until soft. Stir in spaghetti-sauce mix, chili powder, and tomatoes.
4. Heat to boiling, stirring constantly; remove from heat. Stir in olives and ¾ cup grated cheese. (Save remaining for Step 5.) Pour over corn-meal mush in baking dish. (This much can be done ahead; chill. Take from refrigerator 30 minutes before baking.)
5. Remove corn-meal mush from pan by turning upside down onto cutting board. Divide in half lengthwise, then cut each half into thirds; cut each piece diagonally to make 12 wedges. Arrange around edge of baking dish, as pictured on page 49; sprinkle saved ¼ cup cheese on top.
6. Bake in hot oven (400°) 1 hour, or until bubbly-hot. Makes 6 servings.

■ SPANISH CHICKEN

2 broiler-fryers, quartered
¼ cup flour
¼ cup salad oil
1½ cups uncooked rice
3 cups water
1 envelope Spanish-rice–seasoning mix
1 large green pepper, cut in 8 rings
1 cup sliced stuffed green olives

1. Shake chicken with flour in paper bag to coat well. Brown, a few pieces at a time, in salad oil in large frying pan; drain.
2. Place rice in a 10-cup shallow baking dish; arrange browned chicken on top.
3. Stir water into chicken drippings in frying pan; blend in Spanish-rice–seasoning mix; heat to boiling. Pour over chicken and rice; cover.
4. Bake in moderate oven (350°) 30 minutes; uncover and lay green-pepper rings and olives on top. Cover and bake 30 minutes longer, or until chicken and rice are tender, and liquid is absorbed. Makes 8 servings.

■ LAMB CASSOULET

2 to 4 pounds stewing lamb
2 teaspoons salt (for lamb)
1 pound (2 cups) dried marrow beans
1 cup grated raw carrots
¼ pound salami, cut in ½-inch cubes
8 slices bacon, diced
1 large onion, chopped (1 cup)
1 clove of garlic, minced
1 can (about 1 pound) tomatoes
1 bay leaf
½ teaspoon leaf savory
½ teaspoon salt

1. Combine lamb and 2 teaspoons salt with cold

water to cover in large kettle. Cover; heat to boiling, then simmer 1 hour, or until lamb is tender.

2. Remove meat from broth and let cool until easy to handle. Strain broth into 4-cup measure; let stand until fat rises to top; skim off fat. Add water to broth, if needed, to make 4 cups. (Save broth for Step 4.)

3. Pick over meat, discarding fat and bones; dice meat; cover; chill.

4. Combine beans and saved broth in large kettle; cover; heat to boiling; cook 2 minutes. Remove from heat; let stand 1 hour. (All this can be done ahead, if you like.)

5. When ready to finish dish, reheat beans to boiling; stir in carrots and salami; cover. Cook 1 hour, or until skins of beans burst when you blow on a few in a spoon.

6. Saute bacon until crisp in large frying pan; remove and drain on paper toweling. Pour drippings into cup; return 2 tablespoonfuls to frying pan. Add onion and garlic; saute just until soft.

7. Stir in tomatoes, seasonings, lamb, and bacon; heat to boiling; stir into beans in kettle. Pour into 16-cup baking dish; cover.

8. Bake in slow oven (325°) 2 hours; uncover;

if mixture seems dry, add a little water. Bake 1 hour longer, or until beans are tender; remove bay leaf before serving. Makes 8 servings.

■ DIXIE DANDY

1 can (1 pound) applesauce
⅛ teaspoon ground ginger
1 can (12 ounces) pork luncheon meat
  Whole cloves
1 can (about 1 pound) sweet potatoes
½ cup apricot jam
½ teaspoon dry mustard
1 tablespoon water

1. Mix applesauce and ginger in shallow 6-cup baking dish.

2. Halve meat lengthwise, then cut each half in 12 squares almost through to bottom; stud squares with cloves. Place on top of applesauce in dish. Slice sweet potatoes and arrange around meat.

3. Combine remaining ingredients in 1-cup measure; spread mixture evenly over meat and potatoes.

4. Bake in hot oven (400°) 30 minutes, or until hot and richly glazed. Makes 4 servings.

Dixie Dandy is a dream of a fast-fix dinner dish, for everything that goes into it—luncheon meat, sweet potatoes, applesauce—even the apricot-jam glaze—comes right from your pantry shelf

■ PARTY LASAGNA

1 pound ground beef
1 medium-size onion, chopped (½ cup)
1 clove of garlic, minced
1 can (about 2 pounds) Italian tomatoes
1 can (6 ounces) tomato paste
¼ cup water
¼ cup chopped celery
2 tablespoons chopped parsley
2 teaspoons salt
1 teaspoon sugar
½ teaspoon mixed Italian herbs
   OR: ½ teaspoon basil
1 bay leaf
1 pound lasagna noodles
1 tablespoon salad oil
2 cups (1 pound) ricotta cheese
   OR: 2 cups (1 pound) cottage cheese
2 packages (8 ounces each) sliced
    mozzarella or pizza cheese
½ cup grated Parmesan cheese

1. Make sauce: Press ground beef into large patty in kettle; brown 5 minutes on each side; break up into chunks; push to one side.
2. Add onion and garlic; saute 2 minutes, or just until soft; stir in tomatoes, tomato paste, water, celery, parsley, and seasonings.
3. Heat to boiling, then simmer, stirring often, 1 hour, or until thick; remove bay leaf. (Sauce may be made ahead, if you wish, then covered and chilled.)
4. While sauce simmers, cook noodles: Slide lasagna noodles, a few at a time so as not to break, into a large kettle of boiling water; add salad oil, and salt, following label directions. (Oil keeps noodles from sticking.) Cook, stirring often with a wooden spoon, 15 minutes, or just until tender. (Do not overcook.) Drain; cover with cold water.
5. Line bottom of a lightly oiled baking dish, 13x9x2, with single layer of drained noodles. (Lift each strip separately from water with slotted spoon and hold over kettle to drain.) Cover with a third each of sauce, ricotta cheese or cottage cheese, mozzarella or pizza cheese, and Parmesan cheese. Repeat to make 3 layers of each, ending with Parmesan cheese.
6. Bake in moderate oven (350°) 30 minutes, or until bubbly-hot. Let set on top of range for 10 minutes, then cut into 8 equal-size servings. Lift out with wide spatula. Makes 8 servings.

■ MACARONI FAVORITE

1 package (8 ounces) elbow macaroni
1 small onion, grated
2 tablespoons butter or margarine
2 tablespoons flour
1½ teaspoons dry mustard
1 teaspoon salt
¼ teaspoon pepper
1½ teaspoons Worcestershire sauce
1¾ cups milk
1 package (8 ounces) sliced Cheddar cheese
1 can (3 or 4 ounces) sliced mushrooms
2 pimientos, diced
3 wedges of ripe tomato, halved
   Melted butter or margarine

1. Cook macaroni in boiling salted water in large saucepan, following label directions; drain; keep hot for Step 3.
2. While macaroni cooks, saute onion lightly in butter or margarine in medium-size frying pan. Stir in flour, mustard, salt, pepper, and Worcestershire sauce; cook, stirring all the time, just until mixture bubbles. Stir in milk slowly; continue cooking and stirring until sauce thickens and boils 1 minute. Stir in half the cheese until melted. (Save remaining for Step 4.)
3. Combine drained macaroni, mushrooms and liquid, and pimientos in buttered shallow 8-cup baking dish; pour cheese sauce over.
4. Arrange tomato wedges in a double row on top of macaroni. Cut saved cheese slices in strips; arrange around tomatoes.
5. Bake in moderate oven (350°) 20 minutes; brush tomatoes with melted butter or margarine. Bake 10 minutes longer, or until cheese melts and bubbles. Makes 6 servings.

Nothing quite matches baked macaroni-and-cheese ▶ in popularity, and here our **Macaroni Favorite** takes a fancy turn with big rosy tomato wedges poking through a melty golden cheese topper

VEGETABLES

■ GOLDEN SQUASH

8 small yellow squashes
1 small onion, grated
4 tablespoons (½ stick) butter or margarine
½ teaspoon salt
¼ teaspoon pepper

1. Wash and trim squashes, then slice crosswise about ¼ inch thick.
2. Saute with onion in butter or margarine in large frying pan, turning carefully so as not to break rounds, 5 to 7 minutes.
3. Sprinkle with salt and pepper; cover pan; cook over low heat, without stirring, 3 to 4 minutes longer, or just until squash is crisply tender.
4. Spoon into heated serving bowl; sprinkle with finely chopped parsley, if you wish. Makes 8 servings.

■ BRAISED ENDIVE

6 small stalks Belgian endive
1 tablespoon lemon juice
½ teaspoon salt
3 tablespoons butter or margarine

1. Wash and trim endive; halve each stalk lengthwise; arrange in single layer in large frying pan.
2. Pour in water just to cover spears. (This is important to keep them white during cooking.) Add lemon juice and salt; cover.
3. Heat to boiling, then simmer 10 minutes, or just until tender when pierced with a fork.
4. Lift out stalks carefully with a slotted spoon; place in heated serving dish. Drain liquid from pan.
5. Add butter or margarine and heat slowly, shaking pan continuously, just until butter bubbles up. (Watch closely, so it doesn't turn too brown.) Pour at once over endive. Makes 4 servings.

■ CELERY PEAS

1 can (about 1 pound) peas
1½ cups diced celery
½ teaspoon sugar
½ teaspoon salt
⅛ teaspoon pepper

1. Drain liquid from peas into medium-size saucepan; add celery. Heat to boiling; cover; cook 5 minutes. Uncover; cook 5 minutes longer, or until liquid is almost completely evaporated.
2. Stir in peas and seasonings; heat slowly, without stirring, just until bubbly-hot. Makes 6 servings.

SALADS

■ TRIPLE MELON SALAD

1 wedge (about 2 pounds) watermelon
Leaf lettuce
½ cantaloupe, pared and sliced
3 cups honeydew melon balls (about ½ large melon)
1 lime, cut into wedges
Fresh mint
Golden Dressing (recipe follows)

1. Pare green skin and rind from watermelon; slice pink meat into triangles.
2. Stand triangles on lettuce-lined salad plates with cantaloupe slices and honeydew balls, dividing evenly.
3. Garnish each with a lime wedge and sprig of mint; serve with GOLDEN DRESSING. Makes 6 servings.

GOLDEN DRESSING—Combine ¼ cup lime juice, ¼ cup honey, ¼ cup salad oil, ½ teaspoon celery seeds, ¼ teaspoon dry mustard, and a dash of salt in jar with tight-fitting lid; shake well to mix. Chill; shake again just before serving. Makes ¾ cup.

■ HOT BROCCOLI SALAD

1 bunch (about 2 pounds) broccoli
1 tablespoon olive oil or salad oil
1 tablespoon lemon juice
1 teaspoon sugar
½ teaspoon salt
⅛ teaspoon pepper

1. Trim and discard outer leaves and tough ends of broccoli; pare and split thick stalks. Cut stalks and flowerets into 2-inch lengths.
2. Arrange stalks on bottom, flowerets on top, in 1-inch depth of slightly salted water in large saucepan. Cook, covered, 15 minutes, or just until crisply tender; drain well.
3. Combine olive oil or salad oil, lemon juice, sugar, salt, and pepper in a cup; pour over hot broccoli; toss lightly to coat well. Serve hot. Makes 8 servings.

■ ONION-RADISH-RING SALAD

1 small head of Boston or leaf lettuce
¼ pound fresh tender spinach, stems removed
½ sweet red onion, sliced and separated into rings
6 radishes, sliced
¼ cup bottled thin French dressing

1. Tear lettuce and spinach into bite-size pieces; place in salad bowl. Top with onion rings and sliced radishes.
2. Pour French dressing over; toss lightly until greens and vegetables are well-coated. Makes 4 servings.

DESSERTS

■ MOCHA DRINK-A-DESSERT

4 tablespoons instant coffee
4 cups cold milk
1 teaspoon grated orange rind
1 pint chocolate ice cream
¼ cup whipping cream, whipped
   Cinnamon-sugar

1. Dissolve coffee in milk in large pitcher; stir in orange rind.
2. Pour into 6 tall glasses; float a scoop of ice cream on each. Top with a spoonful of whipped cream; sprinkle with cinnamon-sugar. Makes 6 servings.

■ LEMON MERINGUE PIE

1 nine-inch pastry shell
1¾ cups sugar (for filling)
4 tablespoons cornstarch
4 tablespoons flour
¼ teaspoon salt
2 cups water
4 eggs
1 teaspoon grated lemon rind
½ cup lemon juice (about 4 lemons)
2 tablespoons butter or margarine
¼ teaspoon lemon extract
½ cup sugar (for meringue)

1. Prepare and bake pastry shell, using packaged piecrust mix or your own favorite one-crust recipe. Cool.
2. Combine 1¾ cups sugar, cornstarch, flour, and salt in medium-size bowl; stir to mix.
3. Heat water to boiling in medium-size saucepan. Lower heat to medium; gradually add sugar mixture, stirring constantly with wire whisk or spoon. Cook, stirring constantly, 5 to 7 minutes, or until mixture holds a line when cut with spoon; remove from heat at once. (Do not let mixture boil.)
4. Separate eggs, putting whites in medium-size bowl, yolks in small bowl. Beat egg yolks slightly with a fork; stir in a generous ½ cup of hot mixture; quickly stir back into mixture in saucepan. Cook, stirring constantly, over medium heat 3 minutes, or until mixture thickens again and mounds softly; remove from heat.
5. Stir in lemon rind and juice, and butter or margarine until completely blended; pour into pastry shell.
6. Beat egg whites with lemon extract until foamy-white and double in volume; beat in ½ cup sugar, 1 tablespoon at a time, until meringue forms soft peaks. Pile on filling, spreading to edge of crust. (This keeps meringue from shrinking.)
7. Bake in moderate oven (350°) 12 minutes,

or until golden. Cool 4 to 5 hours before cutting. Makes 1 nine-inch pie.

■ BLUEBERRY TURNOVERS

1 package piecrust mix
1 can (1 pound, 4 ounces) blueberry-pie filling
¼ teaspoon mace
1 tablespoon milk
2 teaspoons sugar

1. Prepare piecrust mix, following label directions, or make two-crust pastry from your own favorite two-crust recipe. Roll out to a rectangle, 18x12, on lightly floured pastry cloth or board; cut into 6 six-inch squares.
2. Combine blueberry-pie filling and mace in small bowl. Spoon a scant ¼ cupful into middle of each square. Fold dough over to make a triangle; press edges together firmly with fork to seal; prick tops to let steam escape.
3. Brush tops with milk; sprinkle lightly with sugar. Place on cooky sheet.
4. Bake in hot oven (400°) 20 minutes, or until golden. Remove from cooky sheet at once; cool slightly on wire rack. Serve warm. Makes 6 servings.

Note: Use any leftover filling as a topping for ice cream or warm cake.

NICE TO ADD

■ CELERY CHIP ROLLS

6 brown 'n' serve club rolls
4 tablespoons (½ stick) butter or margarine
   Celery salt

1. Split rolls; spread with butter or margarine, then sprinkle lightly with celery salt.
2. Arrange, not touching each other, on ungreased cooky sheet.
3. Bake in moderate oven (350°) 25 minutes, or until crisply golden. Serve piping-hot. Makes 1 dozen.

■ CHEDDAR PUFFS

2 cups biscuit mix
½ cup grated Cheddar cheese (half a 4-ounce package)
¾ cup milk
   Paprika

1. Combine biscuit mix and cheese in medium-size bowl; stir in milk. Mix, following label directions for biscuits.
2. Spoon into greased muffin-pan cups; sprinkle lightly with paprika.
3. Bake in hot oven (400°) 15 minutes, or until golden. Serve hot. Makes 12 puffs.

WARM-WEATHER cooking calls for a big inviting meal-in-a-bowl salad—bright enough to tempt appetites, hearty enough to satisfy them. And the kinds you can concoct seem almost endless.

Cooked meats and cold cuts; fresh and canned fish; all kinds of cheeses; vegetables, both cooked and raw; fruits; macaroni, rice, and the bean family—all take to salad-bowl fixing like a breeze.

The perfect salad, of course, begins with your choice of cool, crisp, glistening greens. We've pictured favorites

Be a salad artist

(pages 62-63) and included tips *(page 67)* on how to turn them into best-ever salads.

The right dressing is important, too, for it's the prime seasoner of your dish. And what variety: Make-your-own, seasoning mixes to fix in a shake, and the bottled ready-to-use kinds.

In these salad menus you'll find hearty chef and cheese bowls that men especially like, popular chicken and tuna, and make-ahead potato and bean combinations that take well to picnicking. With each are ideas for hot bread, dessert, and beverage refresher to round out the meal.

Western Chef's Salad *(recipe on page 59)* with ▶ its sprinkle-on topper of pine nuts and wheat germ is keyed to a man's taste. Little loaves of bread are made the easy way with a mix

Plan dinner around a big bowl salad

	MAIN DISH	GO-WITHS • BREAD	DESSERT	NICE TO ADD
HEARTY WITH MEAT AND CHEESE (*pictured on page 57*)	★Western Chef's Salad	★Dill Dressing ★Your-own Salad Bread	Strawberry Sundaes ★Sugar Sparklers	Hot Coffee

Lots of meat, cheese, and crisp vegetables slant this big bowl salad to a man's taste. Fix everything ahead, wrap, and chill, if you like, then toss just before serving with enough dressing to coat—not drench—the greens. To go along, try these midget loaves of bread made with hot-roll mix. Everybody gets his own to slice and butter

	MAIN DISH	GO-WITHS • BREAD	DESSERT	NICE TO ADD
CHICKEN WITH A TWIST	★Royal Chicken Salad	★Creamy Boiled Dressing ★Corn-bacon Sticks	★Saucy Apple Dumplings	Jellied Madrilène Buttered Peas Chocolate Milk

While chicken salad makes good eating any time, this version calls for several summery flavor touches. First simmer a stewing chicken, cut up, and let season in a boiled curry dressing. At serving time toss with cantaloupe, grapes, and crunchy almonds. For a refreshing starter, chill madrilene until firm enough to spoon up

	MAIN DISH	GO-WITHS • BREAD	DESSERT	NICE TO ADD
RATES HIGH WITH MEN (*pictured on page 60*)	★Caesar Salad	★Hot Steak Bunwiches	★Orange Fruit-cup Frosty	Iced Coffee

No salad chapter would be complete without one dinner planned around this classic. And with husky steak sandwiches, it's a man's idea of a perfect meal. For beef, choose flank (a snap to carve, for it's all meat) and broil it quickly to keep in all its savory juices. Only other go-withs needed are a simple dessert and beverage

	MAIN DISH	GO-WITHS • BREAD	DESSERT	NICE TO ADD
ALL-AMERICAN WINNER	★Picnic Potato Salad ★Stuffed-egg Daisies	Sliced Bologna ★Zippy Rye-bread Stacks	★Tutti-frutti Parfaits	Milk

Most popular of all summer choices for eating indoors or out—that's potato salad and cold meat. For attractive serving, mound salad in a bowl (recipe tells how), then circle with tomatoes and stuffed eggs. Make rye-bread stacks ahead, wrap, and chill until serving time. Dessert is ice-cream cones heaped with frozen fruit cream

	MAIN DISH	GO-WITHS • BREAD	DESSERT	NICE TO ADD
DIFFERENT WAY WITH COLD CUTS (*pictured on page 64*)	★Cornucopia Salad Bowl	★Grilled Cheese Sandwiches	★Heavenly Plum Kuchen	Dill Pickles Lemonade

For variety, convenience, good eating, and thrift, it's hard to beat cold cuts. Here sliced salami rolled into cone shapes tops a big salad of sweet corn, hominy, and other vegetables in a nippy dressing. With it, serve melty cheese sandwiches "grilled" in the oven—an easy way to fix lots. Plum dessert's just plain heavenly. Do try it

	MAIN DISH	GO-WITHS • BREAD	DESSERT	NICE TO ADD
VERSATILE TUNA IS THE STAR	★Marine Salad Bowl	Fresh Tomato Wedges ★Caraway-butter Roll-ups	★Angel Crumb Pie	Iced Tea

Chunks of tuna mixed with mild-flavor yellow squash and tangy green olives in a coleslaw dressing, then topped with slices of hard-cooked egg, make this hearty salad headliner. With tomato wedges and crusty rolls—the refrigerated kind for easy baking—it's a quick-fix main course. Finish with lemon pie—this one is scrumptious!

MAIN DISHES

■ WESTERN CHEF'S SALAD

8 cups broken mixed salad greens
   (romaine and iceberg lettuce)
½ pound sliced smoked beef tongue, cut in
   thin strips
¼ pound sliced process American cheese, cut in
   thin strips
¼ pound sliced process Swiss cheese, cut in
   thin strips
1 small green pepper, cut in thin rings
1 small sweet red pepper, cut in thin rings
1 small cucumber, pared and sliced
10 radishes, sliced thin
6 cauliflowerets, sliced thin
6 thin slices Bermuda onion, separated into rings
½ cup pitted ripe olives
2 tablespoons wheat germ (from a 12-ounce jar)
2 tablespoons pine nuts (also called pignolia)
   Dill Dressing *(recipe follows)*

1. Fill a large salad bowl with mixed greens.
   Sprinkle most of the sliced tongue, cheeses,
   peppers, cucumber, radishes, cauliflower,
   onion rings, and olives over; toss lightly.
   Arrange remaining on top of salad.
2. Just before serving, sprinkle wheat germ
   and pine nuts over salad; toss with DILL
   DRESSING. Makes 6 servings.
DILL DRESSING—Combine 1 teaspoon sugar, 1
teaspoon salt, ¼ teaspoon pepper, 1 teaspoon
chopped fresh dill, ½ cup salad oil or olive oil,
and 3 tablespoons wine vinegar or cider vinegar
in a small jar with tight-fitting cover; shake to
mix well. Makes about ¾ cup. If dressing is
served at the table in a fancy bottle, add a frond
or two of fresh dill.

■ ROYAL CHICKEN SALAD

1 stewing chicken (about 5 pounds), not cut up
3½ cups water
2 teaspoons salt
6 peppercorns
   Handful of celery tops
1 carrot, scraped and sliced
   Creamy Boiled Dressing *(recipe follows)*
1½ cups cantaloupe cubes
1 cup halved green grapes
1 cup thinly sliced celery
½ cup slivered almonds
1 head of Boston or leaf lettuce
   Paprika

1. Simmer chicken in water with salt, peppercorns, celery tops, and carrot in kettle,
   covered, 1½ to 2 hours, or until tender.
2. Remove from broth and let cool just until
   easy to handle. (Strain broth and save for
   soup for another meal.) Slip skin from
   chicken; remove meat from bones in large

chunks and cut into cubes. (You should have
about 4 cups.)
3. Place chicken in medium-size bowl; toss with
   just enough CREAMY BOILED DRESSING to coat
   well; cover; chill.
4. When ready to serve, stir cantaloupe, grapes,
   celery, and almonds into chicken mixture;
   toss with enough of remaining dressing to
   coat well.
5. Line a salad bowl with lettuce; spoon salad
   in center; sprinkle with paprika. Makes 6
   servings.
CREAMY BOILED DRESSING—Combine 2 tablespoons sugar, 1 tablespoon flour, ½ teaspoon
salt, and ¼ teaspoon curry powder in small
saucepan; stir in 1 egg, beaten; ½ cup water;
and ¼ cup cider vinegar. Cook slowly, stirring
constantly, 5 minutes, or until thick. Remove
from heat; stir in 1 tablespoon butter or margarine until melted. (This dressing keeps well in
a tightly covered jar in the refrigerator.)
Makes ¾ cup.

◄ **Caesar Salad** is the all-time favorite of salad-making show-offs. Into the bowl first goes the dressing, then greens cleaned with loving care and extras of your choice. The grand finale—tossing. Recipe tells how

■ CAESAR SALAD

4 tablespoons olive oil or salad oil
3 tablespoons wine vinegar or cider vinegar
2 tablespoons lemon juice
1 clove of garlic, minced
1 teaspoon salt
⅛ teaspoon coarsely ground pepper
1 large head of romaine
1 egg
¼ cup freshly grated Parmesan cheese
1 can anchovies
1½ cups Crisp Croutons (recipe follows)

1. Combine olive oil or salad oil, wine vinegar or cider vinegar, lemon juice, garlic, salt, and pepper in the bottom of a large salad bowl.
2. Separate romaine leaves; wash and dry well. (This is important so moisture will not dilute dressing.) Cut out any coarse ribs; then break leaves in bite-size pieces into bowl. (You should have about 12 cups.)
3. Place egg in boiling water in small saucepan; cover; remove from heat and let stand for 1 minute to coddle. Remove from water at once.
4. Top greens with Parmesan cheese and anchovies (more or less to suit your taste, for they are salty); break coddled egg over all.
5. Toss salad with servers, spooning from bottom of bowl each time, until greens are evenly coated with dressing. Sprinkle with CRISP CROUTONS; toss to coat well. Serve at once. Makes 6 servings.

CRISP CROUTONS—Cut 3 slices slightly dry bread into small cubes; spread in a single layer in a shallow baking pan. Bake in slow oven (300°) 15 minutes, or until crisply golden. Makes 1½ cups.

■ PICNIC POTATO SALAD

6 large potatoes, cooked, peeled, and cut into small cubes
3 hard-cooked eggs, shelled and chopped
¾ cup chopped dill pickles
¾ cup sliced radishes
½ cup chopped green onions
1 teaspoon salt
¼ teaspoon pepper
1¼ cups mayonnaise or salad dressing
1 head of chicory or curly endive
Stuffed-egg Daisies (recipe follows)
Cherry tomatoes

1. Combine potatoes, eggs, pickles, radishes, green onions, salt, and pepper in large bowl. Stir in mayonnaise or salad dressing, mixing with a spoon until thoroughly blended. (Mixture will be moist.) Chill at least 2 hours to blend and mellow flavors.
2. When ready to put salad together, break chicory or endive into bite-size pieces in large salad bowl; mound potato salad into a cone on top. (It will pat quickly into shape with 2 spoons.) Surround the cone with STUFFED-EGG DAISIES and cherry tomatoes. Makes 6 servings.

To carry to a picnic: Cover lightly with transparent wrap or foil. Or cover, then set bowl in a shallow box and pack crumpled paper around it to hold it steady.

STUFFED-EGG DAISIES

Hard-cook and shell 6 eggs. Halve crosswise, or make "daisy" design this way: Holding each shelled egg upright, draw a guideline around middle with tip of knife, then make even sawtooth cuts into egg above and below the line all the way around. Carefully pull halves apart. Remove yolks and mash in small bowl. Blend in 2 tablespoons mayonnaise or salad dressing, 1 teaspoon prepared mustard, and salt and pepper to taste. Place a small stuffed green olive in each egg-white half, then fill with yolk mixture; chill. Makes 6 servings.

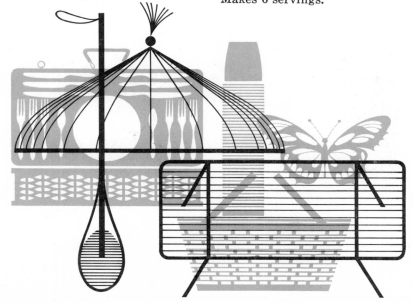

Know your salad greens

1. **CHINESE CABBAGE**—Long frilly leaves. Shred or chop
2. **GREEN CABBAGE**—Familiar choice for slaw
3. **SPINACH**—Vitamin-rich, delightfully fresh-flavored
4. **RADISHES**—A spring garden first—crisp and mildly bitey
5. **RED CABBAGE**—Also called "purple." Ideal for slaw

6. **BIBB LETTUCE**—Tiny head with deep green leaves
7. **MUSHROOMS**—Slice raw into salad for gourmet touch
8. **GREEN ONIONS**—Also called scallions. They're nippy
9. **ICEBERG, or HEAD, LETTUCE**—Great favorite—cuts neatly
10. **WATER CRESS**—Peppy and pungent

Favorites are all here, from frilly soft-leaf Boston lettuce to chunky crisp iceberg. Mix them up in your salad bowl, for a contrast of two greens is good; three, even better. When you shop, look for these leaders

11. BOSTON, or BUTTER, LETTUCE—Head resembles a rose
12. ENDIVE—Grown in Belgium. Try slicing the delicate stalks
13. PARSLEY—A perfect mixer, refreshingly mild. Chop or cut
14. ROMAINE—Long crisp green leaves—a salad-bowl winner
15. SALAD, or LEAF, LETTUCE—Pale green ruffly leaves

16. RED ONIONS—Sweet and mild with a purple tinge. Sometimes displayed braided, rope-style
17. DILL—Fragile, feathery herb with a subtle flavor. Chop it
18. ESCAROLE—Crisp curly-leaf head. A good buy
19. CHICORY, or CURLY, ENDIVE—Feathery, mildly bitter

■ CORNUCOPIA SALAD BOWL

2 cans (16 ounces each) hominy, drained
1 can (12 or 16 ounces) whole-kernel corn, drained
1 cup diced celery
½ cup sliced green onions
6 tablespoons bottled thin French dressing
½ teaspoon salt
¼ teaspoon pepper
1 package frozen Italian green beans
1 head of Boston or leaf lettuce
½ cup prepared sandwich spread
1 package (8 ounces) sliced salami

1. Combine hominy, corn, celery, green onions, 4 tablespoons of the French dressing, salt, and pepper in large bowl; toss well to mix; chill.
2. Cook green beans, following label directions; drain. Combine in small bowl with remaining 2 tablespoons French dressing; chill.
3. When ready to serve, line a large shallow bowl with lettuce; shred any remaining and place in bottom of bowl. Stir sandwich spread into hominy mixture; mound on top of shredded lettuce.
4. Fold salami slices into cornucopia shapes, fastening with wooden picks; arrange in a circle on top. Pile marinated green beans in center; garnish with a twist of pimiento, if you wish. Makes 6 servings.

◀ Sweet golden corn and snowy hominy seasoned brightly are the starter vegetables for this **Cornucopia Salad Bowl.** Big cones of spicy salami, centered with tangy green beans, add a colorful top

■ MARINE SALAD BOWL

2 cans (about 7 ounces each) tuna, drained and flaked
1 cup chopped raw yellow squash
½ cup sliced stuffed green olives
½ cup bottled coleslaw dressing
1 head of escarole
3 hard-cooked eggs, sliced

1. Combine tuna, squash, olives, and dressing in medium-size bowl; toss to coat well. Cover; chill.
2. When ready to serve, shred escarole; place in a salad bowl. Pile tuna mixture in middle; top with egg slices. Makes 6 servings.

GO-WITHS • BREADS

■ YOUR-OWN SALAD BREAD

¼ cup grated Parmesan cheese
2 tablespoons chopped chives
1 package hot-roll mix
1 egg
2 tablespoons melted butter or margarine

1. Stir cheese and chives into hot-roll mix in medium-size bowl. Prepare with egg, following label directions for richer dough. Knead; let rise; knead again. Shape into 14 balls, following label directions.
2. Place 2 balls each in 7 buttered toy-size loaf pans, 5x3x2. Let rise in warm place away from draft 30 minutes, or until double in bulk; brush with butter or margarine.
3. Bake in moderate oven (375°) 20 minutes, or until golden-brown.
Note: If you do not have these toy-size loaf pans, shape dough into 15 balls and arrange in 3 rows of 5 balls each in buttered shallow baking pan, 13x9x2. When baked, break rolls apart. Makes 7 small loaves or 15 rolls.

■ CORN-BACON STICKS

1 package corn-muffin mix
3 slices crisp bacon

1. Prepare corn-muffin mix, following label directions. Crumble bacon fine and fold in.
2. Spoon into well-buttered small corn-stick pans to fill about half full. (It'll take about 1 teaspoonful for each.) Or use well-buttered small muffin-pan cups.
3. Bake in moderate oven (350°) 15 to 20 minutes, or until golden. Serve piping-hot. Makes about 3 dozen.

■ HOT STEAK BUNWICHES

1 flank steak (about 2 pounds)
  Salt and pepper
12 buttered, toasted, split round buns

1. Make shallow diagonal cuts 1 inch apart on one side of steak (to keep meat from curling). Place, scored side down, on broiler rack.
2. Broil, following range manufacturer's directions, 3 minutes; turn; broil 3 to 4 minutes longer for rare. Season with salt and pepper; cut at once on the diagonal into thin slices. (If meat has to stand, keep slices close together, like uncut steak, to hold in juices.)
3. Fold each slice in half; pop into a split hot bun. Makes 6 servings, 2 buns each.

■ ZIPPY RYE-BREAD STACKS

¾ cup (1½ sticks) butter or margarine
6 tablespoons prepared horseradish
18 slices rye bread (about 1 loaf)

1. Cream butter or margarine with horseradish in small bowl. Spread generously on 12 slices bread; leave remaining 6 slices plain.
2. Stack each 2 buttered slices, spread side up; top with plain slice. Cut each into thirds. Makes 18 stacks.

■ GRILLED CHEESE SANDWICHES

½ cup (1 stick) butter or margarine, melted
12 slices white bread
12 slices process American cheese (about ¾ pound)

1. Line a large cooky sheet with clean brown paper; brush with part of the melted butter or margarine.
2. Lay 6 slices bread in single layer on buttered paper; top each with 2 slices cheese and another slice bread; cut in half. Brush tops with remaining melted butter or margarine.
3. Bake in very hot oven (475°) 5 minutes, or until tops are golden-brown and cheese is melted. Serve piping hot. Makes 6 servings.

■ CARAWAY-BUTTER ROLL-UPS

3 tablespoons butter or margarine
1 package refrigerated plain or buttermilk biscuits
  Caraway seeds

1. Melt butter or margarine in baking pan, 8x8x2.
2. Shape each biscuit between palms of hands to make a 3-inch-long stick; roll in melted butter in pan to coat well; sprinkle with caraway seeds.
3. Bake in very hot oven (475°) about 10 minutes, or until golden-brown; serve piping hot. Makes 10.

DESSERTS

■ SUGAR SPARKLERS

    3 cups sifted flour
    1 teaspoon baking powder
    ½ teaspoon salt
    ¾ cup (1½ sticks) butter or margarine
    1 cup sugar
    2 eggs
    1 teaspoon vanilla

1. Measure flour, baking powder, and salt into sifter.
2. Cream butter or margarine with sugar until fluffy in large bowl; beat in 1 egg. Separate remaining egg and beat in yolk, then vanilla. (Save egg white for Step 4.)
3. Sift in dry ingredients, a quarter at a time, blending well to make a stiff dough. Chill 1 hour, or until firm enough to roll.
4. Divide dough into quarters; roll, one at a time to ⅛-inch thickness on greased cooky sheet. (Set cooky sheet on damp towel to keep it from slipping.) Cut into diamonds or squares with pastry wheel or sharp knife. Brush with saved slightly beaten egg white; sprinkle lightly with sugar, if you wish.
5. Bake in moderate oven (350°) 10 minutes, or until firm and shiny golden. Separate cookies carefully on cooky sheets; cool on wire racks. Makes about 6 dozen.

■ SAUCY APPLE DUMPLINGS

    1 egg
    ⅔ cup milk
    3 cups biscuit mix
    ¾ cup sugar
    1 teaspoon cinnamon
    ¼ teaspoon nutmeg
    6 medium-size tart apples, pared and cored
    6 tablespoons (¾ stick) butter or margarine
       Lemon-sugar Glaze (recipe follows)

1. Beat egg slightly with milk in 1-cup measure. Add all at once to biscuit mix in large bowl; stir just until biscuit mix is evenly moist.
2. Turn out onto lightly floured pastry cloth or board; knead lightly. Divide dough in 6 parts; roll out, one at a time, to an about-8-inch square.
3. Mix sugar, cinnamon, and nutmeg in cup. Place an apple in middle of each pastry square; fill center with spice mixture, then dot with butter or margarine, dividing evenly.
4. Fold pastry up and around apples; moisten edges, then pinch to seal. Place dumplings, not touching, in buttered baking pan, 13x9x2.
5. Bake in very hot oven (450°) 10 minutes;

remove from oven; reduce heat to moderate (350°). Brush generously with LEMON-SUGAR GLAZE; pour remaining over.
6. Bake, brushing often with syrup in pan, 40 minutes longer, or until apples are tender and pastry is richly golden. Serve warm with cream, if you wish. Makes 6 servings.

LEMON-SUGAR GLAZE—Combine 1½ cups sugar, ¼ cup light corn syrup, ½ cup water, and 2 tablespoons butter or margarine in small saucepan. Heat to boiling, then cook, stirring once or twice, 5 minutes, or until slightly thickened. Stir in 2 tablespoons lemon juice and 1 teaspoon vanilla. Makes about 1½ cups.

■ ORANGE FRUIT-CUP FROSTY

    3 tablespoons quick-cooking tapioca
    2 tablespoons sugar
       Dash of salt
 2½ cups water
    1 can (6 ounces) frozen concentrated orange juice
    1 orange, pared and sectioned
    1 banana, peeled and sliced
    ½ cup halved seedless grapes
    ½ cup sliced hulled strawberries
       OR: ½ cup fresh red raspberries
    1 tablespoon lemon juice

1. Stir tapioca, sugar, and salt into 1 cup of the water in small saucepan.
2. Heat slowly, stirring constantly, until mixture comes to a full rolling boil; pour into a medium-size bowl.
3. Stir in orange juice until melted, then remaining 1½ cups water. Cool 15 minutes; stir; cover; chill.
4. When ready to serve, stir in orange sections, banana slices, grapes, strawberries or raspberries, and lemon juice. (Mixture will be slightly thickened.) Serve in cups or glasses to eat with a spoon. Makes 6 servings.

■ ANGEL CRUMB PIE

    1 nine-inch Crumb Crust (recipe follows)
    1 envelope unflavored gelatin
    ½ teaspoon salt
    1 cup sugar
    5 eggs, separated
    ½ cup lemon juice
    ¼ cup water
    ½ teaspoon grated lemon rind

1. Make, bake, and cool CRUMB CRUST.
2. Combine gelatin and salt with ½ cup sugar in top of double boiler. (Save remaining ½ cup sugar for Step 4.) Stir in egg yolks, lemon juice, and water; beat until foamy.
3. Cook, stirring constantly, over hot, *not boiling* water, until gelatin dissolves and mixture coats a metal spoon. Remove from heat; stir in lemon rind; chill just until mixture

mounds slightly on spoon and holds its shape.

4. Beat egg whites until foamy-white and double in volume in large bowl; beat in saved ½ cup sugar, 1 tablespoon at a time, until meringue forms soft peaks. Gently fold in chilled, slightly thickened gelatin mixture.
5. Spoon into cooled crust; sprinkle lightly with 2 tablespoons saved graham-cracker–crumb mixture. (*See below.*) Chill until firm. Makes 1 nine-inch pie.

CRUMB CRUST—Mix 1 cup packaged graham-cracker crumbs, ¼ cup sugar, ⅛ teaspoon ground cardamom, and 4 tablespoons (½ stick) melted butter or margarine in small bowl. Press all but 2 tablespoons over bottom and sides of a 9-inch pie plate. (Save rest for topping.) Bake in moderate oven (350°) about 8 minutes. Cool.

■ TUTTI-FRUTTI PARFAITS

1 can (1 pound) fruit cocktail, drained
1 cup tiny marshmallows
1 cup dairy sour cream
6 cup-shape ice-cream cones

1. Combine drained fruit cocktail, marshmallows, and sour cream in medium-size bowl; stir lightly to mix.
2. Spoon into ice-cream cones; freeze several hours, or until firm. Makes 6 servings.

■ HEAVENLY PLUM KUCHEN

½ cup (1 stick) butter or margarine
1 cup sugar
1¼ cups sifted flour
½ teaspoon salt
½ teaspoon cinnamon
¼ teaspoon baking powder
1 pound fresh plums, washed, halved, and pitted
  OR:1 can (1 pound, 4 ounces) purple plums, drained and pitted
1 egg
1 cup cream for whipping

1. Cream butter or margarine and sugar in medium-size bowl.
2. Measure flour, salt, cinnamon, and baking powder into sifter; sift into creamed mixture, blending until crumbly.
3. Measure out ⅓ cup; press remaining evenly into bottom and about 1 inch up sides of an ungreased 10-inch pie plate or baking pan, 8x8x2. Arrange plum halves, rounded side up, in a single layer in shell; sprinkle with saved butter-flour mixture.
4. Bake in moderate oven (375°) 15 minutes; remove from oven, but leave heat on.
5. Beat egg slightly in small bowl; stir in cream; pour over plums. Bake 25 to 30 minutes longer, or until custard is set.
6. Cool completely on wire rack; cut into wedges or squares to serve plain or with ice cream. Makes 6 to 9 servings.

Tips for a perfect salad

Like painting, making a salad is truly an art, yet so simple with the wealth of greens and go-withs available every month of the year. When you plan a salad, consider color and mix the soft pastels of the greens with the vivid hues of fruits or vegetables. Blend flavors—tart with sweet, sharp with mild. And contrast textures—soft with crisp, raw with cooked. With these few rules in mind, you're on your way to a salad creation as inviting to look at as it is to taste.

The perfect salad begins with perfect greens. When you get them home, clean and store them this way:

• Trim stem ends and any droopy leaves. Wash solid heads under running cold water, let leafy heads soak for a few minutes or keep water running through leaves to wash away any soil or sand.

• Drain well for too much moisture not only promotes spoilage, but dilutes the dressing enough to make a soggy, rather than a crisp, salad. Before putting washed greens away, dry in either of these two ways: Wrap loosely in a clean towel and shake or pat dry. Or put them in a wire salad basket and hang to drain. *(Hint: The French stand in the open and twirl the basket high and wide.)*

• Store cleaned greens in your refrigerator vegetable crisper. Or, if the salad is to be made up soon, break leaves—don't cut with knife or scissors—into bite-size pieces and place in a bowl big enough for easy tossing. Then cover and chill for an hour or so until crisply cold. A transparent plastic bag is handy, too, for holding ready-fixed greens you plan to use the same day.

• Choose your dressing carefully. A thin French dressing goes well with a plain- or mixed-greens salad bowl, a thicker French dressing, or mayonnaise or salad dressing with fruit, fish, vegetable, or meat salads. Keep the dressing simple, or add seasoning touches your family likes best. Mixed salad herbs, crumbled blue or grated Parmesan cheese, a dash of curry powder, chopped dill pickles, or snips of spring-green chives are just a few suggestions.

• Be miserly with the dressing, adding just enough to coat and season the salad. Like too much moisture, too much dressing tends to make a heavy salad.

• Use a light touch when tossing salad, reaching well into the bottom of the bowl each time. Toss until each green leaf literally glistens and is evenly coated with dressing.

• Serve your salad as soon as it is dressed. It looks and tastes best then—crisp and inviting. Salads do not wait well.

OUR star here is fish—ready-to-cook fresh or frozen fillets and steaks, versatile canned tuna and salmon, popular shrimps and crab. Like meat, fish is a perfect source of proteins, a big booster for minerals and vitamins. It's a good mixer with potatoes, rice, and cheese—and a good buy, for it's practically all "meat." Best of all, when cooked properly, its delicate fresh flavor is hard to beat.

Today supermarkets everywhere display a selection hardly dreamed of just a few years ago. If you're a new cook, try different kinds. Learn to cook them the way you like fish when

Delicious dinners for no-meat days

you eat out. The tricks are simple to give that different flavor.

Recipes here tell how to stuff and bake a whole fish, oven-cook frozen fillets, turn shrimps into a hearty soup meal, and dress up tuna and crab into company-easy dishes. Also here are vegetable, salad, and dessert ideas to round out each menu, plus a simple guide to pan-frying and broiling fish —and lots of sauce ideas.

With fish, no-meat meals can be feature meals in your house.

◀ **Golden Fish Bake** (recipe on page 71) starts with your choice of fillets, seasoned and baked in a rich creamy sauce. To go along, plan a crisp vegetable salad and French fried potatoes

Family favorites with fish

	MAIN DISH	VEGETABLE • SALAD	DESSERT	NICE TO ADD
FRIDAY FAVORITE *(pictured on page 68)*	★Golden Fish Bake in Cream	Buttered Green Peas ★Rainbow Vegetable Salad	★Double-date Cake	French Fried Potatoes (frozen kind)
	Here, good-for-you fish "steaks" bake flaky-tender in a creamy sauce topped with golden crumbs. Buttery green peas make a pretty garnish for the dish. You can		crisp the potatoes in oven along with fish, if you wish. And for a sweet top-off, do make this date cake. It's rich-rich and keeps moist to its last scrumptious crumb	
FISHERMAN'S CATCH	★Baked Stuffed Fish	Broccoli with Pecan Butter Green Salad Bowl	★Cinnamon-blush Pears with Cream	Cream of Celery Soup Jumbo Corn Chips
	If there is a fisherman in your house, please him with this treat from his catch. Or buy about a 3-pound fish. Stuffed whole with a cheese-and-dill dressing, it bakes		beautifully tender. For vegetable, cook broccoli, then top with melty butter and a few chopped pecans. The spiced-pear dessert is a bake-easy to cook along with fish	
COMPANY-STYLE TREAT	★Deviled Tuna	Mashed Potatoes ★Apple Beets	★Five-minute Plum Whip with ★Sunshine Sauce	★Bouillon Imperial ★Dill Puffs
	This tuna dish looks pretty fancy, yet it calls for foods you are likely to have on hand, and goes together and bakes real fast. When you have some extra time, do		try these batter-type puffy dill buns. Served hot with butter, they are wonderful —will make any meal a success. Dessert, like its name, is a real quickie to make	
FANCY CREOLE FIXINGS *(pictured on page 72)*	★Mardi Gras Gumbo Fluffy Rice	★Avocado-orange Salad	★Southern Pecan Pie	Toasted Sliced French Bread
	In the style of our sunny South, this meal starts with a thick peppery tomato soup with lots of mild-flavor shrimps. Ladle around a mound of fluffy rice, then serve		with a fresh fruit salad. For a crunchy extra, butter and toast thick slices of French bread. Sweet ending? Another favorite—pecan pie. It's sheer confection!	
"MEAT LOAF" FROM THE SEA	★Gourmet Sea-food Ring	Crisp Potato Chips ★Casserole Creamed Limas	★Chocolate Nut Parfait	Marinated Mixed Vegetable Salad Hot Biscuits
	King crab and tuna, delicately seasoned and baked in a ring mold, make a pretty platter when turned out and filled with curry-creamed limas that cook alongside		mold in oven. For the salad-relish, season cooked frozen mixed vegetables with French dressing, then chill. Dessert's a fix-ahead rich fancy that holds well, too	
LET YOUR OVEN TAKE OVER	★Salmon Loaf ★Savory Egg Sauce	Mashed Potatoes ★Fruit Ring Cabbage Slaw	★Sugar-crunch Squares	Stewed Tomatoes Hot Tea
	Flavor-rich salmon can be the starter for many main-dish favorites, and this time it's made into a moist fluffy loaf to serve with creamy sauce. A ring of dainty man-		darin-orange segments crowns its cole-slaw salad partner. Bake dessert—similar to crumb cake—along with salmon, or time it to come from the oven at the last minute	

70

MAIN DISHES

■ GOLDEN FISH BAKE IN CREAM

2 packages (1 pound each) frozen cod, haddock,
   or flounder fillets
  OR: 2 pounds fresh cod, haddock, or flounder
     fillets
4 tablespoons flour
2 teaspoons salt
¼ teaspoon pepper
1 cup milk
2 cups coarse soft bread crumbs (4 slices)
4 tablespoons (½ stick) butter or margarine
1 tablespoon chopped parsley
1 cup dairy sour cream

1. Cut frozen or fresh fillets into serving-size
   pieces; coat with mixture of flour, salt, and
   pepper. Arrange in single layer in baking
   dish, 13x9x2; pour milk over.
2. Bake, uncovered, in moderate oven (350°)
   45 minutes.
3. Toast crumbs lightly in butter or margarine
   in medium-size frying pan. Stir parsley into
   sour cream. Remove fish from oven; spoon
   cream mixture over; top with toasted
   crumbs.
4. Bake 10 minutes longer, or until sour cream
   is set. Garnish with lemon slices and parsley,
   and spoon buttered hot green peas at either
   end of dish, as we did in our picture on page
   68, if you wish. Makes 6 servings.

■ BAKED STUFFED FISH

Buy 1 dressed, split, whole white fish (striped
bass, sea bass, haddock, cod, or bluefish), weighing about 3 pounds. Place half, skin side down,
in greased large shallow baking dish; spread
DILL-CHEESE STUFFING *(recipe follows)* over.
Place other half, skin side up, over stuffing;
fasten with skewers or wooden picks. Brush top
with 2 tablespoons melted butter or margarine;
sprinkle with salt and pepper. Bake in moderate
oven (350°) 1 hour, or until fish flakes easily.
Makes 4 to 6 servings.

DILL-CHEESE STUFFING—Combine 3 cups soft
bread crumbs (6 slices); 1 cup (½ pound)
cottage cheese; ½ cup chopped dill pickle; and
1 small onion, chopped (¼ cup) in medium-size
bowl. Stir in 1 slightly beaten egg, 1 teaspoon
salt, and ¼ teaspoon pepper with a fork, tossing
lightly just to mix. Makes about 3 cups.

■ DEVILED TUNA

2 tablespoons butter or margarine
2 tablespoons flour
1 teaspoon dry mustard
½ teaspoon salt
⅛ teaspoon pepper
1½ cups milk
1 tablespoon lemon juice
1 can (about 7 ounces) tuna, drained and flaked
¾ cup coarsely crumbled saltines (9 crackers)
4 hard-cooked eggs, shelled
  Parsley

1. Melt butter or margarine in medium-size
   saucepan. Stir in flour, mustard, salt, and
   pepper; cook, stirring all the time, just until
   mixture bubbles. Stir in milk slowly; continue cooking and stirring until sauce thickens and boils 1 minute.
2. Remove from heat; stir in lemon juice, tuna,
   and ½ cup cracker crumbs. (Save remaining
   crumbs and 1 egg for topping and garnish.)
3. Chop remaining 3 eggs coarsely; stir into
   tuna mixture. Pour into buttered shallow 4-
   cup baking dish or 9-inch pie plate; sprinkle
   saved ¼ cup cracker crumbs over top.
4. Bake in moderate oven (350°) 20 minutes,
   or until crumbs are golden. Quarter saved
   egg lengthwise; arrange on top to form a
   petal design; center with a sprig of parsley.
   Makes 4 servings.

◄ Shrimps, clams, and tomatoes blend invitingly here in **Mardi Gras Gumbo**, a thick peppery soup to serve around snowy rice. Rest of meal: Crusty bread, orange-avocado salad, and pecan-rich pie

■ MARDI GRAS GUMBO

1 medium-size onion, chopped (½ cup)
1 clove of garlic, minced
4 tablespoons (½ stick) butter or margarine
2 envelopes instant vegetable broth
  OR: 2 vegetable-bouillon cubes
1 can (about 1 pound) tomatoes
1 can (about 1 pound) cut okra
1 can (about 7 ounces) minced clams
1 can (12 ounces) mixed vegetable juices
1 teaspoon salt
1 teaspoon sugar
¼ teaspoon bottled red-pepper seasoning
1 tablespoon cornstarch
½ cup cold water
2 cans (about 5 ounces each) deveined shrimps, rinsed
  Buttered hot rice

1. Saute onion and garlic in butter or margarine just until soft in kettle or large saucepan. Stir in vegetable broth or cubes, tomatoes, okra, clams, vegetable juices, and seasonings; heat to boiling; simmer for 10 minutes.
2. Blend cornstarch into water until smooth in cup; stir into soup mixture. Cook, stirring constantly, until soup thickens slightly and boils 3 minutes. Stir in shrimps; cook 2 to 3 minutes longer, or just until heated through.
3. Spoon mounds of buttered hot rice into heated soup plates or bowls; ladle hot soup around rice, dividing evenly. Makes 6 generous servings.

■ GOURMET SEA-FOOD RING

4 slices white bread, cut in ½-inch cubes
1 can (3 or 4 ounces) chopped mushrooms
1¼ cups milk
1 can (about 6 ounces) king crab meat
1 can (about 7 ounces) tuna
2 eggs
2 tablespoons chopped parsley

1. Heat bread cubes, mushrooms and liquid, and milk to scalding in small saucepan.
2. Drain and flake crab meat, removing any bony tissue. Drain and flake tuna. Combine in medium-size bowl with eggs and parsley; beat bread mixture, then blend in. Spoon into *well-greased* 5-cup ring mold.
3. Bake in moderate oven (350°) 45 minutes, or until top is firm and golden.
4. Let stand 5 to 10 minutes; turn out onto heated serving platter; fill center with CAS- SEROLE CREAMED LIMAS *(recipe on page 74)*, if you wish. Makes 6 servings.

■ SALMON LOAF

1 can (1 pound) salmon
4 tablespoons (½ stick) butter or margarine
¼ cup milk
1 cup coarsely crumbled saltines (12 crackers)
3 eggs, separated
2 tablespoons chopped parsley
1 tablespoon grated onion
1 tablespoon lemon juice
½ teaspoon Worcestershire sauce
½ teaspoon salt
⅛ teaspoon pepper
  Savory Egg Sauce *(recipe follows)*

1. Grease a loaf pan, 9x5x3. Fold a sheet of waxed paper and fit into bottom and up sides of pan, leaving a 1-inch overhang; grease paper. (Liner makes loaf easy to unmold.)
2. Drain liquid from salmon into medium-size saucepan; add butter or margarine and milk; heat just until butter melts. Stir in saltines; let stand 5 minutes.
3. Flake salmon, removing any large bones and skin; fold into crumb mixture. Beat egg yolks in small bowl; blend into salmon mixture with parsley, onion, lemon juice, Worcestershire sauce, salt, and pepper.
4. Beat egg whites just until they form soft peaks in medium-size bowl; fold into salmon mixture. Pour into prepared pan.
5. Set in shallow baking pan; place on oven shelf; pour in boiling water to depth of 1 inch.
6. Bake in moderate oven (350°) 40 minutes, or until thin-blade knife inserted in middle comes out clean.
7. Remove pan from water at once; let stand 5 minutes. Loosen loaf from sides of pan with knife, then lift up paper to loosen, and unmold onto heated platter; peel off waxed paper. Slice and serve with SAVORY EGG SAUCE. Makes 6 servings.

SAVORY EGG SAUCE—Blend ⅓ cup milk into ¾ cup mayonnaise or salad dressing in small saucepan. Heat slowly, stirring constantly, just until hot. (Do not boil.) Remove from heat; stir in 2 hard-cooked eggs, chopped, and 2 tablespoons chopped dill pickle. Makes about 1½ cups.

VEGETABLES

■ APPLE BEETS

4 large beets
1 can (8 ounces) applesauce
2 tablespoons butter or margarine
¼ teaspoon salt
¼ teaspoon nutmeg

1. Cook beets in boiling salted water in medium-size saucepan 25 minutes, or until tender. Drain; remove skins.
2. Return beets to saucepan; mash with a potato masher. Stir in applesauce, butter or margarine, salt, and nutmeg; heat just until bubbly. Makes 4 servings.

■ CASSEROLE CREAMED LIMAS

1 package (10 ounces) frozen baby lima beans
1 medium-size onion, peeled
1 large lettuce leaf
2 tablespoons butter or margarine
¼ teaspoon curry powder
1 can condensed cream of mushroom soup

1. Place frozen limas in 4-cup baking dish; grate onion over; top with lettuce leaf; cover.
2. Bake in moderate oven (350°) 45 minutes.
3. Remove lettuce; stir in butter or margarine and curry powder, then soup. Return to oven; bake 15 minutes longer, or until bubbly-hot. Makes 6 servings.

SALADS

■ RAINBOW VEGETABLE SALAD

6 cups broken mixed salad greens (lettuce, romaine, escarole)
1 cup drained sliced pickled beets (from a 1-pound jar)
2 medium-size carrots, scraped and grated
Bottled blue-cheese dressing

1. Place salad greens in a large salad bowl. Make a ring of beets, overlapping, in center; fill with a cone of grated carrots.
2. When ready to serve, toss with salad dressing. Makes 6 servings.

■ AVOCADO-ORANGE SALAD

1 small head of iceberg lettuce
1 medium-size ripe avocado, peeled and sliced
3 oranges, pared and sectioned
1 small onion, sliced thin and separated into rings
Celery-seed Dressing (recipe follows)

1. Line 6 small salad bowls with lettuce leaves; break remaining into bite-size pieces, dividing evenly among bowls.
2. Arrange avocado slices, orange sections, and onion rings on top. Drizzle each with about 1 tablespoon CELERY-SEED DRESSING. Pass extra dressing, if you like. Makes 6 servings.
CELERY-SEED DRESSING—Combine 1 teaspoon grated onion, ½ teaspoon salt, ½ teaspoon dry mustard, ½ teaspoon paprika, ½ teaspoon celery seeds, ½ cup salad oil, ¼ cup light corn syrup, and 3 tablespoons vinegar in jar with tight-fitting cover. Shake to blend, then shake again just before serving. Makes about 1 cup.

■ FRUIT RING CABBAGE SLAW

8 cups finely chopped cabbage (about 2 pounds)
2 tablespoons sugar
2 tablespoons lemon juice
¼ teaspoon salt
⅛ teaspoon pepper
2 tablespoons mayonnaise or salad dressing
2 tablespoons cream
1 can (about 11 ounces) mandarin-orange segments, drained

1. Toss cabbage with sugar in large bowl; chill 30 minutes, or until serving time.
2. Sprinkle lemon juice, salt, and pepper over. Blend mayonnaise or salad dressing and cream in a cup; stir into cabbage mixture.
3. Spoon into serving bowl; top with a ring of mandarin-orange segments; sprinkle with paprika, if you wish. Makes 6 servings.

DESSERTS

■ DOUBLE-DATE CAKE

1 package (8 ounces) pitted dates
1 cup boiling water
½ cup (1 stick) butter or margarine
1 cup sugar
1 teaspoon vanilla
1 egg
1⅔ cups sifted flour
1 teaspoon baking soda
¼ teaspoon salt
½ cup chopped pecans
Date Frosting (recipe follows)

1. Grease baking pan, 8x8x2; line bottom with waxed paper; grease paper.
2. Chop dates. (Kitchen scissors do a quick job.) Combine with boiling water, butter or margarine, sugar, and vanilla in medium-size heavy saucepan; heat to boiling. Cook, stirring constantly, 10 minutes, or until mixture thickens slightly. Remove from heat; cool.
3. Beat egg in small bowl; blend into cooled date mixture.
4. Sift flour, baking soda, and salt into date mixture, a little at a time, blending well; stir in pecans. Pour batter into prepared pan.
5. Bake in moderate oven (350°) 1 hour, or until top springs back when lightly pressed with fingertip. Remove from oven; while still hot, spread with DATE FROSTING.
6. Cool completely in pan, then cut into small squares, for it's real rich. Serve plain, or top with a spoonful of whipped cream, if you like. Makes 1 eight-inch square cake.

DATE FROSTING—Chop 1 package (8 ounces) pitted dates. Combine with 1 cup boiling water, ½ cup (1 stick) butter or margarine, and 1 cup sugar in medium-size heavy saucepan. Cook, stirring constantly, 20 minutes, or until mixture is very thick. Remove from heat and stir in ½ cup chopped pecans. Cool to lukewarm. Makes enough to cover top of 1 eight-inch square cake. *Note:* This cake freezes perfectly, or wrap any that's left over and keep in refrigerator.

■ CINNAMON-BLUSH PEARS

6 firm ripe pears
½ cup sugar
½ cup water
1 tablespoon red cinnamon candies

1. Wash pears, leaving stems on. Pare to within 1 inch of bottom; stand in a deep baking dish.
2. Combine sugar and water in 1-cup measure; pour over pears; sprinkle with cinnamon can-

dies; stir gently to mix; cover baking dish.
3. Bake in moderate oven (350°), basting every 15 minutes with syrup in dish, 45 minutes, or until tender. Serve warm, plain or with cream. Makes 6 servings.

■ FIVE-MINUTE PLUM WHIP

2 eggs, separated
¼ teaspoon salt
¼ teaspoon cream of tartar
¼ cup sugar
1 can (about 1 pound) purple plums, drained
1 tablespoon lemon juice
Red food coloring
Sunshine Sauce (recipe follows)

1. Beat egg whites, salt, and cream of tartar until foamy-white and double in volume in medium-size bowl. (Save egg yolks for making sauce.) Beat in sugar, 1 tablespoon at a time, until meringue forms soft peaks.
2. Cut plums in small pieces, discarding pits. Beat fruit into meringue, a few pieces at a time; continue beating until meringue is stiff enough to hold its shape. Beat in lemon juice and just enough red food coloring to tint meringue a delicate pink. Spoon into sherbet glasses; top with SUNSHINE SAUCE. Makes 4 servings.

SUNSHINE SAUCE—Beat 2 egg yolks until thick and lemon-colored in small bowl. Beat in 2 tablespoons sugar, 1 tablespoon at a time, then beat in 2 tablespoons lemon juice and 2 tablespoons light or table cream. Continue beating until fluffy. Makes ½ cup.

■ SOUTHERN PECAN PIE

1 stick piecrust mix
4 eggs
1 cup sugar
½ teaspoon salt
1½ cups dark corn syrup
1 teaspoon vanilla
¼ cup flour
1 cup pecan halves

1. Prepare piecrust mix, following label directions, or make pastry from your own favorite 1-crust recipe. Roll out to a 12-inch round on lightly floured pastry cloth or board; fit into a 9-inch pie plate; trim overhang to ½ inch; turn under flush with rim; flute.
2. Beat eggs slightly in medium-size bowl; blend in sugar, salt, corn syrup, and vanilla; stir in flour. Pour into prepared shell; arrange pecan halves in circles on top.
3. Bake in moderate oven (350°) 45 minutes, or until center is almost set but still soft. (Do not overbake, for filling will set as it cools.) Cool on wire rack at least an hour before cutting. Makes 1 nine-inch pie.

■ CHOCOLATE NUT PARFAIT

½ cup (1 stick) butter or margarine
1 cup 10X (confectioners' powdered) sugar
3 eggs, separated
1½ squares unsweetened chocolate, melted
½ teaspoon vanilla
½ cup vanilla-wafer crumbs (about 10 wafers)
½ cup finely chopped walnuts

1. Cream butter or margarine with sugar until fluffy in medium-size bowl. Beat in egg yolks, 1 at a time, beating after each until mixture is thick; slowly stir in melted chocolate and vanilla.
2. Beat egg whites until they form soft peaks in medium-size bowl; fold into chocolate mixture until no streaks of white remain.
3. Combine wafer crumbs and walnuts in 1-cup measure; layer with chocolate mixture, dividing evenly, into 6 parfait glasses or custard cups. Chill several hours, or overnight. Serve plain, as it needs no topping. Makes 6 servings.

■ SUGAR-CRUNCH SQUARES

Cake
2¼ cups sifted flour
3 teaspoons baking powder
1 teaspoon salt
½ cup (1 stick) butter or margarine
1 cup sugar
1 egg
1 teaspoon vanilla
¾ cup milk
Topping
½ cup flour
½ cup sugar
¼ teaspoon cinnamon
4 tablespoons (½ stick) butter or margarine

1. Make cake: Sift flour, baking powder, and salt onto waxed paper.
2. Cream butter or margarine with sugar until fluffy in medium-size bowl; beat in egg and vanilla.
3. Blend in dry ingredients, alternately with milk, just until smooth. Pour into greased baking pan, 9x9x2.
4. Bake in moderate oven (350°) 20 minutes; remove from oven. (Leave heat on.)
5. Make topping: While cake bakes, combine flour, sugar, and cinnamon in small bowl; cut in butter or margarine with pastry blender until mixture is crumbly.
6. Sprinkle over partly baked cake; return to oven. Bake 15 minutes longer, or until golden and top springs back when lightly pressed with fingertip.
7. Cool at least 5 minutes on wire rack; cut into squares; serve oven-warm or cold. Makes 9 servings.

NICE TO ADD

■ BOUILLON IMPERIAL

1 can (12 ounces) mixed vegetable juices
1 cup water
1 vegetable-bouillon cube

1. Combine ingredients in small saucepan; heat to boiling, stirring just until bouillon cube dissolves.
2. Pour into heated cups. Serve plain or float a few paper-thin slices of carrot, cucumber, turnip, or radish, cut into flower shapes with a truffle cutter or knife, on top, if you like. Makes 4 servings.

■ DILL PUFFS

1 envelope active dry yeast
  OR: 1 cake compressed yeast
¼ cup very warm water
1 cup (½ pound) cream-style cottage cheese
2 tablespoons sugar
1 tablespoon instant minced onion
2 teaspoons dill weed
1 teaspoon salt
¼ teaspoon baking soda
1 egg
2⅓ cups sifted flour
  Butter or margarine

1. Sprinkle or crumble yeast into very warm water in large bowl. (Very warm water should feel comfortably warm when dropped on wrist.) Stir until yeast dissolves.
2. Heat cheese just until lukewarm; stir into yeast mixture; stir in remaining ingredients except flour and butter or margarine; mix well.
3. Beat in flour gradually, scraping down sides of bowl, until completely blended; beat vigorously about 20 strokes. (Dough will be sticky and heavy.)
4. Cover with a clean towel; let rise in warm place, away from draft, 1 hour, or until double in bulk.
5. Stir dough down; divide evenly among 8 greased 5-ounce custard cups. Cover with towel; let rise in warm place, away from draft, 45 minutes, or until double in bulk.
6. Bake in moderate oven (350°) 25 minutes, or until puffs are golden-brown and give a hollow sound when tapped. Remove from cups; brush tops lightly with butter or margarine; serve hot. Makes 8 rolls.

Note: Make puffs ahead, if you like, then reheat just before serving this way: Place in a paper bag, sprinkle bag with a few drops water, then close tightly. Slide into hot oven (400°) 3 to 5 minutes.

WHEN YOU COOK FISH

Gentle handling, quick cooking—these are the keys to pan-frying or broiling fish golden-brown outside, moist and flavorful within. For either, start with cleaned small whole or split fish, fillets, or steaks

Pan-fry your catch this way:

Dip fish in a slightly beaten egg in a pie plate, then in fine dry bread, cracker, or potato-chip crumbs in second pie plate. Pat coating on well. Lay breaded fish on a foil-covered rack; let dry 15 minutes

Heat ¼ inch melted shortening, salad oil, or bacon drippings in frying pan. Slide fish, a few pieces at a time, into hot fat. Cook over medium heat, turning just once, 3 to 8 minutes on each side, depending on thickness of cut

Test for doneness? Fish will flake easily with a fork, crumb coating will be crisp and golden-brown. Lift out with slotted spatula onto heated platter. Serve plain, or with lemon or a sauce of your choice

Broil your catch this way:

Arrange fish, not touching, on greased foil-covered broiler rack or pan. Brush with salad oil, melted butter or margarine, or bottled French dressing. Slide pan into broiler about 4 inches from heat

Broil fillets or split fish without turning, 6 to 10 minutes. Cook fish steaks, turning once, 5 to 8 minutes on each side. Broil whole fish, turning just once, 5 to 10 minutes on each side, depending on thickness

Test for doneness? Fish will flake easily with a fork, the same as in pan-frying. Season with a squeeze of lemon juice; transfer carefully to heated platter. Serve plain or with a sauce of your choice

SAUCES FOR FISH

Make it with butter or margarine

● WATER-CRESS BUTTER—Stir 2 tablespoons chopped water cress and 1 tablespoon lemon juice into 4 tablespoons (½ stick) melted butter or margarine. Makes about ¼ cup.

● PARMESAN-PARSLEY BUTTER—Stir 1 tablespoon each grated Parmesan cheese and chopped parsley into 4 tablespoons (½ stick) melted butter or margarine. Makes about ¼ cup.

● ALMOND BUTTER—Stir 2 tablespoons canned slivered almonds, plain or toasted, into 4 tablespoons (½ stick) melted butter or margarine. Makes about ¼ cup. (Also delicious with pecans. Use same amounts of other ingredients.)

Splurge with sour cream

● CUCUMBER CREAM—Blend 2 tablespoons mayonnaise or salad dressing, 2 tablespoons lemon juice, 1 tablespoon sugar, ¼ teaspoon salt, dash of pepper, and the finely chopped white part (no seeds) of 1 pared cucumber into 1 cup dairy sour cream. Makes about 1½ cups.

● HORSERADISH CREAM—Stir 1 tablespoon each prepared horseradish and chili sauce, 1 teaspoon prepared mustard, and a dash of salt and pepper into 1 cup dairy sour cream. Makes about 1 cup.

● MOCK HOLLANDAISE—Stir 2 beaten egg yolks, 1 tablespoon lemon juice, 1 teaspoon sugar, and salt and pepper to taste into 1 cup dairy sour cream in small saucepan. Heat slowly just until thick. Makes about 2 cups.

Dip into the mayonnaise jar

● CAPER SAUCE—Stir ¼ cup light or table cream and 1 tablespoon drained chopped capers into ¼ cup mayonnaise or salad dressing. Makes about ½ cup.

● TARTARE SAUCE—Stir 3 tablespoons chopped sweet pickle, 1 tablespoon chopped parsley, and 1 teaspoon grated onion into ½ cup mayonnaise or salad dressing. Makes about ⅔ cup.

● SOUFFLE SAUCE—Fold ½ cup mayonnaise or salad dressing and 1 tablespoon lemon juice into 1 stiffly beaten egg white. Spoon over cooked fish; slide into heated broiler for 2 to 3 minutes, or until puffed and golden. Makes about 1 cup.

Start with cream sauce

● PLAIN CREAM SAUCE—Melt 2 tablespoons butter or margarine in small saucepan. Stir in 2 tablespoons flour, ¼ teaspoon salt, and a dash of pepper; cook, stirring all the time, just until mixture bubbles. Stir in 1 cup milk slowly; continue cooking and stirring until sauce thickens and boils 1 minute. Makes 1 cup.

● ONION-CURRY—Blend ½ cup mayonnaise or salad dressing, 1 teaspoon grated onion, and ½ teaspoon curry powder into 1 cup PLAIN CREAM SAUCE. Makes about 1½ cups.

● ZIPPY CHEESE—Melt 1 cup grated Cheddar cheese (¼ pound) into 1 cup PLAIN CREAM SAUCE in small saucepan; stir in ¼ teaspoon dry mustard. Makes about 1¼ cups.

THERE'S many a way to cushion our budget and still feed our family right. Of course, we can't change prices, but we *can* make what we pay out go further. And this chapter will help show you how.

Each of these 12 dinner plans centers around the meat dish, for here is where the biggest chunk of our food money goes. Several are appetizingly handsome roasts—yes, even roasts on a budget—that hide one or more good buymanship secrets. For example, when meat is on special, buy a cut

These dinners pamper your pocketbook

big enough for more than one meal, with a planned-over dish in mind. (See Chapter 2.) And do get acquainted with more of the thriftier cuts and how to cook them properly.

Other tips to smart shopping: Make a list, but keep it flexible to take advantage of specials. Buy fresh produce in season. Read can labels and choose sizes and quality suited to your needs. And don't forget convenience foods—the mixes and instants —for your time, too, is worth money.

◀ **Australian Beef Platter** *(recipe on page 82)*, with all its colorful vegetables, makes a handsome dish yet hides its budget-smart secrets well. It's easy cooking, too, for everything goes in the same pan

Twelve budget-best specials

	MAIN DISH	VEGETABLE ● SALAD	DESSERT	NICE TO ADD

DINNER'S IN ONE DISH
(pictured on page 78)

★Australian Beef Platter

Green Salad with Grapefruit Sections French Dressing

Coffee-cream Angel Cake

★Sesame-seed Sticks Red Pepper Relish

Hankering for beef? Try this bountiful platter of thrifty boneless rump, chuck, or round, tenderized then roasted the same as gourmet ribs. Its five hearty vegetables

cook along with it in the oven—another savings plus. For dessert, flavor sweetened whipped cream with instant coffee, spoon over wedges of store-bought angel cake

---

HOMESPUN AND HEARTY

★Dappled Dumpling Fricassee

Buttered Green Beans and Carrots

★Steamed Pudding Ambrosia
(pictured on page 93)

★Cranberry-apple-raisin Relish

There's plenty of good eating in a stewing chicken with its rich broth dividend to turn into creamy gravy. It takes just 20 minutes to steam the parsley-flecked dump-

lings puffy-light, but be sure chicken and gravy are bubbling before spooning batter on top. And remember: The key to perfect dumplings is no peeking during cooking

---

EASY-DO VEAL FANCY
(pictured on page 83)

★Veal-tomato Milanese

Buttered Broccoli Mixed Salad Greens with Radish Slices

Cinnamon Plums Sugar Cookies

Potato Chips

This Italian-style dish starts with penny-wise cube veal steaks, or tenders, pan-cooked until richly golden. Stack each on a tomato half on toast, top with strips of

mozzarella or pizza cheese, and broil until melty. To go along, plan a green vegetable, crisp salad, and dessert of canned plums heated with a smidgen of cinnamon-sugar

---

QUICK-BAKE SEA FOOD

★Herb Baked Scallops Tartare Sauce

Baked Potatoes Creamed Onions and Peas

★Viennese Upside-down Cake

Coleslaw ★Tomato-bouillon Appetizer

Meaty fresh or frozen scallops, dressed with a simple buttery herb sauce, headline this oven-easy meal that cooks with almost no watching. Start the potatoes first, for

they take about an hour. Stir up dessert a rich chocolate-cake mix atop a sweet red-cherry sauce—to bake along with the main dish. It's extra-delicious served oven warm

---

WHEN LAMB IS THE SPECIAL

★California Lamb Roast ★Lamb Pan Gravy

Browned Potatoes ★Lady Cabbage with Peas

★Jellied Rainbow Dessert

★Peach Savories

Watch for specials on leg of lamb—half of one if your family is small, a whole leg for a dividend meal or two. Today's star calls for the shank or butt end roasted with a

garlic-spread seasoner just mild enough to please even the no-garlic set. For dessert, layer contrasting gelatin cubes into cups, then top with a creamy pudding mix sauce

---

PENNY-SMART BUYING

★Sliced Tongue in ★Orange-raisin Sauce

Mashed Potatoes ★Panned Carrots

Minted Chocolate Pudding (from a mix)

Sliced Cucumber Salad

When nutritious smoked tongue is on special, splurge and buy a big one, for it can be served in so many ways. Here it's sliced hot to eat with a tangy fruit sauce. What's

left will keep well for sandwiches or a supper meat-and-salad plate. For a change, try these skillet-cooked buttery carrots seasoned very lightly with onion and sugar

	MAIN DISH	VEGETABLE • SALAD	DESSERT	NICE TO ADD
FRENCH FLAIR ON A BUDGET	*Beef Jardiniere with *Marrow Dumplings	Salad Bowls with Sliced Onions Roquefort Dressing	*Three-Fruits Cobbler	Hot Biscuits (refrigerated kind)

Buy flavorful beef chuck or shank, along with a marrow bone or two for the dainty dumpling balls, to make this French specialty. Simmer meat ever so slowly, then top with dumplings to steam puffy-moist—they're deliciously different. If you have never made marrow balls, be sure to chill before cooking so they'll hold their shape

GOOD-FOR-YOU GOOD BUY	*Julienned Liver Saute	Mashed Potatoes *Continental Green Beans	Baked Lemon Chiffon Pudding (from a mix)	Romaine with Coleslaw Dressing

It's good meal-planning to serve nutritious liver often and thrifty-priced beef or lamb choices give you the same goodness as calf's liver. Here it's cut into strips, browned, then simmered in an herb-tomato sauce for just a wink. A tip to remember when cooking this delicate meat: Watch closely—overcooking toughens it

PRETTY ENOUGH FOR COMPANY	*Scandinavian Ragout	Tomato-lettuce Salad Egg Dressing	*Cherry Log	*Jellied Fruit Cup Toasted Caraway Rye Bread Slices

This inviting casserole stars Swedish meat balls, potatoes, cucumbers, and corn baked together in a rich dill-seasoned sauce, yet each keeps its own special shape and fla- vor. To make salad topper, blend chopped hard-cooked egg into French dressing. Dessert sponge roll is a companylike treat with a cherry filling and snowy frosting

SAVE-A-PENNY STEAK	*London Broil	*Creamy Hashed Potatoes Buttered Beets	*Apple Crisp Pie (pictured on page 91)	Horseradish Sauce (for meat) *Hot Spiced Mocha

Take advantage of good-buy flank—it's all meat, no waste—to give your family a steak treat. Broil quickly—rare to medium is best—then slice and serve plain or with sour cream mixed with a bit of horserad-ish. Evaporated milk makes the easy dress-up for potatoes. Dessert, with big chunks of apples in buttery syrup, bakes in foil

LOOKS LAVISH, COSTS LITTLE (pictured on page 87)	*Glazed Stuffed Pork Roast *Savory Pork Gravy	Baked Sweet Potatoes *Zucchini Scallop	Pears Helene	Spiced Pineapple Chunks (canned variety)

Fresh pork shoulder is a reliable budget buy, and a large one will give you a bonus meal or two. Our roast here is boned (your meatman will do it for you), then stuffed with a tangy orange dressing and roasted crusty brown. For dessert, scoop vanilla ice cream into chilled pear halves, then drizzle with warm chocolate sundae sauce

GROUND BEEF IN SPICY GRAVY	*Skillet Sauerbraten	Boiled Potatoes in Jackets Buttered Limas	*Peach Tart	Lettuce Wedges Russian Dressing

Versatile ground beef goes fancy here, for it tastes teasingly like old-world sauer-braten, yet needs no long seasoning or cooking. Shape meat into a giant patty, then simmer in a sweet-sour sauce. To serve, cut in wedges, spoon sauce over. For a perfect top-off, try this cream-filled pie capped with peaches and a tart glaze

MAIN DISHES

■ AUSTRALIAN BEEF PLATTER

4 medium-size parsnips
4 medium-size onions
4 medium-size potatoes
4 medium-size carrots
1 large acorn squash
5 to 6 pounds boneless beef rump, chuck, or round
   Instant unseasoned meat tenderizer
2 tablespoons salad oil
   Beef-vegetable Gravy (recipe follows)

1. Prepare all vegetables this way: Pare parsnips, halve lengthwise, then cut crosswise into 3-inch chunks. Peel onions. Pare potatoes and cut each in half. Scrape carrots and cut diagonally into 2-inch chunks. Quarter squash, scoop out seeds and membrane, but do not pare.
2. Parboil parsnips and onions together, and potatoes, carrots, and squash together in lightly salted boiling water in two kettles, 15 minutes. Drain, saving 3 cups of the potato-carrot-squash liquid for making BEEF-VEGETABLE GRAVY.
3. Moisten roast and sprinkle with meat tenderizer, following label directions. Place on rack in large shallow roasting pan. If using a meat thermometer, insert bulb into center of roast.
4. Arrange vegetables in separate piles around meat; brush lightly all over with salad oil; sprinkle with pepper, if you wish.
5. Roast in slow oven (325°), allowing about 20 minutes per pound if you like beef pink with lots of juice. Thermometer should register 140°. During roasting, turn vegetables and baste once or twice with drippings in pan. Vegetables and roast should be done at the same time.
6. Remove roast to heated serving platter; lift out vegetables with a slotted spoon and arrange in separate piles around roast. Keep hot while making gravy. Makes 4 servings with enough meat and gravy left over for a casserole or to make into hot sandwiches for another day.

BEEF-VEGETABLE GRAVY—Remove rack from roasting pan. Tip pan and let fat rise in one corner; skim off all fat into a cup, leaving juices in pan. Return 4 tablespoons fat to pan; blend in 4 tablespoons flour; cook, stirring all the time, just until mixture bubbles. Stir in saved 3 cups potato-carrot-squash liquid slowly; continue cooking and stirring, scraping baked-on juices from bottom and sides of pan, until gravy thickens and boils 1 minute. Season to taste with salt and pepper, if needed; darken with a few drops bottled gravy coloring, if you wish. Makes 3 cups.

■ DAPPLED DUMPLING FRICASSEE

1 stewing chicken (about 5 pounds), cut up
4 cups water (for chicken)
1 large onion, sliced
1 cup chopped celery and leaves
1 medium-size carrot, scraped and sliced
2 teaspoons salt
¼ teaspoon pepper
½ cup cold water (for gravy)
6 tablespoons flour
   Dappled Dumplings (recipe follows)

1. Combine chicken, 4 cups water, onion, celery and leaves, carrot, salt, and pepper in large kettle or Dutch oven with tight-fitting cover. Cover; heat to boiling, then simmer 1½ to 2 hours, or until chicken is tender.
2. Remove from broth; cool slightly; slip off skin, if you wish. Strain and measure broth; add water, if needed, to make 5 cups. Press vegetables through strainer into broth; return to kettle; heat to boiling.
3. Stir ½ cup cold water into flour in cup to make a smooth paste; stir into hot broth. Cook, stirring constantly, until gravy thickens and boils 1 minute. Season with salt and pepper to taste, if needed.
4. Return chicken to gravy in kettle; heat slowly to boiling while stirring up DAPPLED DUMPLINGS.
5. Drop batter in 12 mounds on top of steaming chicken. Cook, covered, 20 minutes. (No peeking, or they won't steam puffy-light.)
6. Arrange chicken and dumplings on a heated serving platter; pass gravy in separate bowl. Makes 6 servings.

DAPPLED DUMPLINGS—Sift 2 cups sifted flour, 3 teaspoons baking power, and 1 teaspoon salt into medium-size bowl. Cut in 2 tablespoons shortening with pastry blender until mixture is crumbly. Stir in ¼ cup chopped parsley and 1 cup milk just until flour is moistened. (Dough will be soft.)

Veal-tomato Milanese calls for cube steaks ▶ to pan-cook, then stack atop toast and tomatoes and crown with melty cheese. Plan a crisp salad and green vegetable to go along

■ VEAL-TOMATO MILANESE

1 egg
1 teaspoon salt
⅛ teaspoon pepper
½ cup cracker crumbs
6 cube veal steaks or veal tenders
    (about 1½ pounds)
¼ cup shortening
    Broiled Tomatoes (recipe follows)
6 slices mozzarella cheese, each cut into 4 strips
6 slices buttered toast, crusts removed

1. Beat egg, salt, and pepper with a fork in pie plate; sprinkle cracker crumbs into second pie plate. Dip veal into egg mixture, then into crumbs, to coat both sides.
2. Saute slowly in shortening in large frying pan 5 to 8 minutes on each side, or until richly golden.
3. While veal cooks, prepare BROILED TOMATOES.
4. Place a cooked veal steak on top of each tomato half; arrange 4 strips of cheese over each to form an X; broil just until cheese is melty.
5. Place toast slices in single layer on heated large serving platter; lift veal-and-tomato stacks onto toast with a broad spatula. Makes 6 servings.

BROILED TOMATOES

3 large ripe tomatoes
2 tablespoons salad oil
1½ teaspoons sugar
½ teaspoon salt
⅛ teaspoon pepper

1. Remove stems from tomatoes; cut tomatoes in half crosswise. Arrange, cut side up, on broiler pan; brush with salad oil.
2. Mix sugar, salt, and pepper in a cup; sprinkle over tomatoes.
3. Broil about 5 inches from heat, 5 minutes, or just until bubbly on top. Makes 6 servings.

■ HERB BAKED SCALLOPS

1 pound fresh sea scallops
  OR: 1 package (1 pound) frozen sea scallops
3 tablespoons butter or margarine
2 tablespoons chopped parsley
1 teaspoon basil
  Salt and pepper

1. Wash fresh scallops under running cold water; drain. Or thaw frozen ones, following label directions, or open carton, empty scallops into a shallow dish, cover lightly, and let stand at room temperature 30 minutes. (Scallops can be put into the oven to bake even though not quite thawed.)
2. Arrange scallops in a shallow baking dish; dot with butter or margarine; sprinkle with parsley, basil, and salt and pepper.
3. Bake in moderate oven (350°) 5 minutes; stir to coat scallops well with butter mixture. Bake 20 minutes longer, or until tender when pierced with a fork. Makes 4 servings.

■ CALIFORNIA LAMB ROAST

½ leg of lamb (4 to 5 pounds)
  Salt and pepper
3 tablespoons flour
2 tablespoons bottled garlic spread
  Lamb Pan Gravy *(recipe follows)*

1. Buy either the butt or shank end. (Butt end has a flat bone near the meaty chop end; shank has a longer leg bone, but both carve nicely.) Cut away all excess fat; sprinkle lamb all over with salt and pepper. Make a paste of flour and garlic spread in a cup; spread evenly over meat.
2. Place meat on rack, skin side up, in roasting pan. If using a meat thermometer, insert bulb so it reaches meaty center without touching bone.
3. Roast in slow oven (325°), allowing 30 minutes per pound, or 2 to 2½ hours for well-done. Thermometer should register 180°.
4. Remove to heated serving platter; keep hot while making gravy. Makes 6 servings with enough meat left to chop, heat in gravy, and serve over rice, or slice and make into hot or cold sandwiches for another meal.

LAMB PAN GRAVY—Remove rack from roasting pan. Tip pan and let fat rise in one corner; skim off all fat into a cup, leaving juices in pan. Return 2 tablespoons fat to pan; blend in 2 tablespoons flour; cook, stirring all the time, just until mixture bubbles. Stir in 2 cups water slowly; continue cooking and stirring, scraping baked-on juices from bottom and sides of pan, until gravy thickens and boils 1 minute. Season to taste with salt and pepper; darken with a few drops bottled gravy coloring, if you wish. Makes 2 cups.

■ SLICED TONGUE IN ORANGE-RAISIN SAUCE

1 smoked beef tongue (about 5 pounds)
¼ cup vinegar
2 tablespoons brown sugar
½ teaspoon thyme
8 whole cloves
  Orange-raisin Sauce *(recipe follows)*

1. Wash tongue in cold water; place in large kettle with water to cover. Add vinegar, brown sugar, thyme, and cloves; cover tightly.
2. Heat to boiling; simmer 2 to 3 hours, or until fork-tender. Let meat stand in liquid in kettle until cool enough to handle, then pour off and discard liquid. Cut skin from meat; cut out fat and small bones.
3. Slice part of meat ¼-inch thick; heat in ORANGE-RAISIN SAUCE. Makes 4 servings with enough left for another meal.

ORANGE-RAISIN SAUCE—Mix ¼ cup firmly packed brown sugar, 1 tablespoon cornstarch, ⅛ teaspoon salt, and ⅛ teaspoon ground cloves in small saucepan. Gradually stir in 1 cup orange juice and 2 tablespoons lemon juice. Cook, stirring constantly, until mixture thickens slightly. Stir in ¼ cup seedless raisins; simmer 5 minutes. Makes about 1¼ cups.

■ BEEF JARDINIERE WITH MARROW DUMPLINGS

1½ pounds lean beef chuck or shank, cubed
1 can (about 1 pound) tomatoes
1 cup water
1 teaspoon sugar
1 teaspoon salt
1 bay leaf
½ teaspoon thyme
¼ teaspoon pepper
    Marrow Dumplings (recipe follows)
4 medium-size carrots, scraped and cut into
    3-inch lengths
1 can (about 1 pound) green peas

1. Brown beef quickly in a few melted trimmings in large frying pan.
2. Stir in tomatoes, water, and seasonings. Cover; simmer 1 hour, or just until meat is tender.
3. While stew cooks, make and chill MARROW DUMPLINGS.
4. Add carrots to hot stew; cook 25 minutes, or until tender. Remove bay leaf. Stir in peas and liquid; arrange MARROW DUMPLINGS on top; cover; cook 5 minutes longer. Makes 4 servings.

MARROW DUMPLINGS

Beef marrow from a 3- to 4-inch beef
    marrowbone (½ cup mashed)
1 egg
1 cup soft bread crumbs (2 slices)
1 tablespoon chopped parsley
½ teaspoon salt
⅛ teaspoon pepper

1. Cut out marrow from bone with a sharp thin-blade knife; mash and place in small bowl. Stir in remaining ingredients until well-blended.
2. Form lightly into marble-size balls. Set in a shallow pan; chill at least 1 hour. (Dumplings hold their shape better when chilled before cooking.) Makes about 12 dumplings.

■ JULIENNED LIVER SAUTE

1 pound beef or lamb liver, sliced
    Flour
1 small onion, chopped (¼ cup)
2 tablespoons bacon drippings
¼ cup chili sauce
1 teaspoon salt
⅛ teaspoon thyme
⅛ teaspoon pepper
¾ cup water

1. Snip out veiny parts and skin from liver. (Scissors do a quick job.) Flour slices lightly, then cut into thin strips with a sharp knife.
2. Brown liver with onion in bacon drippings

in medium-size frying pan. Stir in remaining ingredients; cover.
3. Simmer 3 minutes, or just until liver loses its pink color. (Overcooking toughens this delicate meat, so watch it carefully and remove from heat at once.)
4. Arrange on heated serving platter; sprinkle generously with chopped parsley, if you wish. Makes 4 servings.

■ SCANDINAVIAN RAGOUT

1 pound ground beef
½ pound ground veal
1 cup soft bread crumbs (about 2 slices)
1 egg
½ cup evaporated milk
1 tablespoon grated onion
1 teaspoon grated lemon rind
1 teaspoon salt (for meat balls)
4 tablespoons shortening
6 medium-size potatoes, pared and cut as for
    French-frying
1 medium-size cucumber, halved lengthwise
    and sliced ¼ inch thick
1 can (12 or 16 ounces) whole-kernel corn
1 tablespoon flour
½ teaspoon salt (for gravy)
⅛ teaspoon pepper
1 cup dairy sour cream
1 tablespoon dill weed

1. Mix beef, veal, bread crumbs, egg, evaporated milk, onion, lemon rind, and 1 teaspoon salt in large bowl; shape into 36 small balls. Brown in shortening in medium-size frying pan; place in mound in one third of greased 12-cup baking dish. (Set frying pan aside for making gravy in Step 4.)
2. Cook potato strips in small amount boiling salted water 5 minutes; transfer with slotted spoon to baking dish, piling in mound to fill second third of dish; save potato water for Step 4.
3. Cook cucumber slices in small amount boiling salted water 3 minutes; drain, adding liquid to potato water. Drain corn, adding liquid to potato-cucumber water, if needed, to make 1 cup. Toss corn with cucumbers; spoon into remaining space in baking dish.
4. Blend flour, ½ teaspoon salt, and pepper into drippings in frying pan; stir in the 1 cup saved vegetable liquid. Cook, stirring constantly, until gravy thickens and boils 1 minute. Stir in sour cream and dill weed; heat just to boiling. Pour over potatoes and meat; tip dish gently from side to side so gravy flows to bottom; cover.
5. Bake in moderate oven (350°) 30 minutes, or until bubbly-hot. Makes 6 servings.

Note: For entertaining, you might like to cut the potatoes into fancy sticks with a ripple-edge vegetable cutter.

■ LONDON BROIL

Buy 1 flank steak, or 1 thin slice boneless chuck, weighing about 2 pounds. Moisten meat and sprinkle with instant unseasoned meat tenderizer, following label directions, if you wish. Place meat on broiler rack; brush lightly with bottled steak sauce. Broil, following range manufacturer's directions, 3 minutes. Turn; brush again with steak sauce; broil 3 to 4 minutes longer for rare. Cut diagonally across the grain into thin slices. Makes 6 servings.

■ GLAZED STUFFED PORK ROAST

    5 to 6 pounds fresh pork shoulder, boned
    1 large onion, chopped (1 cup)
    4 tablespoons (½ stick) butter or margarine
1¼ cups water
    1 can (6 ounces) frozen concentrated
        orange juice
    1 package (8 ounces) ready-mix bread
        stuffing (4 cups)
    ¼ teaspoon ground sage
    ¼ cup firmly packed brown sugar
    1 teaspoon prepared mustard
        Savory Pork Gravy (recipe follows)

1. Remove skin and trim excess fat from pork.
2. Saute onion in butter or margarine just until soft in medium-size frying pan. Stir in water and ¼ cup concentrated orange juice. (Save remaining for Step 4.) Heat to boiling; pour over bread stuffing and sage in medium-size bowl, toss lightly with a fork to moisten well.
3. Stuff into pocket in pork, packing in well to fill and give meat a rounded shape. Tie with string at 1-inch intervals; place on rack in shallow roasting pan. If using a meat thermometer, insert bulb into meaty portion, not stuffing.
4. Roast in slow oven (325°) 2 hours. Heat saved concentrated orange juice with brown sugar and mustard in small saucepan; brush half of mixture on top of meat. Roast, basting 2 or 3 more times with remaining mixture, 1 to 1½ hours longer, or until meat is tender and richly glazed. Thermometer should register 185°.
5. Remove to heated serving platter; keep hot while making gravy. Makes 6 servings with enough left for a casserole.

SAVORY PORK GRAVY—Remove rack from roasting pan. Tip pan and let fat rise in one corner; skim off all fat into a cup, leaving juices in pan. Return 2 tablespoons fat to pan; blend in 2 tablespoons flour; cook, stirring all the time, just until mixture bubbles. Stir in 2 cups water slowly; continue cooking and stirring, scraping baked-on juices from bottom and sides of pan, until gravy thickens and boils 1 minute. Season with 2 teaspoons salt and 1 teaspoon vinegar. Strain into gravy dish to remove any bits of stuffing. Makes 2 cups.

■ SKILLET SAUERBRATEN

    2 pounds ground beef
    2 teaspoons salt
    ¼ teaspoon pepper
    ¼ teaspoon ground cloves
    ¼ cup wine vinegar (for meat)
    1 medium-size carrot, scraped and sliced
    1 large onion, sliced
    1 large stalk celery, sliced
    1 bay leaf
    ¾ cup water
    ½ cup wine vinegar (for gravy)
    2 tablespoons brown sugar
    3 gingersnaps
    ½ cup hot water

1. Season ground beef with salt, pepper, cloves, and ¼ cup vinegar; shape into a big patty in large frying pan. Add carrot, onion, celery, and bay leaf.
2. Combine water, ½ cup vinegar, and brown sugar in 2-cup measure; pour over meat and vegetables; cover. Simmer, basting often, 1 hour. Remove meat to heated platter; keep hot.
3. Soften gingersnaps in hot water in measuring cup; stir into liquid in frying pan. Heat, stirring constantly, until slightly thick. Remove bay leaf; pour gravy over meat. Makes 6 servings.

Tangy orange dressing and a sparkling fruit sauce ▶ turn fresh shoulder into this inviting **Glazed Stuffed Pork Roast**. Go-withs are spicy pineapple chunks and a zesty top-range "casserole" of squash and tomatoes

VEGETABLES

■ CREAMY HASHED POTATOES

6 tablespoons bacon drippings or
    butter or margarine
6 cups diced raw potatoes (about 6 medium-size)
1 medium-size onion chopped (½ cup)
1 teaspoon salt
¼ teaspoon pepper
1 small can evaporated milk (⅔ cup)

1. Melt drippings or butter or margarine in large frying pan; stir in potatoes, onion, salt, and pepper. Cover; cook over low heat 10 minutes.
2. Uncover; stir from bottom of pan, then saute over low heat, turning often, 15 minutes, or until potatoes are tender and browned. Pour evaporated milk over; heat, stirring gently, 1 to 2 minutes longer. Makes 6 servings.

■ LADY CABBAGE WITH PEAS

4 cups finely shredded cabbage (about ¾ pound)
¾ cup boiling water
3 tablespoons butter or margarine
½ teaspoon salt
¼ teaspoon pepper
½ cup evaporated milk
1 can (about 1 pound) green peas, drained

1. Place cabbage in large saucepan; pour boiling water over. Cover; cook over high heat, 10 minutes, or just until crisply tender and water is almost all evaporated.
2. Season with 2 tablespoons butter or margarine, salt, and pepper; pour evaporated milk over, stirring lightly to mix. Heat slowly just until piping-hot.
3. While cabbage heats, season peas with remaining 1 tablespoon butter or margarine in small saucepan; heat just to boiling.
4. Spoon cabbage into heated serving bowl; pile peas in a mound in center. Makes 6 servings.

■ PANNED CARROTS

2 tablespoons bacon drippings
8 medium-size carrots, scraped and sliced thin
1 small onion, grated
1 teaspoon sugar
½ teaspoon salt
⅛ teaspoon pepper

Heat bacon drippings in heavy frying pan; stir in remaining ingredients. Cover; cook slowly, stirring often, 10 to 15 minutes, or until carrots are tender. Makes 4 servings.

■ CONTINENTAL GREEN BEANS

1 can (about 1 pound) cut green beans
1 small onion, sliced
½ cup condensed cream of chicken soup
2 tablespoons mayonnaise or salad dressing

1. Heat beans and liquid with onion just to boiling in medium-size saucepan; drain; keep hot.
2. Blend chicken soup with mayonnaise or salad dressing in small saucepan; heat just until bubbly-hot. (Do not boil.)
3. Spoon beans and onion into heated serving bowl; pour sauce over. Makes 4 servings.

■ ZUCCHINI SCALLOP

6 small zucchini (about 1 pound), washed, trimmed, and sliced thin
3 tablespoons butter or margarine
1 teaspoon sugar
1 teaspoon salt
½ teaspoon mixed Italian herbs
⅛ teaspoon pepper
1 can (1 pound) tomatoes

1. Saute zucchini lightly in butter or margarine 5 minutes in large frying pan. Sprinkle with sugar, salt, Italian herbs, and pepper; pour tomatoes over; stir gently to blend.
2. Cover; cook over low heat 15 minutes, or until zucchini is crisply tender. Makes 6 servings.

DESSERTS

■ STEAMED PUDDING AMBROSIA

2¼ cups sifted flour
4 teaspoons baking powder
1 teaspoon salt
½ teaspoon ground cardamom
4 tablespoons (½ stick) butter or margarine
1 cup sugar
2 eggs
¾ cup milk
1 teaspoon vanilla
1 cup flaked coconut
1 teaspoon grated orange rind
    Orange Sauce (recipe follows)

1. Grease an 8-cup tube mold well; sprinkle lightly with sugar; tap out any excess.
2. Measure flour, baking powder, salt, and cardamom into sifter.
3. Cream butter or margarine and sugar until fluffy in large bowl; beat in eggs.
4. Sift in dry ingredients, adding alternately with milk; beat well after each addition; stir in vanilla. Fold in coconut and orange rind.
5. Pour into prepared mold; cover with foil, transparent wrap, or double thickness of waxed paper; fasten with string to hold tightly.
6. Place on a rack or trivet in kettle or steamer; pour in boiling water to half the depth of pudding mold; cover tightly.
7. Steam 2 hours, or until a long thin metal skewer inserted near center comes out clean. (Keep water boiling gently during entire cooking time, adding more boiling water, if needed.)
8. Cool mold 5 minutes; loosen pudding around edge with knife; unmold onto serving plate; cool slightly. Spoon warm ORANGE SAUCE over, arranging mandarin-orange segments from the sauce on top. Makes 8 servings.
ORANGE SAUCE—Combine ½ cup sugar, 2 tablespoons cornstarch, and ⅛ teaspoon salt in medium-size saucepan. Stir in 1 cup water; cook over medium heat, stirring constantly, until sauce thickens and boils 3 minutes. Stir in 1 can (about 11 ounces) mandarin-orange segments, 1 teaspoon grated orange rind, ½ cup orange juice, and 3 tablespoons butter or margarine. Heat just until bubbly. Makes 2 cups.

■ VIENNESE UPSIDE-DOWN CAKE

4 tablespoons (½ stick) butter or margarine
¾ cup firmly packed light brown sugar
⅛ teaspoon salt
1 can (1 pound, 4 ounces) unsweetened pitted red tart cherries
1 package devil's-food cake mix

1. Melt butter or margarine in baking pan, 9x9x2; stir in brown sugar and salt. Heat slowly, stirring constantly, just until bubbly; remove from heat.
2. Drain cherries, saving liquid for cake. Spoon cherries over sugar mixture in pan.
3. Prepare devil's-food cake mix, following label directions, and using liquid from cherries as part of liquid called for on package. Pour over cherries in pan.
4. Bake in moderate oven (350°) 1 hour, or until top springs back when lightly pressed with fingertip.
5. Cool on wire rack 5 minutes; cover pan with serving plate; quickly turn upside down, then carefully lift off baking pan. Cut into squares; serve warm, plain or with milk, cream, or ice cream. Makes 9 servings.

■ JELLIED RAINBOW DESSERT

1 package (3 ounces) raspberry-flavor gelatin
1 package (3 ounces) lime-flavor or lemon-flavor gelatin
2 cups hot water
2 cups cold water
    Creamy Custard Sauce (recipe follows)

1. Dissolve each flavor gelatin in 1 cup hot water in separate small bowls; stir 1 cup cold water into each. Pour into separate shallow pans, 8x8x2.
2. Chill several hours, even overnight, or until very firm.
3. Cut each into cubes; layer flavors, alternately, into chilled large bowl or individual dessert dishes. Pour CREAMY CUSTARD SAUCE over. Makes 6 servings.
CREAMY CUSTARD SAUCE—Prepare 1 package custard-flavor dessert mix, following label directions, and using 3 cups milk in place of 2¼ cups called for on package. Cool, then chill well. Makes 3 cups.

■ THREE-FRUITS COBBLER

1 can (1 pound, 6 ounces) blueberry-pie filling
1 tart apple, pared, cored, and sliced thin
1 envelope orange-muffin mix (2 to a package)
2 tablespoons light brown sugar

1. Spread half of pie filling in a shallow 6-cup baking dish. Arrange apple slices in single layer over top; cover with remaining filling.
2. Bake in moderate oven (350°) 20 minutes, or until bubbly around edge.
3. While fruits heat, prepare muffin mix, following label directions; spoon evenly on top of hot fruits, then sprinkle evenly with brown sugar.
4. Bake 25 minutes longer, or until top is golden and wooden pick inserted in center comes out clean. Serve warm with milk or light cream, if you wish. Makes 6 servings.

■ CHERRY LOG

Cake

¾ cup sifted cake flour
1 teaspoon baking powder
¼ teaspoon salt
4 eggs
¾ cup sugar
1 teaspoon vanilla
2 tablespoons 10X (confectioners' powdered) sugar

Filling

1 package vanilla-flavor pudding mix
   Milk
2 tablespoons butter or margarine
1 teaspoon vanilla
   Red food coloring
¼ cup chopped maraschino cherries

Frosting

½ cup cream for whipping
1 tablespoon 10X (confectioners' powdered) sugar
   Chocolate curls

1. Grease baking pan, 15x10x1; line with waxed paper cut ½ inch smaller than pan.
2. Make cake: Measure flour, baking powder, and salt into sifter.
3. Beat eggs until foamy in medium-size bowl; gradually beat in sugar until mixture is thick; stir in vanilla. Sift dry ingredients over and fold in until no dry flour remains. Pour batter into prepared pan, spreading evenly.
4. Bake in hot oven (400°) 12 minutes, or until top springs back when lightly pressed with fingertip.
5. Cut around cake about ½ inch from edge with sharp knife; invert pan onto clean towel dusted with 10X sugar; remove waxed paper. Starting at one end, roll up cake; wrap in towel; cool completely on wire rack. (Or, to keep roll perfectly round, try this cooling trick: Tie cake roll in towel at both ends with string; hang onto handle of cupboard door until cool.)
6. Make filling: Prepare pudding mix with milk, following label directions; remove from heat. Stir in butter or margarine and vanilla. Blend in a few drops red food coloring to tint a delicate pink; fold in cherries; cool. (Cake and filling can be made ahead, ready to be put together about 1 hour before serving.)
7. Make frosting: Beat cream until stiff in medium-size bowl; beat in 10X sugar.
8. Unroll cake carefully; spread evenly with cooled filling; reroll. Frost with whipped cream, sprinkle top with chocolate curls. (To make them, shave thin slices from a square of unsweetened chocolate with a vegetable parer.) Chill roll about 1 hour, or until serving time.
9. Slice crosswise. Makes 6 to 8 servings.

■ APPLE CRISP PIE

1 recipe Plain Pastry (recipe follows)
   OR: 1 stick piecrust mix
3 or 4 large baking apples (about 2½ pounds)
1 cup sugar
2 tablespoons plus ½ cup flour
½ teaspoon nutmeg
½ cup (1 stick) butter or margarine
2 tablespoons lemon juice

1. Make PLAIN PASTRY, or prepare piecrust mix, following label directions. Roll out to a 12-inch round on lightly floured pastry cloth or board; fit into a 9-inch pie plate. Trim overhang to ½ inch; turn under flush with rim; flute to make a stand-up edge.
2. Pare, quarter, and core apples, then halve each quarter crosswise to make chunks. (There should be about 7 cups.) Place in large bowl.
3. Mix ½ cup sugar, 2 tablespoons flour and nutmeg in cup. Mix remaining ½ cup sugar and ½ cup flour in small bowl; cut in butter or margarine with pastry blender until mixture is crumbly. Set aside for next step.
4. Sprinkle sugar-spice mixture over apples; toss lightly to mix. Spoon into prepared shell; drizzle with lemon juice. Sprinkle flour-butter mixture evenly over top.
5. Cover pie loosely with foil, pressing it around rim to hold in place. Place on large cooky sheet for easy handling.
6. Bake in hot oven (425°) 1 hour; remove from oven; lift off foil. (Apples will be tender and sparkly golden.) Cool pie on wire rack. Serve plain, or with Cheddar cheese or ice cream. Makes 1 nine-inch pie.

PLAIN PASTRY

1¼ cups sifted flour
1 teaspoon salt
½ cup shortening
3 to 4 tablespoons cold water

1. Sift flour and salt into medium-size bowl; cut in shortening with pastry blender until mixture is crumbly.
2. Sprinkle water over, a tablespoon at a time; mix lightly with a fork just until pastry holds together and leaves side of bowl clean. Makes enough for 1 single-crust 9-inch pie shell with fluted edge. (To make a two-crust 9-inch pie, just double all ingredients.)

Pie lovers rate this **Apple Crisp Pie** a best-ever. ▶ Husky chunks of fruit, nestled in a buttery syrup, bake invitingly plump and juicy under a golden crumb topping. Recipe gives a special baking hint

■ PEACH TART

Rich Pastry *(recipe follows)*
1 package vanilla-flavor pudding mix
2 tablespoons brown sugar
1½ cups milk
1 tablespoon butter or margarine
½ teaspoon vanilla
1 can (1 pound) sliced cling peaches, drained
¼ cup red currant jelly, melted

1. Prepare RICH PASTRY. Roll out to a 12-inch round on lightly floured pastry cloth or board; fit into a 9-inch pie plate. Trim overhang to ½ inch; turn under flush with rim; flute edge. Prick shell all over with a fork.
2. Bake in hot oven (425°) 15 minutes, or until golden; cool on wire rack.
3. Combine pudding mix, brown sugar, and milk in medium-size saucepan. Cook, following label directions; stir in butter or margarine and vanilla. Pour into cooled tart shell. Chill until serving time.
4. Arrange sliced peaches in a ring on top; drizzle currant jelly over. Makes 1 nine-inch pie.

RICH PASTRY—Sift 1¼ cups sifted flour; ½ teaspoon salt, and ¼ teaspoon mace into a medium-size bowl; cut in ⅓ cup shortening with pastry blender until mixture is crumbly. Beat 1 egg with fork in cup; toss lightly with flour mixture until dough clings together in a ball and leaves side of bowl clean. Makes 1 nine-inch shell.

NICE TO ADD

■ SESAME-SEED STICKS

1 package refrigerated sesame dinner rolls
2 tablespoons butter or margarine, melted

1. Separate rolls into individual pieces; roll each into a pencil-thin strip with hands on pastry cloth or board (no flour needed).
2. Place on cooky sheet; brush with melted butter or margarine.
3. Bake in hot oven (400°) 13 minutes, or until golden. Serve hot. Makes 12 sticks.

■ CRANBERRY-APPLE-RAISIN RELISH

1 can (1 pound) whole-fruit cranberry sauce
1 tart apple, pared, cored, and diced
½ cup seedless raisins
1 tablespoon sweet-pickle relish

1. Break up cranberry sauce with a fork in medium-size bowl. Stir in apple, raisins, and sweet-pickle relish.
2. Let stand at room temperature at least an hour to blend flavors. Makes 3 cups. (This relish will keep well in a covered jar in the refrigerator.)

■ TOMATO-BOUILLON APPETIZER

2 cups tomato juice
1 can condensed beef broth
¼ teaspoon seasoned salt
1 lemon, sliced thin

1. Combine all ingredients, except lemon, in small saucepan; heat just to boiling.
2. Pour into cups; float a slice of lemon on each. Makes 4 servings.

■ PEACH SAVORIES

1 can (about 1 pound) cling peach halves
1 tablespoon bottled savory sauce
1 teaspoon vinegar
⅛ teaspoon salt

1. Combine peaches and syrup with remaining ingredients in medium-size frying pan. Simmer, turning peaches once, 5 minutes.
2. Let stand at least 30 minutes to season, or make a day ahead and chill. Makes 6 servings.

■ JELLIED FRUIT CUP

1 package strawberry-flavor gelatin
1 cup hot water
1¼ cups cold water
3 tablespoons lemon juice
1 can (about 8 ounces) fruit cocktail
1 orange, pared and sectioned

1. Dissolve gelatin in hot water in medium-size bowl; stir in cold water, lemon juice, fruit cocktail and syrup, and orange sections.
2. Chill 3 to 4 hours, or until softly set.
3. When ready to serve, stir lightly. Spoon into sherbet glasses. Makes 6 servings.

■ HOT SPICED MOCHA

6 cups milk
½ cup instant cocoa mix
¼ cup instant coffee
Cinnamon—sugar

1. Heat milk to scalding in medium-size saucepan; stir in instant cocoa and coffee. Remove from heat; beat until foamy.
2. Pour into serving cups; sprinkle with cinnamon-sugar. Serve hot. Makes 6 servings.

Coconut, orange rind, and a measure of spicy cardamom are the flavor secrets of this handsome **Steamed Pudding Ambrosia** *(recipe on page 89)*. Mandarin oranges make its golden sauce and crown ▶

*I*T pays to keep a few fast-cook meal ideas tucked away for days when dinner has to be readied in a rush. And it can be—smooth as clockwork—with a few tricks and some simple know-how.

Each of the meals that follows is proof, for none takes longer than 45 minutes. All depend on our modern instants, mixes, canned and frozen wonders for speed, plus a plan to streamline fixing. Here's how: Jot

When there's little time to dinnertime

down your menu—meat, vegetables, salad, and dessert. Then start with whatever takes longest to cook. Most often it's meat, but if it's a baked dessert, pop it into the oven first. And don't forget that the heat is there, so use it to melt butter, crisp rolls, or warm plates, as needed. Other tips to remember: Gather everything you need from the refrigerator on a tray, and do all cutting, slicing, and chopping at once. Both save minutes, steps —and cleanup, too.

More short cuts go with the menus and recipes. Do try them, for your speed may even top ours.

Paprika Swordfish *(recipe on page 97)* takes just ▶ about 20 minutes to broil richly golden. Serve with cucumbers, lemon, and tartare sauce. Citrus fruits capped with sweet onion rings make salad-starter

Short order specials

	MAIN DISH	VEGETABLE • SALAD	DESSERT	NICE TO ADD
30-MINUTE FISH BROIL (*pictured on page 95*)	*Paprika Swordfish Tartare Sauce	*Vegetables Parisienne Savory French Fries *Cucumbers Vinaigrette	Lemon Turnovers (frozen kind)	*Salad Fruit Cup Parker House Rolls

Fish is a natural for a jiffy-fix dinner, and here thick steaks broil to a golden turn while frozen French fries, sprinkled with seasoned salt for a flavor fillip, heat and crisp in the oven. When the main course comes out, slide frozen turnovers in to bake. For salad-cup starter, use canned fruits or the kind from your dairy case

	MAIN DISH	VEGETABLE • SALAD	DESSERT	NICE TO ADD
45-MINUTE VEAL GRILL	*Broiled Veal-vegetable Platter	Buttered Rice *Marinated Green Beans and Cauliflower	Butter-pecan Ice Cream Sugar Cookies	Toasted French Bread

Spread veal cutlet generously with bottled blue-cheese salad dressing, then broil—it will come out richly golden and as juicy as steak. Onions cook with it; other platter-mates go in later. Season green beans for salad early, for they should stand awhile to blend flavors. With quick-cooking rice, "potato" of the meal cooks in 10 minutes

	MAIN DISH	VEGETABLE • SALAD	DESSERT	NICE TO ADD
30-MINUTE STEW WONDER	*Jiffy Dinner Stew	Romaine-and-onion Salad Italian Dressing	*Purple Plum Compote	*Toasted Anise-butter Cakes Tea

With ground beef and sausages as its cook-fast meats, this dish takes just 30 minutes. To shape beef mixture quickly, pat in a square and cut into patties to brown, then cook with frozen green beans, seasoned tomatoes, and canned potatoes. While stew simmers, fix salad, cook plums, and spread topping on cake for broiling

	MAIN DISH	VEGETABLE • SALAD	DESSERT	NICE TO ADD
40-MINUTE HAM BOUNTY (*pictured on page 101*)	*Southern Ham Bake	Chopped Lettuce Salad Coleslaw Dressing	*Cherry-date Cobbler	Cream of Pea Soup Cereal Croutons

Brown a cut-up slice of ham, layer with canned sweet potatoes and pineapple in a dish, and it's ready for the oven. Marsh-mallows go on at the last minute to melt and toast. Stir up dessert to bake while you are eating the main course, heat canned pea soup with evaporated milk for a creamy opener, fix salad—dinner's on

	MAIN DISH	VEGETABLE • SALAD	DESSERT	NICE TO ADD
30-MINUTE LIVER DRESS-UP (*pictured on page 99*)	*Liver and Bacon Saute	*Creamed Vegetables Cranberry Sauce Corn Relish	Ginger-apple Cake	Honeydew Slices with Lemon Sherbet Poppy-seed Rolls

This go-steady pair makes a perfect short-order choice, for it's ready in 15 minutes. For a vegetable dish, heat canned potatoes and onions while frozen peas cook, then blend all in a quick creamy sauce. For dessert, bake gingerbread from a mix, cut in squares while hot, top each with a dollop of cream cheese, then warm applesauce over all

	MAIN DISH	VEGETABLE • SALAD	DESSERT	NICE TO ADD
35-MINUTE COMPANY CHICKEN (*pictured on page 99*)	*Chicken Royale	*Garden Bean Bowl Lettuce Wedges Blue-cheese Dressing	*Raspberry Cream Shortcakes	*Appetizer Bouillon Thin Pretzel Sticks

Quick-to-cook white meat of chicken, pork-luncheon-meat sticks, and noodles in a creamy sauce make this top-of-the-range casserole. While chicken simmers, there's time to fix salad and appetizer, and cook frozen beans. For dessert, packaged dessert shells, frozen raspberries, and whipped cream make the prettiest shortcakes—fast

MAIN DISHES

■ PAPRIKA SWORDFISH

2 pounds swordfish, cut about ½ inch thick
3 tablespoons butter or margarine, melted
  Paprika
  Salt and pepper
1 lemon, cut in wedges
  Parsley

1. Cut swordfish into 6 serving-size steaks; place in single layer on buttered broiler pan. Brush with about half the melted butter or margarine; sprinkle with paprika, salt, and pepper.
2. Broil, following range manufacturer's directions, 10 to 12 minutes; turn; brush with remaining butter or margarine, then sprinkle again with paprika, salt, and pepper. Broil 10 to 12 minutes longer, or until lightly golden and fish flakes easily with a fork.
3. Lift onto heated serving platter; garnish with lemon wedges and parsley. Serve with TARTARE SAUCE, if you wish (*recipe on page 77*). Makes 6 servings.

■ BROILED VEAL-VEGETABLE PLATTER

1½ to 2 pounds veal cutlet, cut ½-inch thick
¼ cup bottled blue-cheese salad dressing
1 Bermuda onion, peeled and cut in 6 slices
4 tablespoons (½ stick) butter or margarine, melted
  Salt and pepper
3 medium-size tomatoes, halved
6 slices bacon
1 can (3 or 4 ounces) whole mushrooms, drained

1. Place veal on broiler rack; brush top thickly with half of blue-cheese salad dressing.
2. Place onion slices on rack with veal; brush with part of melted butter or margarine; sprinkle with salt and pepper.
3. Broil, 4 to 6 inches from heat, 7 to 8 minutes. Turn veal and onion slices; brush veal with remaining blue-cheese dressing.
4. Place tomato halves, bacon slices, and mushrooms alongside veal and onion on rack. (If rack has too open a grid, put mushrooms in a small foil pan.) Brush tomato halves, onion slices, and mushrooms with remaining butter or margarine; sprinkle with salt and pepper.
5. Continue to broil, turning bacon once, 7 to 8 minutes longer, or until veal is richly golden, bacon is crisp, and tomatoes and mushrooms are heated through.
6. Arrange meats and vegetables on heated serving platter. Carve veal diagonally into ½-inch-thick slices. Serve with lemon wedges, if you like. Makes 6 servings.

■ JIFFY DINNER STEW

½ pound sweet Italian sausages, sliced 1 inch thick
1 pound ground beef
2 teaspoons bottled steak sauce
2 cans (about 1 pound each) stewed tomatoes
2 cans (1 pound each) whole potatoes, drained
1 package frozen Italian green beans
1 teaspoon salt
3 tablespoons flour
3 tablespoons cold water

1. Brown sausages quickly in large frying pan; push to one side.
2. While sausages brown, pat ground beef lightly into a 1-inch-thick square; cut into thirds, then each third into quarters to make 12 patties. Brown on one side in same frying pan; turn; brush with steak sauce. Spoon all fat from pan.
3. Pour tomatoes around meats; add potatoes. Separate frozen beans by tapping package on counter; add to meat mixture; sprinkle with salt. Cover; cook 10 minutes.
4. Blend flour and cold water to a smooth paste in a cup; stir into stew; cover. Cook 10 minutes longer, or until beans are tender. Makes 6 servings.

■ SOUTHERN HAM BAKE

1 slice ready-to-eat ham, cut about ¾ inch thick
1 can (1 pound, 4 ounces) pineapple chunks
½ cup firmly packed brown sugar
1 can (about 1 pound) whole sweet potatoes
12 marshmallows

1. Cut ham into 6 serving-size pieces; brown in large frying pan.
2. Drain syrup from pineapple into 2-cup measure. (There will be about 1 cup.) Stir in brown sugar until dissolved; pour over ham; heat to boiling.
3. Pile ham in middle of an 8-cup baking dish; arrange sweet potatoes around edge. Tuck pineapple chunks in between potatoes; pour hot syrup over.
4. Bake in hot oven (400°) 15 minutes. Remove from oven and place marshmallows around edge; bake 5 minutes longer, or until marshmallows are toasty-brown. Makes 6 servings.

■ LIVER AND BACON SAUTE

½ pound sliced bacon
1½ pounds beef or lamb liver, sliced thin
⅓ cup flour
½ teaspoon salt
⅛ teaspoon pepper

1. Fry bacon just until crisp in large frying pan; drain on paper toweling. Pour all but 2 tablespoons drippings from pan.
2. Shake liver slices in mixture of flour, salt, and pepper in paper bag to coat well. Brown quickly, a few slices at a time, in same frying pan. (Add more drippings, if needed.) Return all liver to pan; lay bacon strips on top; cover; steam 1 minute; serve at once. Makes 6 servings.

■ CHICKEN ROYALE

3 whole chicken breasts (2½ to 3 pounds), split
2 cups water
1 slice of onion
  Handful of celery tops
1 teaspoon salt
4 peppercorns
1 package (8 ounces) noodles
1 can (7 ounces) pork luncheon meat
2 tablespoons butter or margarine
1 can (about 11 ounces) chicken gravy

1. Combine chicken breasts, water, onion, celery tops, salt, and peppercorns in large saucepan. Simmer, covered, 20 minutes, or until chicken is tender.
2. While chicken simmers, cook noodles in large amount boiling salted water, following label directions; drain; place in greased shallow 8-cup baking dish.
3. Cut pork luncheon meat into 12 sticks; saute in butter or margarine in large frying pan; arrange in clusters on top of noodles. (Keep casserole warm in heated oven while browning chicken and heating gravy.)
4. Drain chicken breasts. (Strain broth and save for soup.) Brown chicken quickly in same frying pan, adding more butter or margarine, if needed; place on noodles.
5. Stir chicken gravy into frying pan; heat to boiling; pour over and around chicken. Makes 6 servings.

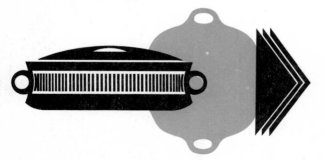

VEGETABLES

■ VEGETABLES PARISIENNE

2 packages (10 ounces each) frozen mixed vegetables
1 tablespoon sugar
1 teaspoon salt
2 tablespoons butter or margarine
2 tablespoons chopped parsley
¼ cup water

Combine all ingredients in medium-size saucepan. Cook, stirring often, 15 minutes, or just until vegetables are tender and liquid is almost evaporated. Makes 6 servings.

■ CUCUMBERS VINAIGRETTE

1 medium-size cucumber
½ teaspoon salt
⅛ teaspoon pepper
2 tablespoons cider vinegar
2 tablespoons water

1. Score cucumber rind with a fork; slice cucumber thin into a medium-size bowl. (There should be about 2 cups.)
2. Sprinkle with salt and pepper; spoon vinegar and water over; toss lightly. Chill. Drain before serving. Makes 6 servings.

■ MARINATED GREEN BEANS AND CAULIFLOWER

1 can (about 1 pound) Blue Lake whole green beans
½ cup bottled thin French dressing
6 cauliflowerets (from 1 small head)
  Lettuce

1. Drain green beans; place in shallow bowl. Drizzle French dressing over; toss lightly to mix. Let stand 15 minutes to blend flavors.
2. Slice cauliflowerets thin; toss with marinated beans. Spoon into lettuce-lined bowl. Makes 6 servings.

■ GARDEN BEAN BOWL

1 package (10 ounces) frozen wax beans
1 package frozen Italian green beans
2 tablespoons butter or margarine

1. Cook wax beans and Italian green beans in separate small saucepans, following label directions; drain.
2. Season each with 1 tablespoon butter or margarine, and salt and pepper. Spoon into separate mounds in heated serving dish. Makes 6 servings.

When time's short, here's a perfect main dish, for **Liver and Bacon Saute** cooks in just 15 minutes. Serve with cranberry sauce and corn relish, and honeydew crescents topped with dips of frosty sherbet

Chicken Royale teams quick-cooking breast of chicken, luncheon meat, noodles, and creamy gravy in a no-bake casserole. Company-fancy iced bouillon appetizer and bright vegetable bowl are jiffy-fix, too

CREAMED VEGETABLES

2 cans (1 pound each) small whole white potatoes
1 can (about 1 pound) small whole onions
3 tablespoons butter or margarine
1 package (10 ounces) frozen peas
1 tablespoon flour
1 cup light or table cream

1. Drain potatoes and onions; place in medium-size frying pan; season with 1 tablespoon butter or margarine. Heat slowly, turning often, 10 minutes, or until heated through.
2. When potatoes heat, cook peas, following label directions; drain. Melt in remaining 2 tablespoons butter or margarine; sprinkle flour over, then stir in cream. Cook, stirring constantly, until sauce thickens slightly and boils 1 minute.
3. Spoon hot potatoes and onions into heated serving dish; pour creamed peas over. Makes 6 servings.

DESSERTS

PURPLE PLUM COMPOTE

½ cup sugar
¼ teaspoon mace
¼ cup water
12 purple plums
2 large oranges

1. Combine sugar, mace, and water in large saucepan; heat to boiling. Add plums; simmer 5 minutes, or just until skins burst.
2. Pare and section oranges; place in serving bowl; pour hot plums and syrup over. Serve warm. Makes 6 servings.

RASPBERRY CREAM SHORTCAKES

6 packaged dessert shells
1 pint vanilla ice cream
1 package (10 ounces) frozen raspberries, partly thawed
Whipped cream in a can

1. Place dessert shells on individual serving plates; fill centers with ice cream.
2. Spoon raspberries over; top with a squeeze of whipped cream from a pressurized can. Makes 6 servings.

CHERRY-DATE COBBLER

1 can (1 pound, 6 ounces) cherry-pie filling
1 envelope (2 to a package) date-muffin mix
Cinnamon-sugar

1. Spread cherry-pie filling in baking pan, 8x8x2. Heat in hot oven (400°) while mixing topping.
2. Prepare muffin mix, following label direc-

tions. Spoon evenly over hot cherries; sprinkle lightly with cinnamon-sugar.
3. Bake in hot oven (400°) 15 to 20 minutes, or until wooden pick inserted in top comes out clean.
4. Cut in serving-size pieces; serve warm, plain or with cream. Makes 9 servings.

NICE TO ADD

SALAD FRUIT CUP

2 cans (1 pound each) mixed orange and grapefruit sections
OR: 1 jar (1 pound, 10 ounces) mixed orange and grapefruit sections
2 thin slices Bermuda onion

1. Chill canned orange and grapefruit sections well. If bought chilled, in a jar from the dairy department, keep in refrigerator until ready to use.
2. Just before serving, spoon fruits into serving dishes. Separate Bermuda onion slices into rings; arrange, dividing evenly, on top. Makes 6 servings.

TOASTED ANISE-BUTTER CAKES

½ teaspoon anise seeds
2 tablespoons butter or margarine
6 slices poundcake

1. Crush anise seeds between a sheet of waxed paper with rolling pin; blend into butter or margarine in cup.
2. Spread lightly on poundcake slices; toast in broiler until golden.
3. Halve each slice or cut into thirds; serve warm. Makes 6 servings.

APPETIZER BOUILLON

2 cans condensed beef bouillon
2 tablespoons lemon juice
1 teaspoon Worcestershire sauce

1. Mix bouillon, lemon juice, and Worcestershire sauce in 4-cup measure.
2. Fill 6 parfait or juice glasses with crushed ice; pour bouillon over. Makes 6 servings.
Note: If you like, place a radish rose in the bottom of each glass before filling with ice. To make, trim root end and leafy top from radish. Cut an X in top, cutting almost to bottom. Chill in bowl of ice and water until cuts open petal-like.

Smoky ham, sweet potatoes, tangy pineapple, and ▶ marshmallows go into this tempting **Southern Ham Bake** (recipe on page 97). Start with creamy soup for an appetizer, then add a simple salad bowl

*W*HAT'S all the whoop-de-do about? Why, cookouts, of course! Fun starts the minute you get the fire going and everybody pitches in.

Ever whiff anything as good as a juicy roast sizzling away as you play sit-down chef in the shade? Ever get a more eager response than when you

Cookouts — the more, the merrier!

call everyone to try your done-just-right masterpiece? Ever discover an easier, happier, more relaxed way to cook for the family or a crowd? No, nothing quite matches cookouts, so here's a whole chapter about them.

We've skipped the easy how-tos for hamburgers, hot dogs, and steak to bring you some special favorites. First comes a beef-roast spectacular that carves beautifully (no bones). Then on to chicken and lamb, each cooked a different way in foil. There's a smoked-pork dinner for rotisserie fans, franks in a skillet for a quick meal, and a whole section of kebabs —for real showmanship. Have fun!

Beef powwow's ready to go. Help yourself to a thick ▶ slice of **Canyon Steak Roast** *(recipe on page 105)* to eat with a husky browned potato, salad, corn, and relishes. Popcorn balls are for the children

Fun's a-cookin' with these outdoor meals

	MEAT	VEGETABLE • SALAD	DESSERT	NICE TO ADD

STEAK POWWOW
(pictured on page 103)

★Canyon Steak Roast   ★Potato Boats
★Double-double Salad

★Picnic Watermelon
★Popcorn Pops

Corn on the Cob
Raw Relishes
Hot Rolls   Milk

It's hard to beat beef for a big outdoor family get-together. This one, a thick cut laced with stuffed olives, is easy chefing, for it cooks on the grill with little watch-ing. Potatoes get a crusty-best topping if broiled a bit in the kitchen range. Dessert teaser for children—jumbo pink popcorn balls—hides a simple cooking-shaping trick

---

ORIENTAL SPECIALTY

★Chicken Kun Koki   ★Oriental Rice Bowl
★Panned Cabbage and Cucumber

★Orange-blossom Sundaes
(pictured on page 113)

Iced Tea
Water-cress Salad

A dainty young visitor from Korea gave us this recipe for chicken to cook first in a soy-and-onion sauce in a foil pan on the grill, then glaze right over the coals. Rice go-with is a must, and this dish is seasoned with celery and almonds in a creamy lime dressing. Dessert's extra–special—home-made ice cream with a sparkly sauce

---

NDER-COVER LAMB ROAST

★Grilled Lamb Roll-up   ★Caldron Potatoes
★Savory Mint Sauce   ★Cookout Salad

★White Mountain Ambrosia
(pictured on page 113)

Sliced Rye Bread
Poundcake

Here's real lazy-day cooking, for foil's both your roasting pan and lid. With meat and sauce wrapped snugly inside, you have only to turn the package atop the grill every half hour or so. Partners are freshly boiled potatoes with a butter-rich season-ing, a simple green salad, and a summery fruit bowl capped with snowy coconut

---

ROTISSERIE SHOW-OFF
(pictured on page 106)

★Ginger Glazed Pork Roast   ★Green-and-gold Squash Saute

Fresh Peach Pie

Lemonade
California Green Salad

Lucky you, if you have a rotisserie for your outdoor grill, for this sparkling chunky pork roast makes quite a show as it twirls round and round. It's a good choice for indoor cooking, too, if your range has a rotisserie attachment. Pota-toes "bake" on same grill—even squash, if there's room. Dessert is a peachy pie

---

DISH-WASHER'S DELIGHT

★Barbecued Franks-in-a-bun

Potato Chips
★Lima Salad Cups

★Apricot Rice-pudding Tart

Iced Tea
Fresh Fruit Basket

Whether you hop in the car to scout a new eating spot or take everything out in the yard, it's hard to find more popular cook-out fare than hot dogs. These heat in a spicy sauce, then go into toasty buns to eat with cup salads of mealy limas mixed with cheese and olives. Dessert treat butters up both pie and pudding fans

---

KEBAB SPEARMAN-SHIP
(pictured on page 109)

★Pick-your-favorite Kebabs   ★Chuck-wagon Beans
★Tomato Bowl

Fresh Bing Cherries
Cookies

Dill Pickles
Limeade

Skewer cooking's really showy and lots of fun, for everyone can get in on the act. Our pictured line-up shows a variety of kebab tempters. Choose one or more, along with their saucy seasoners, then set up the makings for each person to spear-cook his own main dish. Rest of meal's the make-ahead kind to bring from the kitchen

MAIN DISHES

■ CANYON STEAK ROAST

1 four-pound piece of sirloin tip, round, or rump
   beef roast
1 jar (about 3 ounces) stuffed small green olives
Instant unseasoned meat tenderizer
1 envelope garlic-olive dip mix

1. If roast is rolled, remove string and layer of fat, if any. Pound meat with a wooden mallet or rolling pin to flatten to 2½- to 3-inch thickness. Make 1-inch-deep cuts, about 2 inches apart, on both sides of meat with thin sharp knife. Push an olive into each cut.
2. Moisten steak and sprinkle with meat tenderizer, following label directions. Coat one side with half of the garlic-olive dip mix.
3. Place meat, dip-mix side down, on grill over hot coals; grill to a rich brown. Sprinkle top with remaining dip mix; turn; grill until meat is done as you like it. Time will depend on heat and distance of meat from coals, but it will average 30 to 35 minutes on each side for rare.
4. Place meat on cutting board; carve diagonally into ½-inch slices. Makes 8 servings.

■ CHICKEN KUN KOKI

3 broiler-fryers (about 2 pounds each),
   quartered
½ cup chopped green onions
½ cup soy sauce
¼ teaspoon pepper
1½ cups water
½ cup honey

1. Make a large shallow pan out of double-thick heavy foil. (Pan should be big enough to hold chicken pieces in a single layer.) Place on grill about 6 inches above hot coals; arrange chicken quarters, skin side down, in pan.
2. Combine green onions, soy sauce, pepper, and water in small saucepan; heat to boiling; pour over chicken. (Sauce should about half cover them.)
3. Cook slowly, turning and basting often with sauce in pan, 1 hour, or just until chicken is tender.
4. Lift chicken out of pan with tongs and place directly on hot grill. Blend honey into sauce in pan; brush over chicken.
5. Grill, turning and brushing with remaining sauce, 10 minutes longer, or until richly glazed. Makes 6 servings.
Note: To cook chicken indoors, simmer in its sauce in frying pan 1 hour, or until tender. Lift out and place on broiler rack; brush with honey glaze; broil until richly browned.

■ GRILLED LAMB ROLL-UP

1 leg of lamb, weighing 6 to 7 pounds
1 clove of garlic, peeled and cut
¼ cup flour
½ teaspoon salt
⅛ teaspoon pepper
Savory Mint Sauce *(recipe follows)*

1. Remove skin and *trim all fat* from top and underside of lamb. (This is important, so roast will not be greasy. When finished, there may be about a pound of cut-off fat.) Figure roasting time at 30 minutes per pound.
2. Rub meat all over with cut garlic, then coat with a mixture of flour, salt, and pepper.
3. Place in center of a large sheet of heavy freezer foil, or double thickness of the wide all-purpose kind. (Foil should be large enough to cover roast loosely with triple folds at top and ends.) Brush all over with SAVORY MINT SAUCE, then wrap loosely, but seal tightly so no sauce will cook out. Set package on grill 6 inches above hot coals.
4. Roast, turning every 30 minutes (you can even hear the juices bubbling inside), for time required. Slit foil across top; remove lamb to cutting board; pour sauce from package into bowl. Slice meat; serve with sauce to spoon over. Makes 8 to 10 servings.
SAVORY MINT SAUCE—Combine ½ cup bottled steak or savory sauce, ¼ cup catsup, 1 tablespoon vinegar, and 2 tablespoons chopped fresh mint in a 1-cup measure. Makes about ¾ cup, or enough for a whole leg of lamb.

■ GINGER GLAZED PORK ROAST

1 smoked pork shoulder butt, weighing about 5
   pounds
½ cup apricot jam
¼ cup orange juice
1 teaspoon ground ginger

1. Cut off thick skin from pork shoulder. If fat layer is thick, trim off about half, then score remaining fat in diamonds or squares.
2. Place pork on spit, following manufacturer's directions. If using a meat thermometer, insert bulb in one end of meat without touching bone. Set spit in position over hot coals; start rotisserie. (You'll need a fire bed big enough to last about 2 hours.)
3. Roast pork, following manufacturer's directions, about 1½ hours. Thermometer should register 160°.
4. Combine jam, orange juice, and ginger in small saucepan; heat slowly on side of grill, then brush pork all over as it turns.
5. Continue to grill, brushing often with sauce, 30 minutes longer, or until pork is richly glazed. Thermometer should register 170°.
6. Remove meat to cutting board; slice thin. Makes 6 to 8 servings.

■ BARBECUED FRANKS-IN-A-BUN

1 medium-size onion, chopped (½ cup)
2 tablespoons butter or margarine
1 can (16 ounces) tomato sauce
1 tablespoon molasses
1 tablespoon vinegar
1 tablespoon prepared mustard
½ teaspoon salt
½ teaspoon basil
12 frankfurters (about 1½ pounds)
12 split frankfurter rolls, toasted and buttered

1. Saute onion in butter or margarine just until soft in large frying pan. Stir in tomato sauce, molasses, vinegar, mustard, salt, and basil. Simmer, uncovered, 5 minutes.
2. Arrange frankfurters in sauce; cover; simmer 10 minutes, or until puffed and bubbly-hot.
3. Place frankfurters in rolls; spoon sauce over. Makes 6 servings.

■ PICK-YOUR-FAVORITE KEBABS

Each of the following kebab recipes calls for this basic sauce. Keep it on hand in a covered jar in the refrigerator to use plain, or combine with extra seasonings suggested in recipes.

ALL-PURPOSE BARBECUE SAUCE

1 cup light molasses
1 cup prepared mustard
1 cup cider vinegar

Combine all ingredients in a 4-cup jar with tight-fitting cover. Shake to mix well. Makes 3 cups.

HERBED LAMB RIBS

4 to 5 pounds breast of lamb
2 cloves of garlic, sliced
2 teaspoons salt
½ teaspoon pepper
Herb Barbecue Sauce (recipe follows)

1. Cut lamb, if needed, into 5- to 6-inch-long strips, each about 3 inches wide.
2. Place in kettle with water to cover; add garlic, salt, and pepper. Cover; simmer 20 minutes, or just until barely tender; drain. (This much can be done ahead, if you like.)
3. Thread lamb on long skewers; brush with HERB BARBECUE SAUCE.
4. Grill over hot coals, turning and brushing

◀ **Ginger Glazed Pork Roast** (recipe on page 105) is a thrifty smoked pork shoulder butt that cooks like ham, tastes like it, too. Sweet potatoes, squash "bowl" and summery salad are its go-withs

often with sauce, 1 hour, or until richly glazed and meat is so tender it almost falls off bones. Makes 6 servings.
HERB BARBECUE SAUCE—Combine 1 cup ALL-PURPOSE BARBECUE SAUCE (see column 1), ½ cup chili sauce; and ½ teaspoon rosemary, crushed, in small saucepan. Makes 1½ cups.

INDONESIAN PORK

2 pounds lean fresh pork shoulder meat, cut in 1-inch cubes
1 jar (1 pound) spiced whole crab apples
Ginger-rich Barbecue Sauce (recipe follows)

1. Place pork cubes in large saucepan with water almost to cover. Cover; simmer 45 minutes, or just until barely tender; drain. (This much can be done ahead, if you like.)
2. Thread pork and crab apples on large skewers, alternating 2 meat cubes to 1 crab apple. Leave room between cubes so meat will brown nicely on all sides. Brush with GINGER-RICH BARBECUE SAUCE.
3. Grill over hot coals, turning and basting often with sauce, 15 minutes, or until pork is tender and well-glazed. Makes 4 servings.
GINGER-RICH BARBECUE SAUCE—Combine 1 cup ALL-PURPOSE BARBECUE SAUCE (recipe at left), ½ cup ginger marmalade, and 1 teaspoon ground ginger in small saucepan. Makes 1½ cups.

SPANISH MEAT-BALL KEBABS

2 pounds ground beef
2 eggs
¼ cup bottled hamburger relish
½ cup flour
2 teaspoons salt
18 large stuffed green olives
Pepper Barbecue Sauce (recipe follows)

1. Mix beef, eggs, hamburger relish, flour, and salt in medium-size bowl.
2. Shape into 18 balls; place in single layer in a shallow pan or tray; cover loosely. Chill 1 to 2 hours, or until firm enough to hold on skewers.
3. Thread meat balls carefully, alternating with olives, on long skewers; brush with PEPPER BARBECUE SAUCE.
4. Grill over hot coals, brushing once or twice with sauce, 10 minutes. Turn carefully; brush again with sauce; grill 10 minutes longer, or until meat is done as you like it. Keep any remaining sauce warm to serve over meat. Makes 6 servings.
PEPPER BARBECUE SAUCE — Combine 1 cup ALL-PURPOSE BARBECUE SAUCE (see column 1), ½ cup tomato juice, and ½ teaspoon cracked or freshly ground pepper in small saucepan. Makes 1½ cups.

LIVER-AND-BACON KEBABS

8 small white onions
1 pound beef, lamb, or calf's liver, thinly sliced
4 slices bacon
1 large sweet red pepper, seeded and cut into 12 squares
1 large green pepper, seeded and cut into 12 squares
   Zippy Barbecue Sauce *(recipe follows)*

1. Peel onions; parboil in boiling salted water in small saucepan 5 minutes; drain.
2. Cut liver slices into strips about the width of sliced bacon. Lay bacon strips on cutting board; top each with 1 or 2 strips of liver.
3. Thread each of 4 long skewers in this order: One onion; 3 squares of pepper (mixed red and green); liver-and-bacon strip, laced accordion style; 3 pepper squares; and 1 onion. Brush with ZIPPY BARBECUE SAUCE.
4. Grill over hot coals, turning and brushing often with sauce, 15 minutes, or just until bacon is crisp. Do not overcook, for it will toughen liver. Time will depend on heat of coals and distance of kebabs from heat. Makes 4 servings.

ZIPPY BARBECUE SAUCE—Combine 1 cup ALL-PURPOSE BARBECUE SAUCE *(page 107)*, ¼ cup catsup, ¼ cup salad oil, and 2 tablespoons Worcestershire sauce in small saucepan. Makes about 1½ cups.

VEGETABLE KEBABS

3 medium-size cucumbers
3 medium-size yellow squashes
½ cup All-purpose Barbecue Sauce *(recipe on page 107)*

1. Trim ends of cucumbers and squashes, but do not pare. Cut each into 1-inch-thick slices.
2. Place in single layer in large shallow pan or use 2 large frying pans; add water to depth of ½ inch; cover; parboil 3 minutes; drain.
3. Thread, alternating cucumber and squash slices, through skin onto long skewers; brush with ALL-PURPOSE BARBECUE SAUCE.
4. Grill over hot coals, turning and brushing often with sauce, 20 minutes, or until tender and glazed. Makes 6 servings.

VEGETABLES

■ POTATO BOATS

8 large potatoes
6 tablespoons (¾ stick) butter or margarine
¼ teaspoon salt
⅛ teaspoon pepper

1. Cook potatoes in boiling salted water in large saucepan 30 minutes, or just until firmly tender. Drain, then peel.
2. Cut each potato crosswise into 5 or 6 thick slices almost through to bottom; arrange on broilerproof platter or in shallow baking pan.
3. Melt butter or margarine with salt and pepper in small saucepan; brush part over potatoes.
4. Broil 6 inches from heat, basting often with remaining butter, 15 minutes, or until golden. Garnish with parsley, if you wish. Take outdoors and set pan on edge of grill to keep hot. Makes 8 servings.

■ CALDRON POTATOES

8 large thin-skin white potatoes
½ cup (1 stick) butter or margarine
1 cup dairy sour cream
4 slices crisp bacon, crumbled
2 tablespoons chopped fresh dill

1. Scrub potatoes well, but do not pare. Cook in boiling salted water in kettle over hot coals just until tender. (Time will depend on size of potatoes, heat and distance from coals.) Drain; return kettle, uncovered, to grill; let steam a few minutes to dry potatoes.
2. Beat butter or margarine until fluffy in small bowl; beat in sour cream.
3. Make a crisscross in top of each potato; squeeze at each end to fluff up. Top with a big spoonful of butter-cream mixture; sprinkle with bacon and dill. Makes 8 servings.

■ SWEET-POTATO PACKS

6 medium-size sweet potatoes
1 tablespoon salad oil
6 tablespoons (¾ stick) butter or margarine
   Seasoned salt

1. Scrub and dry sweet potatoes well. Rub skins with salad oil; wrap each tightly in foil; set on grill over hot coals.
2. Grill, turning often, 1 hour, or until soft when pressed between fingers. (Protect fingers with a pot holder.)
3. Cut a crisscross in top through foil; squeeze potato firmly at each end to fluff up; turn foil back to form a serving dish. Top each with butter or margarine; sprinkle lightly with seasoned salt. Makes 6 servings.

For fun, there's nothing like a kebab party. Line-up here: **Herbed Lamb Ribs, Indonesian Pork,** and **Vegetable, Spanish Meat-ball,** and **Liver-and-bacon Kebabs.** *(Recipes for all are here and on page 107)*

■ ORIENTAL RICE BOWL

    1 cup uncooked rice
    4 tablespoons (½ stick) butter or margarine
 1½ tablespoons lime juice
    1 cup thinly sliced celery
    1 small onion, grated
    ½ cup toasted slivered almonds (from a 5-ounce
        can)
    ½ cup mayonnaise or salad dressing

1. Cook rice, following label directions. Stir
   in butter or margarine and lime juice; toss
   lightly with a fork. Cool to room temperature.
2. Fold in celery, onion, almonds, and mayonnaise or salad dressing. Spoon into serving
   bowl—no need to heat or chill. Makes 6
   servings.

■ PANNED CABBAGE AND CUCUMBER

    4 tablespoons salad oil
    6 cups finely shredded green cabbage
    1 large cucumber, pared, seeded, and
        chopped (2 cups)
    ½ cup water
        OR: ½ cup canned chicken broth
        Salt and pepper
    ½ cup dairy sour cream
    ½ teaspoon sesame seeds

1. Heat salad oil in your largest frying pan;
   stir in cabbage and cucumber; saute, stirring often, 2 minutes, or just until cabbage
   starts to turn bright green.
2. Pour water or chicken broth over; cover.
3. Heat to boiling, then steam 7 minutes, or
   until vegetables are crisply tender. Season
   with salt and pepper.
4. Spoon sour cream on top; sprinkle with
   sesame seeds. Serve right from its skillet
   cooker. Makes 6 servings.

■ GREEN-AND-GOLD SQUASH SAUTE

    4 medium-size zucchini
    2 medium-size yellow squashes
    2 medium-size onions, sliced and separated
        into rings
    4 tablespoons (½ stick) butter or margarine
    1 teaspoon salt
    ¼ teaspoon pepper
    ¼ cup water

1. Wash and trim ends of zucchini and yellow
   squashes; cut into ½-inch thick chunks.
2. Saute onion rings in butter or margarine
   just until soft in large heavy frying pan;
   push to one side.
3. Place zucchini and squash chunks in same
   pan; sprinkle with salt and pepper; pour
   water over; spoon onion rings on top.
4. Cover; steam 20 minutes, or until crisply
   tender. Garnish with chopped pimiento, if
   you wish. Makes 6 servings.

■ CHUCK-WAGON BEANS

    4 slices bacon, diced
    1 large onion, chopped (1 cup)
    2 cans (about 1 pound each) baked beans
    1 tablespoon molasses
    1 tablespoon vinegar
    ½ teaspoon dry mustard
    ¼ teaspoon cinnamon
   12 pitted dried prunes

1. Saute bacon slowly in large frying pan; stir
   in onion and cook just until soft.
2. Place beans in a 6-cup baking dish or bean
   pot; stir in bacon-onion mixture, molasses,
   vinegar, mustard, and cinnamon. Cut up
   prunes with scissors and stir into beans.
3. Bake, uncovered, in moderate oven (350°)
   1 hour, or until bubbly-hot. Makes 6 servings.

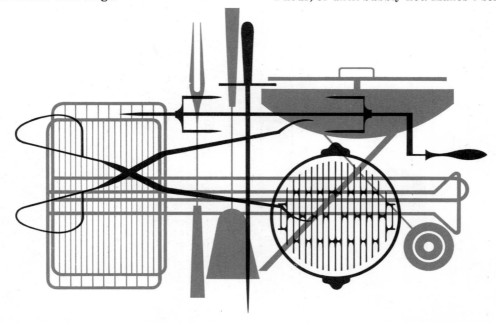

SALADS

■ DOUBLE-DOUBLE SALAD

1 small head of romaine
1 small head of iceberg lettuce
¼ pound sharp Cheddar cheese, cubed
¼ pound Monterey Jack cheese, cubed
   OR: ¼ pound Muenster cheese, cubed
6 small thin carrots, trimmed and scraped
6 white radishes, trimmed and scraped
   Piquant Dressing (recipe follows)

1. Break romaine and lettuce into bite-size pieces in salad bowl, leaving a shallow well in center. Arrange cheese cubes around well.
2. Bunch carrots and radishes, tip ends up, to form a bouquet; place in center well. (Cheese cubes will hold bouquet in place.)
3. Toss with PIQUANT DRESSING just before serving. Makes 8 servings.

PIQUANT DRESSING—Combine ⅔ cup salad oil, ⅓ cup wine vinegar or cider vinegar, 2 teaspoons sugar, ½ teaspoon dry mustard, and ½ teaspoon salt in jar with tight-fitting cover. Shake well to mix, then shake again just before serving. Makes 1 cup.

■ COOKOUT SALAD

1 large head of romaine
1 cucumber, pared and sliced
3 hard-cooked eggs, shelled and chopped
1 cup cherry tomatoes, halved
   Bottled Italian salad dressing

1. Break romaine into bite-size pieces in a large salad bowl. Arrange cucumber slices, then hard-cooked eggs in rings on top; fill center with cherry tomatoes.
2. Toss with just enough salad dressing to coat greens well. Makes 8 servings.

■ LIMA SALAD CUPS

2 packages (10 ounces each) frozen Fordhook lima beans
2 cups sliced celery
¼ cup thin French dressing
¼ pound unsliced process American cheese, cut in small cubes
12 pitted ripe olives, sliced
   Lettuce

1. Cook lima beans, following label directions, adding celery during last 5 minutes' cooking. Drain; place in medium-size bowl.
2. Pour French dressing over; toss lightly to mix; chill.
3. Just before serving, add cheese and olives; toss lightly. Serve in lettuce-lined waxed paper cups or bowls. Makes 6 servings.

■ TOMATO BOWL

1 clove of garlic, minced
1 teaspoon salt
1 teaspoon sugar
¼ teaspoon pepper
2 teaspoons prepared mustard
¼ cup olive oil or salad oil
2 tablespoons cider vinegar
6 firm ripe tomatoes, sliced
¼ cup chopped parsley

1. Combine garlic, salt, sugar, pepper, mustard, olive oil or salad oil, and vinegar in jar with tight-fitting cover; shake to mix well.
2. Place tomato slices in large shallow serving bowl; sprinkle with parsley; pour dressing over. Let stand at room temperature at least 20 minutes to blend flavors. Makes 6 servings.

DESSERTS

■ PICNIC WATERMELON

Buy a ripe whole watermelon. (A ripe one will give a dull thumping sound when tapped.) Cut off a slice across top equal to ⅓ of melon; lift off. Run knife around inside of rind of larger piece to loosen melon from edge about 3 inches down. Cut fruit down middle, then slice crosswise into pieces; pry out with knife. Cut sections from small piece the same way; pile all back into melon shell. Chill. Serve plain or with salt. Figure about 8 generous servings from 1 watermelon.

■ POPCORN POPS

⅔ cup light corn syrup
⅔ cup sugar
½ teaspoon salt
⅛ teaspoon red food coloring
   Few drops peppermint extract
8 cups unsalted freshly popped popcorn

1. Combine corn syrup, sugar, salt, red food coloring, and peppermint extract in small saucepan. Heat slowly, stirring constantly, 3 to 5 minutes, or just until sugar dissolves.
2. Pour syrup over popped corn in kettle; toss with wooden spoon until evenly coated. Place kettle over medium heat; cook, stirring constantly, 5 minutes, or until corn kernels start to stick together.
3. Divide into 4 mounds on waxed paper, foil, or transparent wrap; shape into large balls. (You'll have no burned fingers here, for corn stays sticky enough to mold when cool.)
4. To serve on a stick, make a deep hole in each ball with knife; insert a long thin dowel stick. Tie with red, white, and blue ribbons, if you wish. (For easy handling, make only one recipe at a time.) Makes 4 pops.

111

■ ORANGE-BLOSSOM SUNDAES

1¼ cups milk
⅔ cup sugar
1 can (6 ounces) frozen concentrated orange
  juice
1 cup cream for whipping
⅛ teaspoon salt
1 tablespoon lemon juice
1 egg white, stiffly beaten
  Burnt-sugar Sauce *(recipe follows)*

1. Combine milk and sugar in medium-size saucepan; heat, stirring constantly, just until sugar dissolves. Remove from heat.
2. Stir in frozen orange juice, cream, salt, and lemon juice. (Mixture may look curdled, but flecks will disappear when frozen.)
3. Pour into pan, 8x8x2, or 2 ice-cube trays; freeze until firm about 1 inch in from edge. Spoon into a chilled large bowl; beat until fluffy-smooth; fold in beaten egg white.
4. Return to pan; freeze 30 minutes; stir again. Freeze 2 to 3 hours longer, or until firm.
5. Spoon into dessert dishes; pour BURNT-SUGAR SAUCE over. Garnish with a ball of crystallized ginger pierced with a kebab stick or pick, if you wish. Makes 6 to 8 servings.

BURNT-SUGAR SAUCE—Heat 1½ cups sugar in medium-size heavy frying pan or saucepan, stirring often with a wooden spoon, just until melted into a golden syrup; remove from heat. Stir in 1 cup boiling water *very slowly*. (Watch it, for mixture will spatter.) Return to heat; cook, stirring constantly, 10 minutes, or until sugar dissolves. (Sauce will be thin, but it will thicken as it cools.) Makes about 1½ cups.

■ WHITE MOUNTAIN AMBROSIA

3 large oranges, pared and sectioned
3 ripe peaches, peeled and sliced
2 red apples, quartered, cored, and cut into
  bite-size pieces
1 can (about 13 ounces) frozen pineapple chunks,
  thawed
½ cup orange juice plus juice from sectioned fruit
1 can (3½ ounces) flaked coconut

Combine fruits and juices in a shallow glass serving bowl; top with a cone of flaked coconut. Chill until serving time. Makes 8 servings.

■ APRICOT RICE-PUDDING TART

½ cup uncooked rice
½ cup sugar (for filling)
2 tablespoons butter or margarine
¼ teaspoon salt
¼ teaspoon ground allspice
1 cup milk
1 cup water
1 package piecrust mix
1 can (1 pound, 13 ounces) apricot halves,
  drained
1 tablespoon cream
1 tablespoon sugar (for topping)

1. Combine rice, ½ cup sugar, butter or margarine, salt, allspice, milk, and water in large saucepan; heat to boiling. Cover; simmer, stirring often with a fork, 30 minutes, or until rice is tender but still moist. Remove from heat.
2. Prepare piecrust mix, following label directions, or make pastry from your own favorite two-crust recipe. Roll out half to a 12-inch round on lightly floured pastry cloth or board; fit into a 9-inch pie plate, leaving overhang to trim later.
3. Spoon rice mixture into shell; arrange apricot halves, rounded side up, on top.
4. Roll out remaining pastry to a rectangle, 12x8. Brush lightly with cream and sprinkle with 1 tablespoon sugar; cut into 10 strips, each about ¾ inch wide. Twist and weave strips over filling to make a crisscross top; trim overhang to ½ inch; turn up over rim and flute.
5. Bake in hot oven (400°) 30 minutes, or until pastry is golden. Cool on wire rack. Serve with cream or a dollop of creamy topping from a pressurized can, if you wish. Makes 1 nine-inch tart.

Velvety ice cream, a glittering sun-gold sauce, and ▶ saucy ginger stick make this cookout-best **Orange-blossom Sundae**. With its snowy cap of coconut, **White Mountain Ambrosia** is as cooling as its name

*I*NVITE folks for Sunday dinner, weekday potluck, or just because you want to share your specialty, for dinner's such a friendly, cozy way to entertain.

In this chapter you won't find a single roast, for they're spotted around in other places. Instead, we have chosen simple dishes with just enough doll-ups to add a party flair, yet none keeps you hustling about the kitchen until the last minute before mealtime.

Chicken, an all-time favorite and a budget-saver, too, comes first. Here meaty pieces bake with the best-tast-

Dinners that say "Welcome!"

ing curry-sparked sauce imaginable. Veal pie, hiding some gourmet touches, is here, and sauerbraten—an Old-World stand-by. All are perfect meat choices to remember when men head your guest list.

Read on to our pretty-as-springtime crab-omelet roll. It may be new to you, but do give it a try on the family first, then splurge with a party for the girls. Pork chops—and even versatile ground beef—have their place in these dinners that say "Welcome, we're glad you came."

Party-perfect Chicken *(recipe on page 117)* rates its ▶ name, for it bakes with only a smidgen of care, looks so glamorous on its platter with rice. Turn to page 125 to see its splurgy coffee-cup dessert partner

Party dinners for casual get-togethers

	MAIN DISH	VEGETABLE • SALAD	DESSERT	NICE TO ADD

EASY-DO CHICKEN FANCY
(pictured on page 115)

★Party-perfect Chicken with ★Curry Glaze — Buttered Rice ★Vegetable Medley ★Spinach-ring Salad — ★Lemon Souffle-ettes *(pictured on page 125)* — ★Melon Crescents *(pictured on page 6)*

The fame of this dish travels fast, and once you serve it, be prepared for recipe requests. Chicken bakes deep and rich with a zesty bacon-curry topping. Mild-flavor rice go-with can cook in the same oven. Fix the dessert spectacular ahead—it'll take chilling. Pop into oven to bake while you eat, then carry to the table piping-hot

---

DINNER'S IN ONE DISH

★Continental Veal Pie — Romaine Salad Bowl with Roquefort Cheese — ★Viennese Chocolate Torte *(pictured on page 125)* — ★Pâté Provencale Toast Squares

It takes so little to give food a gourmet lift, and this veal pie is a good example. Meat is budget-tagged shoulder, simmered with hot sausage in a ready-mix sauce, then baked with a crispy crust decked with pastry cutouts, continental style. Go old-world the whole way and serve this choco-laty Viennese dessert. It's plain lavish!

PRETTY AS SPRINGTIME
(pictured on page 118)

★Crab Roulade with ★Shrimp Sauce ★Fluted Mushrooms — ★Peas Parisienne ★Salad Relish Tray ★Louis Dressing — ★Queen's Coconut Cake Tea — ★Strawberry-lime Cup Hot Biscuits

Call it luncheon or dinner, for it's dainty, yet hearty enough for either—and a con-versation-starter when you are entertain-ing the girls. Crab salad is the filling for the heavenly-light omelet roll with shrimp sauce to spoon over. Top buttered peas with "petals" of sliced radishes; finish with the queen of cakes and cups of tea

---

SUNNY PORK PLATTER

★Spicy Glazed Pork Chops with Apricots — ★Garden Pepper Pie ★Green Beans Vinaigrette — ★Coffee-almond Sparkle Sundaes ★Oatmeal Dandies — ★Shrimp Cocktail with ★Guacamole Sauce

Pork chops rate high as a meat choice, and here they are baked with a tangy apricot glaze. And do try this new way with crisp sweet red and green peppers, for the big bright squares, nestled in a creamy cus-tard, bake inside a corn-meal crust along-side pork. Shrimps, topped with a zippy avocado dressing, make an inviting starter

---

GOOD CHOICE FOR MEN

★Old-world Sauerbraten — Boiled Potatoes ★Caraway Cabbage — ★Rich-rich Cheesecake — Buttered Green Beans Dark Rye Bread

Here's a meat men order when they eat out. It's really simple to cook but it does take time to season, so buy beef at least three days ahead of your dinner. Fluffy boiled potatoes and savory cabbage are "musts" with sauerbraten. And to end this feast with rich-as-rich creamy cheesecake is nothing short of pure gourmet dining

---

GOURMET HAMBURGER TREAT

★Burger-tomato Towers — ★Cheese Potatoes ★Carrot Rings with Peas — ★Parfait Straw-berry Shortcakes — ★Senegalese Soup ★Molded Relish Salad

Ground beef moves right up to the party front here. Thick patties "broil" juicy-tender atop the range, then team with grilled tomatoes and perky mushroom kebabs for the prettiest company main dish. Go-withs all have fancy touches— even dessert of crispy-thin biscuits layered with berries and cream in big goblets

MAIN DISHES

■ PARTY-PERFECT CHICKEN

Curry Glaze *(recipe follows)*
2 broilers-fryers (about 3 pounds each),
   quartered
6 tablespoons flour
½ teaspoon salt
1 teaspoon ground ginger
6 tablespoons (¾ stick butter or margarine
   Buttered hot rice

1. Make CURRY GLAZE.
2. Cut away backbones and any small rib bones
   from chickens. (Kitchen scissors do a fast
   neat job.) Pull off skin, if desired. Shake
   chicken pieces in mixture of flour, salt, and
   ginger in paper bag to coat well.
3. Melt butter or margarine in large shallow
   baking or roasting pan. Roll chicken in
   melted butter to coat well, then arrange,
   skin side up, in single layer in pan.
4. Bake, uncovered, in hot oven (400°) 20 minutes, or until starting to turn golden. Spoon
   about half of CURRY GLAZE on top of chicken
   to make a thick coating; bake 20 minutes.
   Spoon on remaining glaze; bake 20 minutes
   longer, or until chicken is tender and richly
   browned.
5. Arrange chicken around a mound of buttered hot rice on serving platter. Garnish
   with lemon cups filled with your own or
   store-bought pepper relish, if you wish.
   Makes 8 servings.

CURRY GLAZE

6 slices bacon, finely diced
1 medium-size onion, chopped (½ cup)
2 tablespoons flour
1 tablespoon curry powder
1 tablespoon sugar
1 teaspoon salt
1 teaspoon bottled steak sauce
2 envelopes instant beef broth
   OR: 2 beef-bouillon cubes
1 cup water
2 tablespoons lemon juice
1 jar (4 ounces) baby-pack strained
   apples-and-apricots
2 tablespoons flaked coconut

1. Fry bacon slowly in medium-size saucepan
   just until fat starts to cook out; stir in
   onion; saute just until soft.
2. Blend in flour, curry powder, sugar, salt,
   and steak sauce; cook, stirring constantly,
   just until mixture bubbles; stir in remaining ingredients.
3. Heat, stirring constantly, to boiling, then
   simmer, uncovered, 15 minutes, or until
   thickened. Makes about 2 cups.

■ CONTINENTAL VEAL PIE

1½ pounds veal shoulder meat, cut in 1-inch cubes
3 tablespoons flour
3 tablespoons olive oil or salad oil
2 Italian hot sausages, sliced ½-inch thick
12 small white onions, peeled
1 envelope (2¼ ounces) spaghetti-sauce mix
   with tomato
3 cups water
12 small carrots, scraped and cut in sticks
6 medium-size zucchini, trimmed and cut in
   sticks
¼ pound fresh mushrooms, sliced
   OR: 1 can (3 or 4 ounces) sliced mushrooms
   and liquid
1 stick piecrust mix
1 egg
1 tablespoon milk
   Few drops bottled red-pepper seasoning

1. Shake veal, a few pieces at a time, with flour
   in paper bag to coat evenly. Brown quickly
   in olive oil or salad oil in heavy kettle or
   Dutch oven; push to one side.
2. Brown sausages in same kettle; push to one
   side; add onions and saute just until lightly
   browned.
3. Combine spaghetti-sauce mix and water in
   4-cup measure. (Mix has tomato right in it,
   so all you need to add is the water.) Stir into
   kettle; cover. Simmer 1½ hours, or until
   veal is tender.
4. Cook carrot and zucchini sticks together in
   boiling salted water in large saucepan 15
   minutes, or just until crisply tender; drain
   thoroughly.
5. Mound veal mixture, cooked vegetables, and
   mushrooms into a round 8-cup baking dish.
6. Prepare piecrust mix, following label directions, or make pastry from your own favorite
   one-crust recipe. Roll out on lightly floured
   pastry cloth or board to a circle 3 inches
   larger than baking dish; cut 4-inch cross in
   center. Fold points of cross back so gravy
   won't darken pastry; lay circle over rolling
   pin and transfer to baking dish. Trim overhang to 1 inch; fold under flush with rim;
   flute.
7. Roll out all trimmings ¼-inch thick; cut into
   fancy shapes with truffle or small cooky
   cutters.
8. Beat egg slightly with milk and red-pepper
   seasoning in a cup; brush part over pie.
   Place cutouts around edge; brush them also.
   Cover center hole with a small piece of foil
   to keep vegetables from drying out during
   baking.
9. Bake in hot oven (425°) 15 minutes; brush
   again with egg mixture. Bake 15 minutes
   longer, or until golden.
10. Remove the foil covering. To serve pie, cut
    pastry into wedge-shape pieces with sharp
    knife. Makes 6 servings.

■ CRAB ROULADE

Crab-salad Filling

2 cans (about 7 ounces each) king crab meat
2 cups finely diced celery
½ cup toasted slivered almonds
    (from a 5-ounce can)
½ cup mayonnaise or salad dressing
¼ cup dairy sour cream
1 tablespoon lemon juice
½ teaspoon salt

Omelet Roll

4 tablespoons (½ stick) butter or margarine
½ cup flour
½ teaspoon salt
    Dash of cayenne
2 cups milk
4 eggs
    Shrimp Sauce (recipe follows)
    Fluted Mushrooms (recipe follows)

1. Make crab-salad filling: Drain and flake crab meat, carefully removing any bony tissue; place in medium-size bowl.
2. Stir in remaining ingredients; toss lightly to mix. Save for Step 9. (If made ahead, chill, then remove from refrigerator and let stand at room temperature for 15 minutes before filling roll.)
3. Make omelet roll: Grease jelly-roll pan, 15x10x1; line with waxed paper; grease paper; dust with flour.
4. Melt butter or margarine in medium-size saucepan; remove from heat. Blend in flour, salt, and cayenne; stir in milk slowly. Cook, stirring constantly, until mixture is very thick and boils 1 minute.
5. Separate eggs, putting whites and yolks in separate medium-size bowls. Beat whites until they form soft peaks. Beat yolks slightly, then *very slowly* beat in hot mixture until well-blended. Fold in beaten whites until no streaks of yellow or white remain. Spread evenly into prepared pan.
6. Bake in slow oven (325°) 40 to 45 minutes, or until golden-brown and top springs back when lightly pressed with fingertip.
7. While omelet roll bakes, make SHRIMP SAUCE and FLUTED MUSHROOMS.
8. Remove omelet roll from pan this way: Loosen around edge with spatula; cover with waxed paper or foil. Place a large cooky sheet or tray on top, then quickly turn upside down. Lift off pan; peel off waxed paper.
9. Spoon crab-salad filling evenly over roll.

◄ Planned just for the girls—that's this pretty-as-springtime platter. **Crab Roulade** is the tenderest golden omelet, baked, then rolled around a zippy crab filling. Rest of meal is just as elegant

(Use a slotted spoon to let any dressing drip back into bowl.) Starting at one end, roll up omelet, jelly-roll fashion, lifting waxed paper or foil as you roll to steady and guide it.

10. Lift roll onto heated serving platter with two wide spatulas. (If serving time is delayed, keep warm in heated oven.) Spoon about ½ cup hot SHRIMP SAUCE over; garnish with FLUTED MUSHROOMS. Cut roll into thick slices with sharp knife. Serve remaining sauce in a separate bowl to spoon over. Makes 6 servings.

SHRIMP SAUCE—Thaw 1 can frozen cream of shrimp soup in top of double boiler over boiling water. Blend in ¼ cup milk; heat until bubbly-hot. Stir in 2 tablespoons chopped parsley. Makes 1½ cups.

FLUTED MUSHROOMS—Wash 6 large fresh mushrooms; cut off stems close to caps. With a sharp thin-blade knife, mark center of each cap. Starting here, make a curved cut about ⅛ inch deep to edge. Repeat around cap to make 8 evenly spaced cuts. Now make a second curved cut just behind each line, slanting knife in so you can lift out a narrow strip. (Cap will now spread open slightly when heated.) Melt 2 tablespoons butter or margarine over medium heat in small frying pan; place mushrooms, cut side down, in pan. Saute 1 to 2 minutes, or until golden; turn; saute 1 minute longer. Skewer each to CRAB ROULADE with a wooden pick threaded with 3 small pickled onions. Makes 6 servings.

■ SPICY GLAZED PORK CHOPS WITH APRICOTS

1 can (1 pound, 14 ounces) whole apricots
1 tablespoon bottled steak sauce
1 teaspoon salt
6 rib or loin pork chops, cut ½ inch thick
1 teaspoon whole cloves

1. Drain syrup from apricots into medium-size saucepan; stir in steak sauce and salt. Heat to boiling; cook, uncovered, 5 minutes, or until syrup thickens slightly. (There should be about 1¼ cups after cooking.) Set apricots aside for heating and glazing in Step 3.
2. Arrange chops in single layer in baking pan, 13x9x2; pour ¾ cup hot syrup over. Do not cover.
3. Bake in moderate oven (375°) 45 minutes; turn chops. Stud apricots with cloves; arrange around chops; pour remaining syrup over.
4. Bake, basting several times with syrup in pan, 30 minutes longer, or until chops are tender and richly glazed. Makes 6 servings.

Note: Any pan juices left over? Save and use to glaze cooked sweet potatoes for another meal.

OLD-WORLD SAUERBRATEN

5 to 6 pounds beef round, rump, sirloin tip, or
    boneless chuck roast
2 cups wine vinegar or cider vinegar
2 cups water
¼ cup firmly packed brown sugar
1 tablespoon salt
½ teaspoon pepper
½ teaspoon ground cloves
1 bay leaf
3 medium-size onions, chopped (1½ cups)
2 large carrots, diced (1½ cups)
1½ cups diced celery
2 tablespoons bacon drippings or shortening
8 gingersnaps, crumbled

1. Place meat in a large glass or pottery bowl;
   pour mixture of vinegar, water, brown
   sugar, seasonings, and vegetables over.
   Cover; store in refrigerator 2 to 3 days,
   turning meat several times to marinate on all
   sides.
2. When ready to cook, remove meat from marinade and pat dry; brown in hot drippings or
   shortening in heavy kettle or Dutch oven.
   Strain vegetables from marinade; add to
   meat in kettle, then pour in liquid to a depth
   of 1 inch.
3. Cover kettle tightly; simmer 3 hours, or
   until meat is very tender. Remove to heated
   serving platter; keep hot while making
   gravy.
4. Strain broth into a 4-cup measure; let stand
   about a minute, or until fat rises to top. Skim
   off fat, returning 4 tablespoons to kettle.
5. Add water to broth, if needed, to make 2
   cups; stir back into kettle; sprinkle crumbled gingersnaps over. Cook, stirring constantly, until gravy thickens and is bubbly-
   hot.
6. Slice meat; serve with gravy to spoon over.
   Makes 8 servings.

BURGER-TOMATO TOWERS

2½ pounds ground beef
1½ teaspoons seasoned salt
2 large firm ripe tomatoes
2 cans (3 or 4 ounces each) whole mushrooms
3 tablespoons butter or margarine

1. Spread ground beef on a sheet of foil or
   waxed paper; sprinkle with seasoned salt;
   shape lightly into a roll, then slice into 8
   thick patties. (Handle meat with a light
   touch, then it will cook tender and juicy.)
2. Place patties in heated large frying pan. (No
   need to add fat.) Turn heat to low; cook 10
   minutes, or until juices appear on top; turn;
   cook 5 to 10 minutes longer, or until done as
   you like them.
3. While meat cooks, remove stem ends from tomatoes; cut each crosswise into 4 thick slices.

Drain mushrooms. (Save liquid for next
step.) Saute tomato slices and mushrooms
in butter or margarine in second large frying pan, turning tomatoes once, just until
heated through.
4. Arrange meat patties on heated serving
   platter. Heat liquid from mushrooms in
   same frying pan; spoon over patties. Top
   each with a tomato slice; garnish with
   mushroom caps. (If small, thread on wooden
   picks, dividing evenly; stick into tomato,
   kebab style.) Makes 8 servings.

VEGETABLES

CHEESE POTATOES

8 baking potatoes, scrubbed and dried
6 tablespoons (¾ stick) butter or margarine
¾ cup milk
1 teaspoon salt
⅛ teaspoon pepper
1 cup grated Cheddar cheese (¼ pound)

1. Bake potatoes in moderate oven (375°) 1
   hour, or until soft when pressed with fingers.
   (Use a hot pad to protect your fingers.)
2. Cut a thick slice lengthwise across top of
   each potato; scoop out middle with a spoon
   into top of large double boiler. (Discard top
   skins, saving shells for Step 4.)
3. Heat butter or margarine with milk, salt,
   and pepper in small saucepan; beat into potatoes, a little at a time, until fluffy-light.
4. Heap hot potato mixture into shells, dividing
   evenly; sprinkle grated cheese over. (If potatoes must stand for a while before stuffing,
   cover double-boiler top and set over simmering water to keep hot.
5. Bake in moderate oven (375°) 10 minutes
   longer, or until cheese melts. Makes 8
   servings.

■ VEGETABLE MEDLEY

2 packages (10 ounces each) frozen green peas
1 cup thinly sliced celery
4 green onions, sliced
½ teaspoon sugar
2 tablespoons butter or margarine
⅛ teaspoon pepper
½ cup cream

1. Cook peas, celery, green onions, and sugar in small amount boiling salted water in medium-size saucepan 10 minutes, or just until peas are tender; drain.
2. Season with butter or margarine and pepper; pour cream over; reheat just until bubbly-hot. Makes 8 servings.

■ PEAS PARISIENNE

2 packages (10 ounces each) frozen green peas
1 teaspoon salt
1 teaspoon sugar
2 tablespoons butter or margarine
1 large lettuce leaf
6 radishes, trimmed and sliced thin
    (about ½ cup)

1. Place peas in 6-cup baking dish; sprinkle with salt and sugar; dot with butter or margarine; top with lettuce leaf.
2. Bake, covered, in slow oven (325°) 1 hour and 15 minutes, or until tender.
3. Remove lettuce; spoon peas into serving dish; arrange radish slices, overlapping, to form a rosette on top. Makes 6 servings.

■ GARDEN PEPPER PIE

Crust
¾ cup sifted flour
½ cup yellow corn meal
1½ teaspoons baking powder
½ teaspoon salt
4 tablespoons shortening
⅓ cup milk

Filling
2 medium-size sweet red peppers
2 medium-size green peppers
1 large onion, chopped (1 cup)
4 tablespoons (½ stick) butter or margarine
3 tablespoons flour
1 teaspoon salt
1 teaspoon oregano
1 egg
¾ cup milk

1. Make crust: Combine flour, corn meal, baking powder, and salt in medium-size bowl; cut in shortening with pastry blender until mixture is crumbly. Stir in milk with a fork just until dough clings together and leaves side of bowl clean.
2. Press evenly over bottom and side of a 10-inch pie plate or 6-cup shallow baking dish.
3. Make filling: Wash peppers; cut out stems, seeds, and membrane; cut peppers into 1-

inch squares. Parboil in small amount boiling salted water in medium-size saucepan 5 minutes; drain well.
4. Saute onion in butter or margarine in same saucepan; stir in drained peppers. Sprinkle with flour, salt, and oregano; toss lightly to mix; spoon into crust-lined dish.
5. Beat egg slightly with milk in 2-cup measure; pour over vegetable mixture.
6. Bake in moderate oven (375°) 40 minutes, or until top is golden and custard is set but still soft in center. Let stand 10 to 15 minutes; cut into wedges. Makes 6 servings.

■ CARAWAY CABBAGE

1 medium-size head of green cabbage (about 3 pounds)
1 teaspoon sugar
1 teaspoon salt
2 tablespoons butter or margarine, melted
1 teaspoon caraway seeds

1. Halve cabbage, then cut each half into 4 wedges. Cook in small amount of boiling water seasoned with sugar and salt in large frying pan, 15 minutes, or just until tender.
2. Lift out with slotted spatula onto heated serving platter, being careful not to break wedges. Spoon butter or margarine over; sprinkle evenly with caraway seeds. Makes 8 servings.

■ CARROT RINGS WITH PEAS

2 pounds of carrots (about 20 medium-size)
1 small onion, chopped (¼ cup)
4 tablespoons (½ stick) butter or margarine
¼ cup chopped parsley
1½ teaspoons salt
¼ teaspoon pepper
2 packages (10 ounces each) frozen green peas
Butter or margarine
Salt and pepper

1. Scrape and quarter carrots; cook in boiling salted water in medium-size saucepan 20 minutes, or until tender; drain; mash.
2. Saute onion in butter or margarine until soft in small frying pan; stir into carrots with parsley, salt, and pepper.
3. Grease 8 four-ounce ring molds; fill with carrot mixture, dividing evenly. (This much can be done ahead, then chilled until 30 minutes before baking time.)
4. Bake in moderate oven (375°) 15 minutes, or until carrot mixture starts to pull away from sides of molds.
5. While carrots bake, cook peas, following label directions; drain; season to taste with butter or margarine, salt and pepper.
6. Unmold a carrot ring onto each heated serving plate; spoon seasoned peas into center. Makes 8 servings.

121

SALADS

■ SPINACH-RING SALAD

2 packages (10 ounces each) fresh spinach
2 pimientos, cut into rings
1 small Bermuda onion, sliced thin and separated
   into rings
½ cup salted peanuts
   Egg Dressing (recipe follows)

1. Remove stems and any coarse leaves from spinach; wash and dry leaves well; tear into bite-size pieces. Arrange with pimiento and onion rings in salad bowl.
2. Just before serving, add peanuts; toss with EGG DRESSING. Makes 8 servings.

EGG DRESSING

¼ cup salad oil
2 tablespoons lemon juice
½ teaspoon salt
½ teaspoon sugar
⅛ teaspoon pepper
2 hard-cooked eggs, shelled and chopped

1. Combine salad oil, lemon juice, salt, sugar, and pepper in jar with tight-fitting cover; shake well.
2. Just before serving, add chopped eggs; shake well again. Makes about ½ cup.

■ SALAD RELISH TRAY

2 stalks Belgian endive
1 package frozen artichoke hearts
¼ cup bottled thin French dressing
1 pimiento, diced
   Louis Dressing (recipe follows)

1. Split endive stalks, then shred each lengthwise into long thin strips with sharp knife. Chill in a bowl of ice and water 1 to 2 hours, or until strips curl.
2. Cook artichoke hearts in medium-size saucepan, following label directions. Drain; place in pie plate; pour French dressing over. Let stand at least 1 hour to marinate.
3. When ready to serve, drain endive well; arrange in mounds around edge of round serving tray. Drain artichoke hearts; spoon in between; garnish with diced pimiento.
4. Fill a small bowl with LOUIS DRESSING; set in center of tray. Makes 6 servings.

LOUIS DRESSING

1 cup mayonnaise or salad dressing
¼ cup chili sauce
¼ cup chopped ripe olives
1 hard-cooked egg, shelled and diced
½ teaspoon Worcestershire sauce
½ teaspoon seasoned salt

Combine mayonnaise or salad dressing, chili sauce, olives, egg, Worcestershire sauce, and salt in small bowl; stir until well-blended. Cover; chill until serving time. Makes 1⅔ cups. (Store any leftover dressing in covered jar in refrigerator for salad another day.)

■ GREEN BEANS VINAIGRETTE

1 can (about 1 pound) Blue Lake whole
   green beans
1 green onion, sliced
½ cup salad oil
¼ cup vinegar
2 teaspoons sugar
½ teaspoon basil
½ teaspoon salt
⅛ teaspoon pepper
1 small head of iceberg lettuce

1. Drain green beans; place in shallow dish; sprinkle onion over.
2. Mix salad oil, vinegar, sugar, basil, salt, and pepper in 1-cup measure; pour over beans; cover. Let stand at least an hour to season and blend flavors.
3. When ready to serve, shred lettuce; place in individual salad bowls, dividing evenly. Arrange seasoned green beans in small bundles on top; spoon dressing from dish over. Makes 6 servings.

DESSERTS

■ VIENNESE CHOCOLATE TORTE

Filling
1 envelope unflavored gelatin
¼ cup cold water
¾ cup brewed coffee
½ cup (1 stick) butter or margarine
¾ cup sugar
2 eggs
⅓ cup dry cocoa (not instant mix)
1 teaspoon vanilla
1 cup (from an about-8-ounce jar) marshmallow
   cream

Cake
1 cup sifted cake flour
¼ cup dry cocoa (not instant mix)
½ teaspoon baking powder
½ cup (1 stick) butter or margarine
½ cup sugar
3 eggs
½ teaspoon vanilla
½ cup finely chopped walnuts

Frosting
2 tablespoons dry cocoa (not instant mix)
2 tablespoons butter or margarine
1 tablespoon brewed coffee
1 cup sifted 10X (confectioners' powdered) sugar
½ teaspoon vanilla
   Whole blanched almonds

1. Make filling: Soften gelatin in water in

small saucepan; stir in coffee; heat slowly, stirring constantly, just until gelatin dissolves; cool.

2. Cream butter or margarine with sugar until fluffy in large bowl; add eggs, 1 at a time, beating in each very well. (Each will take about 3 minutes.) Stir in cocoa and vanilla; slowly add cooled gelatin mixture; fold in marshmallow cream.

3. Line the bottom of an 8-inch layer-cake pan with waxed paper; pour in gelatin mixture. Chill 2 hours, or until firm.

4. Make cake: Measure flour, cocoa, and baking powder into sifter.

5. Cream butter or margarine with sugar until fluffy in medium-size bowl; beat in eggs, 1 at a time, then vanilla. Sift in dry ingredients, stirring just until well-blended; stir in walnuts. Pour into greased 9-inch layer-cake pan.

6. Bake in slow oven (300°) 35 minutes, or until cake starts to pull away from side of pan. Cool in pan on wire rack 10 minutes; remove from pan; cool completely.

7. Split cake crosswise with sharp thin-blade knife to make 2 thin layers; place 1 on serving plate.

8. Run a spatula around edge of molded filling to loosen from pan; turn out onto cake layer on plate; peel off waxed paper. Top with second layer. Chill while making frosting.

9. Make frosting: Combine cocoa, butter or margarine, and coffee in small saucepan; heat, stirring constantly, just until butter or margarine melts; remove from heat. Stir in 10X sugar and vanilla; beat until smooth. (Frosting will be thin.) Pour immediately over top of cake, spreading to edge with spatula; rim top with whole blanched almonds.

10. Chill until ready to serve. (It will hold well if made even a day ahead.) Slice in thin wedges. Makes 1 nine-inch layer cake.

■ COFFEE-ALMOND SPARKLE SUNDAES

2 cups firmly packed brown sugar
¼ cup dark corn syrup
3 tablespoons water
1 tablespoon lemon juice
¾ teaspoon salt
1 tablespoon butter or margarine
1 teaspoon vanilla
2 pints coffee ice cream
¼ cup toasted blanched almonds

1. Mix sugar, corn syrup, water, lemon juice, and salt in medium-size saucepan. Heat slowly, stirring just until sugar dissolves; add butter or margarine.

2. Heat to boiling; cook, without stirring, to 230° on candy thermometer. (A little syrup will spin fine threads when dropped from tip of spoon.)

3. Remove from heat; stir in vanilla; cool.

4. Scoop ice cream into dessert dishes; spoon sauce over; top with almonds. Makes 6 servings.

■ OATMEAL DANDIES

1½ cups sifted flour
½ teaspoon baking soda
½ teaspoon salt
1 cup shortening
1¼ cups firmly packed brown sugar
1 egg
¼ cup milk
1¾ cups quick-cooking rolled oats
1 cup chopped walnuts

1. Measure flour, baking soda, and salt into sifter.

2. Cream shortening and brown sugar until fluffy in large bowl; beat in egg.

3. Sift in dry ingredients, a third at a time, adding alternately with milk; stir until well-blended. Fold in rolled oats and walnuts.

4. Bake in moderate oven (375°) 12 minutes, or until golden. Remove from cooky sheets; cool completely. Makes about 3½ dozen.

■ LEMON SOUFFLE-ETTES

5 eggs
1 teaspoon baking powder
¼ teaspoon salt
5 tablespoons sugar
2 teaspoons grated lemon rind
3 tablespoons lemon juice

1. Prepare cup bakers this way: Coat 8 straight-side 4-ounce demitasses with softened butter or margarine (or use straight-side custard cups). Make a 2-inch stand-up collar for each cup this way: Fold a 6-inch-wide piece of foil in half lengthwise; wrap around cup, overlapping ends. Mold foil tightly at handle; fasten top with a paper clip, bottom with cellophane tape. Coat inside of collar with butter or margarine; dust each cup lightly with sugar, then tap out any excess.
2. Separate eggs, putting whites into large bowl, yolks into medium-size bowl.
3. Beat egg whites with baking powder and salt just until they form soft peaks.
4. Beat egg yolks well; gradually beat in sugar, 1 tablespoon at a time, until very thick, then slowly beat in lemon rind and lemon juice.
5. Fold egg-yolk mixture gently into beaten egg whites until no streaks of yellow or white remain. Spoon mixture into prepared cups, dividing evenly. Set cups in shallow baking pan; chill not longer than 45 minutes.
6. When ready to bake, place pan on oven shelf; pour boiling water into pan to depth of 1 inch. (Be sure cups do not touch.)
7. Bake in slow oven (325°) 35 minutes, or until puffy-light, dry and firm on top. Remove collars; serve at once. Makes 8 servings.

■ QUEEN'S COCONUT CAKE

3 cups sifted cake flour
4 teaspoons baking powder
1 teaspoon salt
¾ cup shortening
1¾ cups sugar
3 eggs
1 teaspoon vanilla
½ teaspoon lemon extract
1¼ cups milk
Lemon-buttercup Filling *(recipe follows)*
Fluffy Frosting *(recipe follows)*
1 can (3½ ounces) flaked coconut

1. Grease bottoms of 3 nine-inch layer-cake pans; line pans with waxed paper; grease paper.
2. Sift cake flour, baking powder, and salt onto waxed paper.
3. Cream shortening with sugar until fluffy in large bowl with spoon or electric mixer at medium speed. Beat in eggs, 1 at a time, beating well after each addition, then beat in vanilla and lemon extract until well-blended.
4. Add sifted dry ingredients, a third at a time, alternately with milk, stirring with a spoon or beating with mixer at low speed, just until blended. Pour into prepared pans, dividing evenly.
5. Bake in moderate oven (350°) 30 minutes, or until centers spring back when lightly pressed with fingertip.
6. Cool in pans on wire racks 5 minutes; loosen around edges with knife; turn out onto racks; peel off waxed paper; cool completely.
7. Put layers together with LEMON-BUTTERCUP FILLING; frost top and side with FLUFFY FROSTING. Sprinkle coconut around side and over top. Makes 1 nine-inch triple-layer cake.

LEMON-BUTTERCUP FILLING

½ cup sugar
3 tablespoons cornstarch
¼ teaspoon salt
2 egg yolks
¾ cup water
⅓ cup lemon juice
2 tablespoons butter or margarine

1. Mix sugar, cornstarch, and salt in medium-size saucepan; stir in egg yolks and water.
2. Cook, stirring constantly, until mixture thickens and boils 3 minutes; remove from heat. Stir in lemon juice and butter or margarine until well-blended; cool completely. Makes enough to fill 1 nine-inch triple-layer cake.

FLUFFY FROSTING

2 tablespoons light corn syrup
2½ tablespoons water
1½ teaspoons vanilla
½ teaspoon lemon extract
2 egg whites
¼ teaspoon cream of tartar
1 pound 10X (confectioners' powdered) sugar, sifted

1. Combine light corn syrup, water, vanilla, and lemon extract in a cup.
2. Beat egg whites with cream of tartar until they stand in firm peaks in medium-size bowl.
3. Beat in 10X sugar, a quarter at a time, alternately with corn-syrup mixture, beating well after each addition, until frosting is creamy-stiff and easy to spread. Makes enough to frost top and side of 1 nine-inch triple-layer cake.

Just look at these spectaculars! **Lemon Souffle-ettes** ▶ bake sky-high in little coffee-cup servers. Triple cocoa-rich layers make the handsome **Viennese Chocolate Torte**. *(You'll find recipes here and on page 122)*

■ RICH-RICH CHEESECAKE

    1 eight-inch Crumb Crust *(recipe follows)*
1½ packages (8 ounces each) cream cheese
 ¾ cup sugar (for cake)
    Dash of salt
 ½ teaspoon vanilla (for cake)
    2 eggs
    1 cup dairy sour cream
    2 tablespoons sugar (for topping)
    1 teaspoon vanilla (for topping)

1. Make and chill CRUMB CRUST.
2. Let cream cheese soften in large bowl. Beat in ¾ cup sugar, salt, and ½ teaspoon vanilla until fluffy; add eggs, 1 at a time, beating well after each addition until creamy-smooth. Pour into CRUMB CRUST.
3. Bake in moderate oven (350°) 50 minutes, or until firm in center; remove from oven; let stand 15 minutes. Reset oven to very hot (450°).
4. Combine sour cream, 2 tablespoons sugar, and 1 teaspoon vanilla in small bowl; spread over top of cake. Return to oven; bake 10 minutes, or just until topping is set. Cool cake on wire rack; chill completely.
5. Loosen cake around edge of pan with knife; release spring and carefully lift off side of pan. Place cake, still on its metal base, on serving plate. Cut into wedges. Makes 1 eight-inch cake.

CRUMB CRUST—Combine 1½ cups packaged graham-cracker crumbs and 2 tablespoons sugar in small bowl; blend in 4 tablespoons (½ stick) melted butter or margarine. Press firmly over bottom and about 2½ inches up side of a heavily buttered 8-inch spring-form pan, or use a 9-inch pie plate, if you prefer. If using a spring-form pan, set on a 12-inch-long piece of double-thick foil; fold up around side to catch any butter mixture that may bubble out as cake bakes. Chill.

■ PARFAIT STRAWBERRY SHORTCAKES

    2 cups biscuit mix
 ¼ cup sugar
 ⅔ cup milk
    3 tablespoons melted butter or margarine
    6 cups strawberries, washed, hulled, sliced, and sweetened to taste
1½ cups cream, whipped

1. Combine biscuit mix and 2 tablespoons sugar in medium-size bowl. (Save remaining 2 tablespoons sugar for topping in Step 3.) Stir in milk, following label directions for biscuits.
2. Turn out onto lightly floured pastry cloth or board; knead lightly 10 times. Roll out to slightly less than ¼-inch thickness, *for biscuits must be thin;* cut out with floured 2-inch cutter to make 32 rounds.

3. Place on ungreased cooky sheet; prick all over with fork. Brush with melted butter or margarine; sprinkle with saved 2 tablespoons sugar.
4. Bake in very hot oven (450°) 8 minutes, or until golden.
5. Layer 4 hot biscuits with strawberries and cream between each, into goblets or deep dessert dishes. Serve at once while biscuits are hot. Makes 8 servings.

NICE TO ADD

■ MELON CRESCENTS

1 ripe casaba or honeydew melon
1 tablespoon lemon juice
  Pomegranate seeds
1 whole lemon, cut into 8 slices

1. Take melon from refrigerator at least an hour before dinnertime, but do not cut. (When too cold, melon seems to lose some of its flavor and fragrance.) Slice into 8 wedges; scoop out seeds, then pare for daintier serving, if you wish.
2. Brush each wedge with lemon juice; place on serving plate. Sprinkle with a few pomegranate seeds; perch a slice of lemon on one end of each wedge, as pictured on page 6. Makes 8 servings.

■ PÂTÉ PROVENÇALE

1 envelope unflavored gelatin
1 can condensed beef bouillon
2 cans (3 ounces each) liverwurst spread
1 can (4½ ounces) deviled ham
1 teaspoon grated onion
1 teaspoon lemon juice

1. Soften gelatin in bouillon in small saucepan; heat over low heat, stirring constantly, just until gelatin dissolves. Measure ¾ cup into a 3-cup mold; chill just until sticky-firm on top.
2. While gelatin sets, blend liverwurst spread, deviled ham, grated onion, and lemon juice into remaining gelatin mixture in saucepan; spoon over sticky-firm gelatin layer in mold. Cover with waxed paper, foil, or transparent wrap; chill about 2 hours, or until firm.
3. To unmold, run a sharp-tip, thin-blade knife around top of mold, then dip mold *very quickly* in and out of a pan of hot water. Cover with serving plate; turn upside down, then gently lift off mold. Garnish plate with a ring of water cress, if you like. Serve with small squares of toast or your favorite crackers. Makes 8 to 12 servings.

Note: Any left over? Use as a sandwich filling.

■ STRAWBERRY-LIME CUP

2 cups (1 pint) strawberries
1 can (about 14 ounces) frozen pineapple chunks, thawed slightly
1 pint lime sherbet
10X (confectioners' powdered) sugar

1. Wash and hull strawberries; pick out 6 of the biggest and prettiest to save for garnish, then halve remaining.
2. Spoon pineapple chunks into 6 sherbet glasses, dividing evenly. Place a small scoop of sherbet in center. Stand halved strawberries, tip ends up, around sherbet.
3. Dip the saved 6 strawberries into 10X sugar to coat well; stand on top of sherbet. Makes 6 servings.

Note: For a dainty touch, circle base of each glass with a ribbon-tied bouquet of flowers, as shown in our picture on page 118.

■ SHRIMP COCKTAIL

1 pound medium-size fresh shrimps
  OR: 1 package (10 to 12 ounces) frozen shrimps in shells
1 teaspoon salt
1 small onion, sliced
2 slices lemon
1 bay leaf
  Shredded lettuce
  Guacamole Sauce *(recipe follows)*

1. Wash, shell, and devein shrimps. (Turn to page 30 for easy directions.)
2. Half-fill a large frying pan with water; season with salt, onion, lemon, and bay leaf; heat to boiling. Add shrimps; reheat until bubbling, then simmer about 5 minutes for fresh shrimps, 15 to 20 minutes for frozen, or just until tender. (Do not overcook, as this toughens them.) Lift out at once with tongs or slotted spoon; chill.
3. Line 6 sherbet glasses with shredded lettuce. Save 6 shrimps for garnish; spoon remaining on lettuce, dividing evenly. Top with GUACAMOLE SAUCE, then with saved shrimps. Makes 6 servings.

GUACAMOLE SAUCE—Halve, pit, peel, and mash 1 medium-size ripe avocado in small bowl. (You should have about 1 cup.) Blend in ¼ cup mayonnaise or salad dressing, 2 tablespoons lemon juice, 1 teaspoon salt, and ¼ teaspoon bottled red-pepper seasoning. (If sauce is covered tightly, it will keep its rich green color for an hour before serving.) Makes about 1½ cups.

■ SENEGALESE SOUP

2 cans condensed cream of chicken soup
3 cups milk
½ teaspoon curry powder
2 tablespoons toasted coconut

1. Combine soup, milk, and curry powder in medium-size saucepan; heat just until bubbly-hot, then beat with rotary beater until creamy-smooth.
2. Pour into 8 small bowls or cups, dividing evenly; sprinkle with coconut. Makes 8 servings.

■ MOLDED RELISH SALAD

1 package (3 ounces) lime-flavor gelatin
1 cup hot water
1 cup cold water
2 tablespoons cider vinegar
1 teaspoon prepared horseradish
1 teaspoon salt
⅛ teaspoon pepper
1 cup chopped green cabbage
½ cup chopped pared cucumber
2 tablespoons chopped green pepper
2 radishes, sliced thin
  Lettuce

1. Dissolve gelatin in hot water in medium-size bowl; stir in cold water, then remaining ingredients, except lettuce, mixing well.
2. Pour into a square pan, 8x8x2, or into 8 individual molds, dividing evenly. Chill 2 hours, or until firm. (Salad can be made ahead and chilled overnight.)
3. Divide in half with a sharp knife, then cut each half crosswise into 4 servings. (Or unmold individual salads.) Place on lettuce-lined plates. Serve plain or with bottled thin French dressing, if you wish. Makes 8 servings.

WITH winter, summer, any time, comes the excuse for entertaining. Around the Christmas holidays, parties just seem to burst out all over, and their happy spirit carries on right through a new year of springtime teas, summer get-togethers, just-for-family turkey feasting, and on to Christmas again.

Whatever your party plans—simple or splashy, for few or for many—we hope you will find the answers to easy,

Holidays are party days

smooth, happy hostessing right here in this chapter.

We begin with a cheery table set to welcome guests to a Christmas open house. There's a supper buffet for a New Year's midnight party. And a tea, pretty as a May day, for 12 or 100. For summer fun — it's a graduation celebration for your teen-ager and an Hawaiian luau for big and little kids of all ages. And, of course, a Thanksgiving feast is the introductory bell-ringer to Christmas all over again.

Getting the holiday spirit? May your party be the prettiest, gayest, and happiest ever!

◀ This holiday open-house buffet introduces our party entertaining with festive food choices—some dainty, some hearty—to please all guests. *(Recipes for the starred dishes, serving 25, start on page 132)*

Festive foods for entertaining

PARTY STARTERS	MAIN DISHES	FANCY GO-WITHS	SWEET ENDINGS

PLAN A HOLIDAY OPEN HOUSE
(pictured on page 128)

★Hot Bouillon Cup
★Twist Crisps
★Danish Cheese Mold
★Ribbon Pâté

★Buffet Glazed Corned Beef with
★Tangy Mustard Sauce
★Pickup Chicken Sticks

★Holiday Sage Bread
Assorted Crackers

★Double-good Apple Cake
Coffee

It's a friendly way to entertain and a simply decorated table will set your party mood so prettily. Our pictured one—spread with a Christmas-red cloth—is banked with candles to radiate a warm welcome. Festive menu—planned for 25—costars corned beef for sandwiches and tiny chicken "drumsticks"—both perfect holders on a buffet table so guests may help themselves whenever they like. Rest of menu includes two fancy appetizer molds with a cheery hot beverage to start the party rolling fast, your own homemade bread, and a luscious triple-layer cake

---

RING IN THE NEW YEAR
(pictured on page 137)

★Tomato Tango
★Hot Sea-food Hors d'oeuvres with Dips
★Cucumber Fans
★Diable Egg Cups
★Ribbons

★Party Meat Balls with
★Creamy Dill Sauce
★Potato-onion Pie-ettes

Assorted Crisp Breads
★Butter Balls
★Winter Garden Salad Tray

★Fruits Finlandia
★Almond Crown Spongecake
Coffee

'T is the season for a party to wish those near and dear a bright new year. So make up your guest list for this favorite buffet gathering. Our menu is planned for 12, but doubles nicely for a larger group. Festive starters include sea-food bites in a chafing dish, tiny sandwiches, and a rosy tomato cup. Main-dish meat balls in a dill-seasoned sauce need a keep-hot server, too, so star your chafing dish a second time. So-simple and so-good potato pies can be baked ahead and reheated. Even the double dessert—fruit and cake—to serve with coffee takes neatly to fixing beforehand

---

HOLD A GRADUATION ROUNDUP

★Tomato Dip
★Cheddar-relish Dip
★Bean-onion Dip
Corn Chips
Potato Chips
Soda Pop   Cola

★Burger Burgoo In-a-kettle
★Zigzag Parmesan Loaves

Celery, Carrot, Green-onion Sticks;
Radishes;
Cauliflowerets
★Merry Mix-up

★Make-your-own Sundaes
★Jiffy Fudge Sauce
★Butterscotch-nut Sauce
★Diploma Cake Roll

Be prepared for a big party, for the guest list has a way of growing and growing as the crowd gets set to celebrate school's big day—graduation. Mother, plan foods that hold well, then step aside and let the teens take over. That's the way they like it best, for with the record player going amid the din of conversation, eating will go on for hours. These refreshments—planned for 12—start with dips and chips with plenty of pop and cola, then on to a bottomless kettleful of hamburger mix to go along with crusty bread slices. For the final blast-off, it's ice cream and a "diploma" cake

GIVE THANKS FOR OUR BOUNTY
(pictured on page 142)

★Frosted Cider Cup
★Sesame Pastry Stacks

★Butter-crisp Roast Turkey
★Celery-rice Stuffing
★Giblet Gravy
★Mashed Potatoes
★Buttered Asparagus and Carrot Sticks
(pictured on page 6)

★Onion "Mums" with Squash Rings
★Mandarin-cranberry Sauce
★Pimiento-corn Relish
★Buttercup Rolls

★Praline Pumpkin Pie
Demitasse

Thanksgiving dinner's always a feast when traditional turkey takes the spotlight, and here it is roasted buttery-golden with a savory rice stuffing and rich brown gravy to spoon over. (And what a joy today's younger, plumper birds are, for they carve into such generous slices.) With it go har- vest vegetables—some old favorites, some new doll-ups. Dessert finale? Of course, it's pumpkin pie, and this one has a soft candylike nut layer hiding beneath its gold- en custard filling. Recipes for eight give fix-ahead tips for getting much of the cook- ing done early so dinner will be just right

GIVE A MAYTIME TEA
(pictured on page 145)

★Butter Triangles
★Banana-nut Sticks
★Pineapple Pinwheels
★Strawberry Pinwheels
★Tea for a Crowd

★Cheese Moons
★Deviled Cucumber Rounds
★Harlequins

★Candied Lemon Rounds
Crystallized Ginger
Whole Cloves
Assorted Mints
Toasted Almonds

★Jewel Creams
★Daisy Teacake
★Strudelettes
★Posy Puffs

It's a gracious way to honor your club president, a bride-to-be, a visiting rela- tive, or just to gather friends together. Your table will set the mood, so spread it with your prettiest cloth and arrange a tea service at either end, if your group is to be larger than 25. The recipes here are planned for 25, with hostess notes on how much to buy, what can be made ahead, how to pack everything on trays to keep it fresh and inviting until serving time—even how to multiply each recipe so it will serve 100 guests. There's a special section, too, on how to make tea for few or for many

GO HAWAIIAN WITH A LUAU

★Mauna Loa Punch
★Fresh Coconut Chips

★Honolulu Ribs with
★Honolulu Sauce
★Shrimps Mandarin
★Fried Rice

★Islands Vegetable Bake
★Flower Salad Bowl
★Lime Dressing

★Paradise Parfaits
★Kona Sundaes
Tea

Bring out the ukes and your old hula rec- ords, hang up some straw hats, lanterns, and travel posters, for going Hawaiian is excuse enough for a party. Set up a low table—boards on bricks work fine—and borrow enough pillows for sitting, for chairs are barred at a luau. Food is a lot easier to fix than you may think and it's fun to plan exotic touches such as the ap- petizer punch bowl nestling in cool green fernery, yet spouting curls of smoking "lava." If your gathering is outdoors, guests can help cook ribs, make sundaes. Recipes are for eight, but double easily

PLAN A HOLIDAY OPEN HOUSE

■ HOT BOUILLON CUP

4 cans condensed tomato soup
2 soup cans water
2 cans (46 ounces each) mixed vegetable
    juices
½ cup lemon juice
2 tablespoons sugar
2 tablespoons Worcestershire sauce

1. Combine all ingredients in kettle; heat slowly to boiling.
2. Pour into a heated large tureen; garnish with parsley, if you wish. Ladle into cups to serve hot. Makes 25 servings, ¾ cup each.

■ TWIST CRISPS

1 cup sifted flour
1½ teaspoons baking powder
½ teaspoon salt
2 tablespoons butter or margarine
½ cup grated sharp Cheddar cheese
⅓ cup cold water

1. Sift flour, baking powder, and salt into medium-size bowl; cut in butter or margarine and cheese with pastry blender until mixture is crumbly. Sprinkle water over; mix lightly with a fork just until pastry holds together and leaves side of bowl clean.
2. Roll out to a rectangle, 12x10, on lightly floured pastry cloth or board. Divide in half lengthwise, then cut each half crosswise into ½-inch-wide strips. Lift, one at a time, and carefully twist; place, 1 inch apart, on ungreased cooky sheets.
3. Bake in hot oven (425°) 10 minutes, or until lightly golden. Remove from cooky sheets; cool on wire racks. Makes 4 dozen.

■ DANISH CHEESE MOLD

2 envelopes unflavored gelatin
½ cup water
1 can (5¼ ounces) Danish Camembert cheese
    OR: 4 wedges (1⅓ ounces each)
      Camembert cheese
½ pound blue cheese
½ teaspoon curry powder
2 eggs, separated
1 cup cream for whipping

1. Soften gelatin in water in 1-cup measure; place cup in pan of hot water; heat until gelatin dissolves.
2. Combine Camembert and blue cheeses in medium-size bowl; beat until well-blended, then beat in curry powder, egg yolks, and gelatin.
3. Beat egg whites until they stand in firm peaks in small bowl. Beat cream until stiff in second small bowl.

4. Fold egg whites, then whipped cream into cheese mixture until no streaks of white remain. Pour into 4-cup mold; cover with waxed paper, foil, or transparent wrap. Chill several hours, or until firm.
5. Unmold onto serving plate. Serve with your choice of crackers. Makes 25 servings.

■ RIBBON PÂTÉ

Aspic
1 envelope unflavored gelatin
2 envelopes instant beef broth
    OR: 2 beef-bouillon cubes
1 cup water
1 tablespoon lemon juice
Cheese Mixture
2 packages (8 ounces each) cream cheese
½ cup dairy sour cream
1 tablespoon grated onion
Ham Mixture
2 cans (4½ ounces each) deviled ham
¼ cup prepared sweet-mustard relish
    (from a 9-ounce jar)
Liver Mixture
2 cans (4½ ounces each) liver pâté
¼ cup mayonnaise or salad dressing
2 tablespoons chopped parsley
Topping
3 pitted ripe olives, sliced

1. Make aspic: Combine gelatin, instant beef broth or bouillon cubes, and water in small saucepan; heat, stirring constantly, just until the gelatin dissolves. Measure ¼ cup into a 6-cup mold; stir in lemon juice. Use remaining ¾ cup aspic to make cheese, ham, and liver mixtures for layering into mold.
2. Make cheese mixture: Blend cream cheese, sour cream, onion, and ¼ cup aspic until creamy-smooth in medium-size bowl.
3. Make ham mixture: Blend deviled ham, mustard relish, and ¼ cup aspic in small bowl.
4. Make liver mixture: Blend liver pâté, mayonnaise or salad dressing, and parsley into the remaining ¼ cup aspic in saucepan. Keep the 3 mixtures at room temperature while layering mold.
5. Make topping: Set mold from Step 1 in a pan of ice and water to speed setting. When aspic layer is just beginning to be sticky-firm, arrange a ring of olive slices on top; let set until sticky-firm.
6. Spoon half of the cheese mixture on top; let set until sticky-firm. Repeat with all of the ham mixture, remaining cheese mixture, then all of the liver mixture, waiting each time until layer on top is sticky-firm.
7. Remove mold from ice and water; cover with waxed paper, foil, or transparent wrap. Chill several hours, or until firm.
8. Unmold onto serving plate. Surround with crisp crackers. Makes 25 servings.

■ BUFFET GLAZED CORNED BEEF

6 pounds corned-beef brisket
10 peppercorns
1 bay leaf
¼ cup firmly packed brown sugar
Tangy Mustard Sauce (recipe follows)

1. Simmer corned beef with peppercorns and bay leaf in water to cover in kettle 3½ to 4 hours, or until tender. Let stand in broth until ready to glaze.
2. Place meat, fat side up, on broiler rack or broilerproof platter; sprinkle brown sugar evenly over top. Broil just until sugar bubbles up.
3. Place meat on carving board; slice thin across grain, then into serving-size pieces. Serve with TANGY MUSTARD SAUCE. Makes 25 servings.

TANGY MUSTARD SAUCE

4 tablespoons (½ stick) butter or margarine
4 tablespoons flour
3 tablespoons dry mustard
1 tablespoon sugar
2 teaspoons salt
Dash of cayenne
2 cups milk
2 eggs
¼ cup vinegar

1. Melt butter or margarine over low heat in medium-size saucepan. Stir in flour, mustard, sugar, salt, and cayenne; cook, stirring constantly, just until mixture bubbles. Stir in milk slowly; continue cooking and stirring until sauce thickens and boils 1 minute.
2. Beat eggs slightly in small bowl; stir in a generous ½ cup hot mixture; quickly stir back into mixture in saucepan. Cook over medium heat, stirring constantly, 1 minute longer.
3. Remove from heat; stir in vinegar. Serve warm or chilled. (Store any left over in a covered container in refrigerator.) Makes 2½ cups.

■ PICKUP CHICKEN STICKS

3 pounds chicken wings (about 25)
1 cup (2 sticks) butter or margarine
1½ cups sifted flour
⅓ cup sesame seeds
1 tablespoon salt
½ teaspoon ground ginger

1. Singe chicken wings, if necessary; cut off and discard tips. Divide each wing in half by cutting through joint with a sharp knife. Wash and drain on paper toweling.
2. Melt butter or margarine in large shallow baking pan. Mix flour, sesame seeds, salt, and ginger in pie plate.

3. Roll chicken pieces, one at a time, in butter in pan, letting any excess drip back. Roll in flour mixture to coat generously, then set aside on sheets of waxed paper until all are coated. Arrange, not touching, in single layer in same pan.
4. Bake in moderate oven (350°) 1 hour, or until tender and richly golden on bottom. Slide pan in heated broiler for 3 to 5 minutes to brown tops. Makes 25 servings.

■ HOLIDAY SAGE BREAD

1 cup milk
3 tablespoons sugar
1 tablespoon salt
1 tablespoon instant minced onion
2 tablespoons butter or margarine
2 envelopes active dry yeast
    OR: 2 cakes compressed yeast
1 cup very warm water
4½ cups sifted flour
2 teaspoons leaf sage, crumbled

1. Scald milk with sugar, salt, instant onion, and butter or margarine in small saucepan; cool to lukewarm.
2. Sprinkle or crumble yeast into very warm water in large bowl. ("Very warm" water should feel comfortably warm when dropped on wrist.) Stir until yeast dissolves, then stir in cooled milk mixture.
3. Stir in flour and sage until well-blended, then beat vigorously, scraping down side of bowl, about 100 strokes. (Dough will be sticky and heavy.)
4. Cover with a clean towel; let rise in warm place, away from draft, 1 hour, or until double in bulk.
5. Stir dough down; spoon into greased 10-cup tube mold or 8-inch angel-food pan.
6. Bake in moderate oven (375°) 1 hour, or until bread gives a hollow sound when tapped. Remove from mold; cool on wire rack. (If you like a soft crust, brush with melted butter or margarine while still hot.) Makes 1 large round loaf.

■ DOUBLE-GOOD APPLE CAKE

2½ cups sifted flour
1½ teaspoons baking soda
½ teaspoon salt
½ teaspoon cinnamon
½ teaspoon nutmeg
1 tablespoon vinegar
1 cup milk
½ cup shortening
1 cup sugar
4 eggs
1 cup apple butter (from a 12-ounce jar)
　Fluffy Filling and Frosting (recipe follows)
1 red apple
1 tablespoon lemon juice
　Walnut halves

1. Grease bottoms of 3 eight-inch layer-cake pans; line with waxed paper; grease paper.
2. Measure flour, baking soda, salt, cinnamon, and nutmeg into sifter. Stir vinegar into milk in 2-cup measure.
3. Cream shortening and sugar until fluffy in large bowl with spoon or electric mixer at medium speed. Beat in eggs, 1 at a time, beating well after each addition.
4. Sift in dry ingredients, a quarter at a time, adding alternately with milk mixture; stir with a spoon or beat with mixer at low speed just until blended. Stir in apple butter. Pour into prepared pans, dividing evenly.
5. Bake in moderate oven (350°) 30 minutes, or until centers spring back when lightly pressed with fingertip.
6. Cool in pans on wire racks 5 minutes; loosen around the edges with knife; turn out onto racks. Peel off paper; cool layers completely.
7. Make FLUFFY FILLING AND FROSTING. Put layers together with filling; cover top and side with frosting.
8. Quarter, core, and slice apple into thin wedges, then dip in lemon juice to keep white. Arrange with walnuts around top and side of cake, as pictured on page 128. Chill until ready to serve. Makes 1 eight-inch triple-layer cake.

FLUFFY FILLING AND FROSTING

1 cup (2 sticks) butter or margarine
1 package (1 pound) 10X (confectioners' powdered) sugar, sifted
¼ cup orange juice
2 tablespoons dark corn syrup
1 teaspoon lemon extract
¼ teaspoon salt
1 cup (8 ounces) cream-style cottage cheese
⅓ cup chopped walnuts
1 teaspoon grated orange rind

1. Cream butter or margarine until soft in medium-size bowl. Beat in 10X sugar, alternately with mixture of orange juice, corn syrup, lemon extract, and salt until thick and easy to spread.

2. Measure ½ cupful into small bowl. Set remaining aside for frosting cake. Stir cottage cheese, walnuts, and orange rind into the ½ cupful until well-blended. Use for filling cake layers. Makes enough to fill and frost 1 eight-inch triple-layer cake.

RING IN THE NEW YEAR

■ TOMATO TANGO

1 can (46 ounces) tomato juice
　Handful of celery tops
2 envelopes instant beef broth
　OR: 2 beef-bouillon cubes
1 bay leaf
1 teaspoon salt
1 teaspoon celery salt
1 teaspoon sugar
⅛ teaspoon pepper
¼ cup finely chopped parsley
2 tablespoons lemon juice
1 lemon, sliced thin

1. Combine 1 cup of the tomato juice with celery tops, beef broth or bouillon cubes, bay leaf, salt, celery salt, sugar, and pepper in small saucepan. Heat to boiling; simmer 5 minutes to blend flavors.
2. Strain into a 6-cup jar; stir in parsley, lemon juice, and remaining tomato juice; chill.
3. Just before serving, pour into a large pitcher or punch bowl; garnish with lemon slices. Makes 12 servings, about ½ cup each.

■ HOT SEA-FOOD HORS D'OEUVRES

4 tablespoons (½ stick) butter or margarine
1 pound frozen deveined shelled raw shrimps
1 clove of garlic, minced
1 pound fresh or frozen raw sea scallops
1 package (8 ounces) frozen cooked codfish balls
1 jar (about 6 ounces) hollandaise sauce
1 jar (about 12 ounces) cocktail sauce
2 tablespoons chopped parsley
Paprika

1. Melt 2 tablespoons butter or margarine in medium-size frying pan. (Save remaining 2 tablespoons for Step 3.) Add frozen shrimps and garlic; simmer, stirring often, 20 to 25 minutes, or until shrimps are tender; keep hot.
2. While shrimps cook, wash fresh scallops under running cold water; drain. (Or partly thaw frozen scallops, following label directions.) Cut any large scallops in bite-size pieces.
3. Melt saved 2 tablespoons butter or margarine in second medium-size frying pan; add scallops. Cook slowly, stirring often, 5 to 8 minutes, or until tender; keep hot.
4. Heat codfish balls, following label directions; keep hot.
5. Heat hollandaise sauce just until piping-hot in top of double boiler over simmering water. (Or make half the recipe for MOCK HOLLANDAISE on page 77.) Heat cocktail sauce to boiling in small saucepan.
6. When ready to serve, pile shrimps, scallops, and codfish balls in separate mounds in chafing dish or keep-hot server; sprinkle parsley over shrimps and paprika over scallops. Spoon hollandaise and cocktail sauces into separate small bowls. Remember to set out cocktail picks for spearing and dunking. Makes 12 servings.

■ CUCUMBER FANS

½ large cucumber
9 thin slices white bread
6 tablespoons (¾ stick) butter or margarine

1. Score rind of cucumber with a fork, then cut cucumber into 12 thin slices.
2. Spread bread with butter or margarine; cut 2 rounds out of each slice with an about-2-inch cutter. (Rounds should be about the same size as cucumber slices.)
3. Make 6 sandwiches, each with 2 cucumber slices between 3 rounds of bread. Place on tray lined with a damp clean towel; cover; chill.
4. When ready to serve, cut each round into quarters to make 4 wedges. Place some on serving plate; keep remaining covered with damp towel to refill plate. Makes 2 dozen.

■ DIABLE EGG CUPS

12 eggs
4 tablespoons mayonnaise or salad dressing
3 teaspoons prepared mustard
Salt and pepper
4 tablespoons (½ stick) butter or margarine
12 thin slices whole-wheat bread
Parsley

1. Hard-cook and shell eggs. Halve each crosswise; scoop out yolks and mash in small bowl.
2. Blend in mayonnaise or salad dressing and 2 teaspoons mustard; season with salt and pepper to taste. Pile back into whites, dividing evenly; place on plate; cover; chill.
3. Cream remaining 1 teaspoon mustard into butter or margarine in second small bowl; spread on bread; cut 2 rounds out of each slice with an about-2-inch cutter. Place on tray lined with a damp clean towel. (If stacked, put waxed paper between layers.) Cover; chill.
4. Just before serving, stand a stuffed-egg half on each round of bread on serving plate; garnish with a sprig of parsley. Makes 2 dozen.

■ RIBBONS

1 package (3 or 4 ounces) cream cheese
2 tablespoons chopped parsley
1 teaspoon Worcestershire sauce
1 can (5 ounces) chicken spread
2 cans (3 ounces each) liverwurst spread
8 slices whole-wheat bread
8 slices white bread
4 tablespoons (½ stick) butter or margarine, softened

1. Blend cream cheese, parsley, and Worcestershire sauce in small bowl. Empty chicken and liverwurst spreads into custard cups.
2. Place bread in 4 rows of 4 slices each, alternating rows of white and whole-wheat, on large cutting board. Spread with butter or margarine.
3. Spread chicken spread on half of whole-wheat bread, and liverwurst spread on remaining. Spread cream-cheese mixture on half of white bread; leave remaining plain.
4. Make 4 sandwiches, each 4 slices high, this way: Whole-wheat with liverwurst; white with cream cheese, cheese side up; whole-wheat with chicken, chicken side up; and plain white, butter side down. Wrap each in waxed paper, foil, or transparent wrap; chill.
5. To serve, trim crusts; halve each sandwich. Cut each half into 6 slices.
6. Arrange some in stacks on serving plate; keep remaining covered with damp towel to refill plate. Makes 4 dozen.

PARTY MEAT BALLS

1½ pounds ground beef
1 pound ground veal
1 can (4½ ounces) deviled ham
1 small can evaporated milk (⅔ cup)
2 eggs
1 tablespoon grated onion
1 cup soft whole-wheat bread crumbs
    (2 slices)
½ teaspoon salt
½ teaspoon allspice
¼ teaspoon pepper
¼ cup shortening
¼ cup water
    Creamy Dill Sauce *(recipe follows)*

1. Combine ground beef and veal, deviled ham, evaporated milk, eggs, onion, bread crumbs, and seasonings in large bowl; mix lightly with a fork just until blended. Shape into about 72 small balls.
2. Brown, a few at a time, in shortening in large frying pan. Drain any fat from pan; return meat balls. Add water; cover. Simmer 20 minutes to blend flavors. (If made ahead, chill after browning, then reheat in frying pan just before serving.)
3. Spoon into a chafing dish or keep-hot server. Pour CREAMY DILL SAUCE over. (There will be just enough to coat meat balls lightly.) Garnish with a sprig of fresh dill, if you like. Makes 12 servings.

CREAMY DILL SAUCE

2 tablespoons butter or margarine
2 tablespoons flour
½ teaspoon salt
1 cup water
1 cup dairy sour cream
1 tablespoon catsup
1 tablespoon dill weed

1. Melt butter or margarine in small saucepan; blend in flour and salt; cook, stirring all the time, just until mixture bubbles. Stir in water slowly; continue cooking and stirring until sauce thickens and boils 1 minute.
2. Stir in sour cream, catsup, and dill weed; heat just to boiling. Makes about 2 cups.

POTATO-ONION PIE-ETTES

1 package piecrust mix
4 medium-size onions, peeled and sliced thin
6 tablespoons (¾ stick) butter or margarine
3 medium-size potatoes, pared and sliced thin
1½ teaspoons salt
¼ teaspoon pepper
2 tablespoons chopped parsley

1. Prepare piecrust mix, following label directions, or make pastry from your own favorite two-crust recipe.

2. Roll out, ⅓ at a time, to ⅛-inch thickness on lightly floured pastry cloth or board; cut each into 4 six-inch rounds, using a saucer for pattern. Fit into 4-inch tart-shell pans or 1-cup custard cups; trim any overhang.
3. Saute onions in butter or margarine until soft in large frying pan; stir in potatoes, salt, and pepper. Cook, stirring constantly, over low heat, 5 minutes; spoon into prepared shells, dividing evenly.
4. Bake in hot oven (400°) 35 minutes, or until pastry is golden and potatoes are tender. Cool on wire rack 5 minutes; remove from pans; sprinkle with parsley.
5. Arrange on heated large serving tray or platter. (They stack nicely without breaking.) Serve hot. Makes 12 tarts.

Note: Tarts can be baked early in the day and removed from pans. Just before serving, place on cooky sheet; heat in moderate oven (350°) 15 minutes, or until hot. Recipe allows 1 tart for each serving, but it's a good idea to make twice this amount. They are deliciously different and each guest will probably want a second.

BUTTER BALLS

A mound of golden balls nestled in a bowlful of crushed ice gives another festive touch to your holiday table, and they are really fun to make. The secret is simple: Just keep everything— bowls of water, wooden paddles, pats of butter or margarine—chilly cold. Here's how to shape them: Cut a stick (¼ pound) butter or margarine into 12 slices. As you cut, drop each slice into a bowl of ice and water; let chill until almost brittle. Have a pair of wooden butter paddles chilling in a second bowl of ice and water. (*Hint:* Two pairs are even better, for one can be chilling while you're using the other.) Place one pat of butter at a time between chilled paddles, and rolling one paddle against the other, form pat into a ball. Work quickly with a light touch. (You may be amazed how fast the job is finished!) As each ball is shaped, drop it into a bowl of ice and water. Keep balls chilled until serving time, then pile on top of a bed of crushed ice in serving bowl. For an added holiday touch, roll part of the balls in finely chopped parsley, dust part lightly with paprika, and leave the rest plain. Then pile each in a separate mound in serving dish. One pound of butter or margarine makes 48 balls.

Everybody loves a ring-in-the-new-year party. These ▶ foods—the make-ahead kinds—need only a few last-minute company-best touches, and hold well on the table. (Recipes for starred dishes start on page 134)

■ WINTER GARDEN SALAD TRAY

5 medium-size carrots
1 package (10 ounces) frozen Fordhook lima beans
1 can (1 pound) whole Blue Lake green beans, drained
2 cans (3 or 4 ounces each) whole mushrooms, drained
1 envelope Italian salad-dressing mix
1 envelope onion salad-dressing mix
 Salad oil
 Vinegar
1 large cucumber
1 large sweet onion
¼ cup vinegar
¼ cup water
1 teaspoon salt
¼ teaspoon pepper
1 jar (about 1 pound) sliced pickled beets, drained

1. Scrape carrots, then cut into 3-inch-long sticks. Cook, covered, in small amount boiling salted water in small saucepan, 10 minutes, or until crisply tender; drain. Cook lima beans, following label directions; drain.
2. Place carrots, limas, green beans, and mushrooms in separate piles in large shallow dish.
3. Prepare Italian and onion salad-dressing mixes with salad oil, vinegar, and water, following label directions for each, then combine and mix well. Pour over vegetables; cover. Chill at least an hour to season and blend flavors.
4. Score rind of cucumber with a fork; slice cucumber thin. Peel and slice onion, then separate into rings. Place each in separate piles in shallow dish. Mix vinegar, water, salt, and pepper in a cup; pour over vegetables; cover. Chill at least an hour to season and blend flavors.
5. When ready to serve, spoon up vegetables, 1 at a time, with slotted spoon; let dressings drain back into dishes. Arrange each, along with pickled beets, in separate piles or rows on a large shallow platter or tray. (Save any Italian-onion salad dressing that's left over in vegetable dish for salad for another meal.) Makes 12 servings.

■ FRUITS FINLANDIA

1 cup dried apricots
2 cups water
⅓ cup quick-cooking tapioca
⅛ teaspoon salt
4 cups orange juice
1 can (about 11 ounces) mandarin-orange segments
1 cup halved seedless grapes (about ½ pound)
1 banana

1. Combine apricots and 1 cup of water in small saucepan. Heat to boiling; remove from heat; cover; let stand about 1 hour.
2. Stir tapioca and salt into remaining 1 cup

water and 1 cup of the orange juice in small saucepan. Heat, stirring constantly, until mixture comes to a full rolling boil; pour into a large bowl; let stand 15 minutes.
3. Stir in remaining 3 cups orange juice, apricots and liquid, mandarin-orange segments and liquid, and grapes; cover. Chill.
4. When ready to serve, slice banana and stir in. Serve in cups or glasses to eat with a spoon. Makes 12 servings.

Note: This delightfully refreshing dessert can be made with many fruits. Use prunes in place of the apricots or add canned sliced cling peaches or fresh orange sections for the mandarin-orange segments. Strawberries, too, give a bright rosy touch, and fresh or frozen pineapple cubes add a tangy flavor.

■ ALMOND CROWN SPONGECAKE

1 cup sifted cake flour
1 teaspoon baking powder
½ teaspoon salt
3 eggs
1 cup sugar
½ teaspoon almond extract
¼ teaspoon vanilla
⅓ cup scalded milk
24 blanched whole almonds
1 tablespoon butter or margarine
 Vanilla Glaze *(recipe follows)*

1. Measure cake flour, baking powder, and salt into sifter.
2. Beat eggs until thick and foamy in large bowl with electric or rotary beater. Beat in sugar, 1 tablespoon at a time, beating well after each addition, until sugar dissolves. (Beating should take about 15 minutes in all.) Stir in almond extract and vanilla.
3. Sift in dry ingredients, ⅓ at a time; fold in with a wooden spoon until no streaks of white remain. Stir in scalded milk quickly.
4. Pour into ungreased 9-inch tube pan; cut through batter with knife to break up any air bubbles.
5. Bake in moderate oven (350°) 35 minutes, or until top springs back when lightly pressed with fingertip.
6. Invert cake in pan on wire rack or hang, upside down, on a bottle; cool completely. Loosen around edge and tube with knife; turn out onto serving plate.
7. Heat almonds in butter or margarine in small frying pan, stirring constantly, until lightly toasted; drain on paper toweling.
8. Spread VANILLA GLAZE over top of cake, letting it drip down side and tube. Place almonds in two rings around top. Makes 1 nine-inch tube cake.

VANILLA GLAZE—Blend 1 cup 10X (confectioners' powdered) sugar, dash of salt, 4 teaspoons milk, and ¼ teaspoon vanilla until smooth in small bowl. Makes ½ cup.

HOLD A GRADUATION ROUNDUP

■ TOMATO DIP

1 package (3 or 4 ounces) cream cheese
1 can condensed tomato soup
¼ cup chopped ripe olives
2 tablespoons chopped parsley
⅛ teaspoon pepper

1. Soften cream cheese in medium-size bowl; blend in soup gradually until mixture is smooth. Stir in olives, parsley, and pepper; chill.
2. Spoon into serving bowl; garnish with ripe olive slices and parsley, if you wish. Makes 2 cups.

■ CHEDDAR-RELISH DIP

1 cup grated Cheddar cheese (¼ pound)
½ cup mayonnaise or salad dressing
¼ cup bottled hot-dog relish

1. Combine all ingredients in small bowl; stir until well-blended; chill.
2. Spoon into serving bowl; garnish with chopped pimiento, if you wish. Makes 1½ cups.

■ BEAN-ONION DIP

1 can (1 pound) pork-and-beans
1 small onion, peeled and quartered
¼ cup molasses
2 tablespoons prepared mustard

1. Combine all ingredients in electric-blender container. Blend at high speed 1 minute, or until smooth; chill. (Or press pork-and-beans through sieve and grate onion, then blend with other ingredients. Dip won't be as smooth, but it will taste just as good.)
2. Spoon into serving bowl; garnish with tiny white onions, if you wish. Makes 2 cups.

■ ZIGZAG PARMESAN LOAVES

2 long loaves Italian bread
½ cup (1 stick) butter or margarine
½ cup grated Parmesan cheese

1. Cut bread into V-shape slices ½-inch thick, cutting from outside toward middle and through bottom crusts. (Keep slices in order.)
2. Melt butter or margarine in small saucepan; stir in Parmesan cheese. Brush generously over each slice, then thread onto 2 long skewers to re-form into loaves; wrap loosely in foil.
3. Bake in moderate oven (350°) 10 minutes, or until heated through. Unwrap loaves and serve on skewers. Makes 12 servings.

■ BURGER BURGOO IN-A-KETTLE

4 pounds ground beef
2 large onions, chopped (2 cups)
2 cups diced celery
2 cloves of garlic, minced
2 tablespoons sugar
4 teaspoons salt
¼ teaspoon pepper
¼ teaspoon leaf marjoram
2 cans (46 ounces each) mixed vegetable juices
2 cups uncooked rice

1. Shape meat into 2 large patties; brown, 1 at a time, in large heavy frying pan, 5 minutes on each side, then break up into chunks; remove.
2. Saute onions, celery, and garlic in drippings in same pan, stirring often, until soft.
3. Combine sugar, salt, pepper, marjoram, and mixed vegetable juices in large kettle; stir in browned meat and onion mixture.
4. Heat to boiling; stir in rice; cover. Simmer, stirring often, 45 minutes, or until rice is tender. Makes 12 servings.

■ MAKE-YOUR-OWN SUNDAES

Set up a separate table with a variety of ice creams, fruits, sauces, and toppings, so each guest can make his own specialty. Pack favorite flavors of ice cream in a big tub of ice. (Two-quart cartons will stay firm for about an hour.) Surround with bananas and bowls of sweetened sliced strawberries, canned crushed pineapple, and maraschino cherries. Buy sundae sauces to pour from pitchers, or make your own JIFFY FUDGE SAUCE and BUTTERSCOTCH-NUT SAUCE *(recipes follow)*. For that final extra, add bowls of coconut, marshmallow cream, and peanuts, along with creamy topping in a pressurized can. Don't forget ice-cream scoops or big heavy-handle spoons, serving bowls (waxed-lined paper ones are good), and plenty of bright colored paper napkins.

JIFFY FUDGE SAUCE

2 cups (12-ounce package) semisweet-chocolate pieces
2 tablespoons butter or margarine
1½ cups light corn syrup
½ cup milk
1 teaspoon vanilla

1. Melt semisweet-chocolate pieces with butter or margarine in top of small double boiler over simmering water.
2. Beat in corn syrup and milk until creamy-smooth; stir in vanilla. Serve warm or cold. Makes about 3½ cups.

Note: This sauce keeps well in a covered jar in the refrigerator. To reheat, place the jar, covered loosely, in a saucepan of water. Heat slowly until sauce is warm.

BUTTERSCOTCH-NUT SAUCE

2 cups firmly packed brown sugar
⅔ cup light corn syrup
4 tablespoons (½ stick) butter or margarine
½ cup evaporated milk
¼ cup water
½ cup chopped walnuts
1 teaspoon vanilla

1. Combine brown sugar, corn syrup, and butter or margarine in medium-size heavy saucepan; heat over low heat, stirring constantly, until butter melts and mixture is well-blended.
2. Heat to boiling; cook to 230° on candy thermometer. (A little syrup will spin fine threads when dropped from tip of spoon.)
3. Remove from heat; stir in evaporated milk, water, walnuts, and vanilla. Serve warm or cold. Makes 2½ cups.

Note: This sauce keeps well in a covered jar in the refrigerator. To reheat, place the jar, covered loosely, in a saucepan of water. Heat slowly until sauce is warm.

■ DIPLOMA CAKE ROLL

½ cup sifted cake flour
¾ teaspoon baking powder
¼ teaspoon salt
3 eggs
½ cup sugar
1 teaspoon vanilla
¼ teaspoon almond extract
   10X (confectioners' powdered) sugar
1 jar (12 ounces) fruit jelly (grape, apple, raspberry, or strawberry)

1. Grease baking pan, 15x10x1; line with waxed paper cut ½ inch smaller than pan; grease paper.
2. Measure flour, baking powder, and salt into sifter.
3. Beat eggs until foamy in medium-size bowl; gradually beat in sugar until mixture is thick; stir in vanilla and almond extract.
4. Sift dry ingredients over and fold in until no streaks of flour remain. Spread batter evenly into prepared pan.
5. Bake in hot oven (400°) 8 minutes, or until top springs back when lightly pressed with fingertip.
6. Cut around cake about ½ inch in from edge of pan with sharp knife; invert pan onto clean towel dusted with 10X sugar; peel off waxed paper. Starting at one end, roll up cake; wrap in towel; cool completely on wire rack. (Or, to keep roll perfectly round, try this cooling trick: Tie cake roll in towel at both ends with string; hang onto handle of cupboard door until cool.)
7. Unroll cake carefully; spread evenly with jelly. (Choose a jelly to match the school color, if possible.) Reroll; dust top with more 10X sugar. Tie a school-color ribbon bow around middle.
8. Slice crosswise into thin rounds. Makes 12 servings. *(Hint:* Better make up two, for cake will be popular.)

■ MERRY MIX-UP

4 cups bite-size shredded-wheat biscuits
4 cups bite-size shredded-rice biscuits
4 cups thin pretzel sticks
8 tablespoons (1 stick) butter or margarine
2 jars (about 5 ounces each) dry toasted peanuts
   Seasoned salt

1. Spread cereals and pretzel sticks in single layer in large shallow roasting pan; slice butter or margarine over.
2. Bake in slow oven (325°), stirring often with a fork to coat well with melted butter, 15 minutes, or until toasty. Stir in peanuts; toast 5 minutes longer. Sprinkle with seasoned salt.
3. Cool, then store in a container with tight-fitting cover. Nibbles will keep fresh for weeks. Just before serving, reheat in a slow oven (325°), if you wish. Makes about 14 cups.

GIVE THANKS FOR OUR BOUNTY

■ FROSTED CIDER CUP

½ pint lemon sherbet
3 cups sweet cider, chilled

Drop a generous spoonful of sherbet into each of 8 small fancy juice glasses; pour chilled sweet cider over. Serve at once. Makes 8 servings.

■ SESAME PASTRY STACKS

1 stick piecrust mix
1 tablespoon melted butter or margarine
1 tablespoon sesame seeds

1. Prepare piecrust mix, following label directions, or make pastry from your own favorite one-crust recipe. Roll out to an 8-inch square on lightly floured pastry cloth or board; brush with melted butter or margarine; sprinkle with sesame seeds.
2. Cut square in half with pastry wheel or knife; place one half, sesame-seed side up, on top of other half. Cut lengthwise into 4 even strips, then cut each strip crosswise into quarters. Place on cooky sheet.
3. Bake in very hot oven (450°) 10 minutes, or until golden. Serve hot. Makes 16 stacks.

■ BUTTER-CRISP ROAST TURKEY

For 8 servings, plus some left over for another meal, buy a cleaned, ready-to-stuff chilled fresh or frozen bird weighing about 12 pounds. In either, you will find the giblets and neck neatly wrapped and tucked into the body or neck cavity.

If your turkey is frozen, follow directions on wrapper for thawing, or do it in either of these ways:

1. Keep in its sealed original wrapper in the refrigerator, allowing 2 days' time.

2. Place bird, sealed in original wrapper, under cold running water for about 2 hours, or until thawed enough to handle easily.

When thawed, rinse turkey inside and out with cold water; drain; pat dry and store, lightly covered, in refrigerator until ready to stuff and roast (not longer than 24 hours). Cook giblets and neck for gravy. (Recipe for GIBLET GRAVY on page 143 tells how.) Or simmer slowly in small amount of slightly salted water until tender. Chop meaty pieces and add to stuffing.

To stuff: Make CELERY-RICE STUFFING *(recipe follows)* ahead, if you like, but do not put into bird until just before roasting time. Then, sprinkle inside of bird with salt; lightly stuff breast cavity. Smooth neck skin over stuffing and skewer to back of bird. Twist wing tips until they rest flat against skewered neck skin. Next stuff body cavity. If your turkey comes "tucked," with legs slipped under a ribbonlike skin band across opening, slide legs out, stuff bird lightly, then slip legs back in place. If your turkey is not a "tucked" type, lace opening together with poultry pins or skewers and string, and truss legs close to body.

To roast: Place stuffed bird in roasting pan; coat all over with softened butter or margarine. (You'll need about ¼ pound [1 stick].) No need to wrap bird in cheesecloth, add water, or cover pan. If you use a meat thermometer, stick it into the meaty part of a thigh.

Roast in slow oven (325°) for time suggested on turkey wrapper, or figure 30 minutes per pound—about 6 hours for a 12-pounder, or 190° to 195° on meat thermometer. During roasting, baste bird every half hour with buttery drippings in pan so skin will roast crispy-golden.

To test for doneness: Start testing 30 minutes before roasting time is up. Protecting your fingers with paper toweling, squeeze meaty part of the thigh. It should feel soft. Now move drumstick up and down; it should twist and move easily. When turkey is done, place it on a heated platter and keep warm while making GIBLET GRAVY *(recipe on page 143).* Turkey slices more easily and neatly if allowed to stand for 20 to 30 minutes. Our turkey platter, pictured on page 142, has a garnish of "carrot flowers" made this way: Scrape a carrot, then shave

lengthwise into paper-thin slices with vegetable parer; cut slices into 4-inch lengths. Stack 4 or 5; insert wooden pick in middle to hold them together; fan out "petals." Chill in a bowl of ice and water to curl.

CELERY-RICE STUFFING

2 cups diced celery
1 large onion, chopped (1 cup)
½ cup (1 stick) butter or margarine
2 cups uncooked rice
2 cans (3 or 4 ounces each) chopped mushrooms
¼ cup chopped celery leaves
2 chicken-bouillon cubes
4½ cups water
2 teaspoons salt
1½ teaspoons poultry seasoning
¼ teaspoon pepper

1. Saute celery and onion in butter or margarine 3 to 5 minutes in large frying pan. Stir in rice; saute slowly, stirring often, 10 minutes, or until rice is golden and vegetables are soft.

2. Stir in mushrooms and liquid, celery leaves, bouillon cubes, water, salt, poultry seasoning, and pepper. Heat to boiling, stirring until bouillon cubes dissolve.

3. Cover; simmer 20 minutes, or until rice is tender and liquid is absorbed. Makes about 9 cups, or enough to stuff a 12-pound turkey.

Note: Make stuffing a day ahead, if you wish, and keep chilled, ready to put into turkey at roasting time—*not before.*

GIBLET GRAVY

2 stalks of celery, sliced
1 medium-size onion, chopped (½ cup)
1 teaspoon salt
4 whole cloves
4 cups water
Turkey giblets and neck
½ cup flour

1. Combine celery, onion, salt, cloves, and water in large saucepan; add turkey giblets (except liver) and neck. Heat to boiling, then simmer 1 hour. Add liver during last 20 minutes' cooking.
2. Strain stock; measure and add water, if needed, to make 4 cups. Chop giblets and neck meat and add to stock. (This much can be done a day ahead and chilled.)
3. After turkey has been removed from roasting pan, tip pan and let fat rise in one corner; pour off all fat into a measuring cup, leaving brown drippings in pan.
4. Return ½ cup fat to pan; blend in flour; cook, stirring all the time, just until mixture bubbles. Stir in the 4 cups stock and giblets; continue cooking and stirring, scraping baked-on juices from bottom and sides of pan, until gravy thickens and boils 1 minute. Makes 4 cups.

■ MASHED POTATOES

8 large potatoes, pared and cut up
½ cup milk
4 tablespoons (½ stick) butter or margarine
Salt and pepper

1. Cook potatoes in boiling slightly salted water in large saucepan 20 minutes, or just until tender; drain well. Place pan over low heat; shake gently for 1 minute to dry and fluff potatoes.
2. Scald milk with butter or margarine in small saucepan. Mash potatoes; beat in milk mixture, a little at a time, until smooth, then beat until fluffy. Season with salt and pepper.
3. Cover pan lightly; place over simmering water to keep hot. Makes 8 servings.

Note: If you have room enough in your oven, you may prefer to keep mashed potatoes hot this way: Spoon into a buttered ovenproof serving dish; dot lightly with 1 tablespoon butter or margarine and sprinkle with paprika. Do not cover. Slide into a slow oven (325°) to keep hot until serving time.

◀ Turkey's the king of the day for any Thanksgiving feast. And with a few plan-ahead, fix-ahead tricks *(they're given in the recipes starting on page 140)*, your dinner can be one to remember most pleasantly

■ BUTTERED ASPARAGUS AND CARROT STICKS

8 medium-sized carrots
2 packages (12 ounces each) frozen asparagus spears
4 tablespoons (½ stick) butter or margarine
2 teaspoons lemon juice
⅛ teaspoon salt
Dash of pepper

1. Scrape carrots and cut into 3-inch-long sticks. Cook in small amount boiling salted water in medium-size saucepan 20 minutes, or just until tender. Drain well.
2. Cook asparagus in small amount boiling salted water, following label directions. Drain well.
3. Arrange vegetables in separate mounds in heated serving dish. Heat butter or margarine with lemon juice in saucepan over low heat just until bubbly. (Watch it, for once it is hot, it turns brown quickly.) Spoon over vegetables; sprinkle with salt and pepper. Makes 8 servings.

■ ONION "MUMS" WITH SQUASH RINGS

8 large yellow onions
2 teaspoons salt
2 medium-size acorn squashes
½ cup (1 stick) butter or margarine, melted
Paprika

1. Peel and trim ends from onions. To make petals, set each onion, flat end down, on a cutting board; make 4 evenly spaced cuts from outside edge almost to center, cutting down just to within ½ inch of bottom. Next, cut each quarter into 4 sections, again slicing not quite to center and bottom.
2. Place onions close together in a single layer in large frying pan. (This much can be done ahead if pan is covered tightly with transparent wrap.) When ready to cook, sprinkle with 1 teaspoon salt; pour in water to depth of 1 inch; cover pan.
3. Trim ends from squashes; cut each crosswise into 4 rings. Scoop out seeds with a teaspoon, but do not pare. Place rings in 2 layers in large frying pan. Sprinkle with remaining 1 teaspoon salt; pour in water to depth of 1 inch; cover pan.
4. Cook both vegetables 15 minutes, or until tender, but still firm enough to hold their shape.
5. Drain squash; arrange in single layer on heated serving platter. Carefully lift out each onion "mum" with slotted spoon; let drain for a few seconds, then place on a squash ring. Spoon melted butter or margarine over; sprinkle "mums" lightly with paprika. Makes 8 servings.

■ MANDARIN-CRANBERRY SAUCE

1½ cups sugar
1½ cups water
4 cups (1 pound) fresh cranberries
1 can (about 11 ounces) mandarin-orange segments, drained

1. Heat sugar and water to boiling in medium-size saucepan; stir in cranberries. Cook, without stirring, 5 minutes, or until skins pop. Remove from heat; cool slightly.
2. Save 3 mandarin-orange segments to thread on pick for garnish, as pictured on page 142; fold remaining into sauce. Chill. Makes about 4 cups.

■ PIMIENTO-CORN RELISH

2 cans (12 or 16 ounces each) whole-kernel corn
2 teaspoons mustard seed
1 teaspoon dry mustard
½ teaspoon salt
½ teaspoon pepper
⅔ cup vinegar
2 tablespoons salad oil
1 large onion, diced
2 pimientos, diced

1. Drain liquid from corn into a small sauce-pan; stir in mustard seed, dry mustard, salt, pepper, vinegar, and salad oil. Heat just to boiling.
2. Combine corn, onion, and pimientos in medium-size bowl. Pour hot liquid over; toss lightly to mix. Cover; chill at least an hour to blend flavors.
3. Spoon into relish dish; garnish with a few onion rings, if you wish. Makes 4 cups.

■ BUTTERCUP ROLLS

¾ cup milk
6 tablespoons sugar
3 teaspoons salt
5 tablespoons shortening
2 envelopes active dry yeast
   OR: 2 cakes compressed yeast
½ cup very warm water
1 egg, beaten
4½ cups sifted flour
6 tablespoons (¾ stick) butter or margarine, melted

1. Scald milk in small saucepan; stir in sugar, salt, and shortening; cool to lukewarm.
2. Sprinkle or crumble yeast into very warm water in large bowl. (Very warm water should feel comfortably warm when dropped on wrist.) Stir until yeast dissolves, then stir in cooled milk mixture and egg.
3. Sift in half of the flour; beat until smooth. Stir in remaining flour to make a soft dough; beat 100 times with a spoon or about 1 minute with an electric beater. (This makes rolls feather-light.)

4. Coat top of dough lightly with soft shortening; cover; place in refrigerator at least 2 hours, or until ready to shape.
5. Punch dough down; turn out onto lightly floured pastry cloth or board; divide in half.
6. Roll out one half to a rectangle, 18x10; brush with 3 tablespoons melted butter or margarine; cut rectangle in half lengthwise. Starting at one side of each piece, roll up, jelly-roll style; slice crosswise into 18 about-1-inch-thick pinwheels. Repeat with remaining half of dough to make 72 pinwheels in all. Place 3 each, cut sides up, in bottom of greased large muffin-pan cups.
7. Cover; let rise in warm place, away from draft, 1 hour, or until double in bulk.
8. Bake in hot oven (400°) 15 minutes, or until golden. Serve hot. Makes 24 rolls.

■ PRALINE PUMPKIN PIE

Praline Layer

1 stick piecrust mix
3 tablespoons butter or margarine
⅓ cup firmly packed brown sugar
⅓ cup chopped pecans

Custard Layer

1 cup evaporated milk
½ cup water
3 eggs
1½ cups canned pumpkin
½ cup granulated sugar
½ cup firmly packed brown sugar
1½ teaspoons pumpkin-pie spice
1 teaspoon salt
½ cup cream, whipped

1. Make praline layer: Prepare piecrust mix, following label directions, or make pastry from your own favorite one-crust recipe. Roll out to a 12-inch round on lightly floured pastry cloth or board; fit into a 9-inch pie plate. Trim overhang to ½ inch; turn under flush with rim; flute.
2. Cream butter or margarine with brown sugar in small bowl; stir in pecans. Press over bottom of prepared shell in an even layer.
3. Bake in very hot oven (450°) 10 minutes; remove; cool on wire rack 10 minutes. Reduce heat to moderate (350°).
4. Make custard layer: Scald evaporated milk with water in small saucepan. Beat eggs slightly in large bowl; stir in pumpkin, granulated sugar, ½ cup brown sugar, pumpkin-pie spice, and salt; beat in scalded milk mixture. Pour into cooled pastry shell.
5. Bake in moderate oven (350°) 50 minutes, or until center is set but still soft. (Do not overbake, for custard will set as it cools.) Cool completely on wire rack.
6. Top with a crown of whipped cream. Makes 1 nine-inch pie.

GIVE A MAYTIME TEA

■ BUTTER TRIANGLES

12 **thin slices fresh white bread (about ¾ loaf)**
12 **thin slices fresh whole-wheat bread**
(about ¾ loaf)
½ **pound (2 sticks) butter or margarine, softened**

1. Arrange breads in consecutive slices as they come from the loaf in a single layer on large cutting board. Spread half the slices evenly and to their crusts, each with a generous tablespoonful softened butter or margarine; put together with unspread slices to make 6 white and 6 whole-wheat sandwiches.

Sunny, sunny May! What a pretty time to hold a tea to honor a special someone. The key to a perfect party—serve-yourself dainties, as few or as many as you wish, that can be made up ahead of time

2. Stack about 3 sandwiches at a time; trim off crusts. Wrap sandwiches in waxed paper or transparent wrap and a damp towel, or in foil; chill at least 2 hours.
3. To serve, cut each stack diagonally into 4 triangles. Makes 4 dozen sandwiches.

Hostess note: If your sandwich trays have to stand, cover lightly with waxed paper, foil, or transparent wrap, then with a slightly damp towel. For 100 guests, make 4 times this recipe.

■ BANANA-NUT STICKS

½ cup shortening
1 cup sugar
2 eggs
2 cups sifted flour
1 teaspoon baking soda
¼ teaspoon salt
3 large bananas, mashed
     (about 1 cup)
½ cup chopped walnuts
1 teaspoon vanilla
8 tablespoons (1 stick) butter
     or margarine, softened

1. Cream shortening and sugar until fluffy in medium-size bowl; beat in eggs, 1 at a time, beating well after each addition.
2. Sift flour, soda, and salt onto waxed paper; stir into creamed mixture just until blended. Stir in mashed bananas, walnuts, and vanilla; pour into greased loaf pan, 9x5x3.
3. Bake in moderate oven (350°) 1 hour, or until wooden pick inserted in middle comes out clean. Cool 5 minutes; turn out onto wire rack; cool completely. Wrap in waxed paper, transparent wrap, or foil; let stand at least 24 hours.
4. Trim crusts from both ends of loaf; slice thin into about 40 slices. Put together, sandwich style, with softened butter or margarine. Cut each sandwich into thirds. Makes one 9x5x3 loaf of bread, or about 5 dozen sandwiches.

Hostess note: If you're serving a large variety of tea sandwiches, you may want to make up only half this loaf into sandwiches for 25 guests. Use the rest for a snack treat. To serve 100 guests, bake 2 loaves.

■ PINEAPPLE PINWHEELS

1 loaf *unsliced* whole-wheat bread
2 jars (5 ounces each) pineapple-cheese spread,
     softened

1. Trim all crusts from loaf of bread, then slice bread lengthwise into 9 or 10 thin slices; cover with a damp towel; let stand for 10 minutes.
2. Spread slices, 1 at a time, with softened cheese spread; roll up, jelly-roll fashion. Wrap tightly in waxed paper, foil, or transparent wrap; chill at least 2 hours.
3. To serve, unwrap and slice each roll crosswise into 7 or 8 pinwheels. Makes 6 to 7 dozen sandwiches.

Hostess note: Most supermarkets do not carry unsliced bread regularly but will be glad to order it for you. Give them at least 2 days' notice of the number of loaves you will need. For 100 guests, make 2 to 3 times this recipe, depending on the varieties of other sandwiches in your tea menu.

■ STRAWBERRY PINWHEELS

2 packages (8 ounces each) cream cheese
2 cups strawberries, washed, hulled, and sliced
2 tablespoons 10X (confectioners' powdered)
     sugar
1 loaf *unsliced* white bread

1. Soften cream cheese in medium-size bowl; gradually blend in strawberries and 10X sugar until smooth and easy to spread.
2. Trim crusts from loaf of bread, then slice bread lengthwise into 9 or 10 thin slices; cover with a damp towel; let stand for 10 minutes.
3. Spread slices, 1 at a time, with cheese mixture, using 3 to 4 tablespoons per slice; roll up, jelly-roll fashion. Wrap tightly in waxed paper, foil, or transparent wrap; chill at least 2 hours.
4. To serve, unwrap and slice each roll crosswise into 7 or 8 pinwheels. Makes 6 to 7 dozen sandwiches.

Hostess note: Use your sharpest knife, for bread must be sliced thin and even. We found it easier to cut crusts from bottom and 2 long sides, leaving top and 2 short sides to hold onto, and then trim the short crusts. When you slice rolls, wipe knife between each cutting so filling will not smear. For 100, make 2 to 3 times the recipe, depending on the varieties of other sandwiches in your tea menu.

■ CHEESE MOONS

1 cup sifted flour
¼ teaspoon salt
1 cup grated sharp Cheddar cheese (¼ pound)
¼ teaspoon Worcestershire sauce
½ teaspoon prepared mustard
½ cup (1 stick) butter or margarine
     Paprika

1. Mix flour, salt, and cheese in medium-size bowl; sprinkle Worcestershire sauce over; add mustard. Cut in butter or margarine with pastry blender; knead lightly in bowl to form a soft dough.
2. Roll, a teaspoonful at a time, into marble-size balls between palms of hands. Place, 2 inches apart, on ungreased cooky sheets. Leave some of the balls plain, sprinkle others lightly with paprika to make both golden and blush-pink toppings when baked.
3. Bake in moderate oven (350°) 15 minutes, or until golden. Makes 3 dozen.

Hostess note: If you work with about a level teaspoonful of dough, this recipe will make 4 dozen. Either size makes a generous number for 25. For 100 guests, you should make the recipe four times. If you plan to serve these hot, keep pans of shaped dough in the refrigerator and bake as needed.

■ DEVILED CUCUMBER ROUNDS

24 thin slices white bread (about 1½ loaves)
1 can (4½ ounces) deviled ham
4 tablespoons (½ stick) butter or margarine,
   softened
2 tablespoons horseradish mustard
2 small cucumbers
12 stuffed green olives, sliced

1. Cut 2 two-inch rounds from each slice of bread with biscuit cutter; spread lightly with mixture of deviled ham, softened butter or margarine, and horseradish mustard. Arrange in single layers on trays; cover with waxed paper or transparent wrap and a damp towel; chill.
2. Just before serving, pare, then score cucumbers deeply with a fork; cut crosswise into thin slices. Place 1 on each deviled-ham round; top with a slice of stuffed olive. Makes 4 dozen sandwiches.

Hostess note: To serve for 100 guests, cut rounds from 6 loaves of bread and spread with 4 times the recipe for deviled-ham mixture. Round sandwiches add a pretty touch to any tray, but they *are* wasteful of bread. When you are serving 100, you may prefer to make square sandwiches: Spread slices from 3 loaves of bread with 4 times the recipe for deviled-ham mixture; trim crusts; cut each slice into quarters; top each with a cucumber and an olive slice.

■ HARLEQUINS

8 thin slices whole-wheat bread (about ½ loaf)
8 thin slices white bread (about ½ loaf)
8 tablespoons (1 stick) butter or margarine,
   softened
Parsley–cream-cheese Filling *(recipe follows)*
Egg Filling *(recipe follows)*

1. Arrange bread in 4 rows of 4 slices each on large cutting board, making first and fourth rows whole wheat, second and third rows white. Spread all with softened butter or margarine.
2. Spread PARSLEY–CREAM-CHEESE FILLING on first (whole-wheat) and third (white) rows; spread EGG FILLING on second (white) row.
3. Place each fourth-row (whole-wheat) slice, buttered side down, on parsley–cream-cheese slice; then stack on egg-spread slice, then on parsley–cream-cheese slice to make 4 four-deck sandwiches. Trim off crusts; wrap each in waxed paper, foil, or transparent wrap; chill.
4. To serve, cut each into quarters, then cut each quarter into 3 thin slices. Makes 4 dozen sandwiches.

PARSLEY–CREAM-CHEESE FILLING—Let 1 package (8 ounces) cream cheese soften in medium-size bowl; blend in 2 tablespoons milk and 1½ cups finely chopped parsley. Makes about 1 cup.

EGG FILLING—Shell and chop 3 hard-cooked eggs fine; combine in small bowl with 3 tablespoons mayonnaise or salad dressing, 1 teaspoon prepared mustard, and ¼ teaspoon salt. Makes about ½ cup.

Hostess note: These sandwiches are wonderful make-aheads; in fact, they can be prepared a whole day ahead, wrapped in waxed paper or transparent wrap and a damp towel, or in foil, and kept chilled. Just before serving, cut as in Step 4. For 100 guests, make 4 times the fillings and buy 2 loaves each of thin-sliced white and whole-wheat breads and 1 pound of butter or margarine.

■ CANDIED LEMON ROUNDS

Slice 3 large lemons very thin. (You should get about 10 slices from each.) Sprinkle ½ cup sugar over bottom of large platter; arrange lemon slices in a single layer over sugar; sprinkle with an additional ½ cup sugar. Let stand at room temperature, turning 2 or 3 times, 2 hours, or until slices are glazed. Remove and lay between sheets of waxed paper, foil, or transparent wrap until serving time. Makes about 25 servings.

■ JEWEL CREAMS

Crust

4 tablespoons (½ stick) butter or margarine
⅓ cup sugar
1 egg
¼ teaspoon vanilla
1 cup sifted flour
¼ teaspoon salt

Filling

½ cup sugar
1 envelope unflavored gelatin
2 eggs, separated
1 cup milk
2 packages (8 ounces each) cream cheese, softened
3 tablespoons lemon juice
1½ cups cream for whipping

Frosting

1 cup 10X (confectioners' powdered) sugar
4 tablespoons (½ stick) butter or margarine
1 tablespoon milk
½ teaspoon vanilla
½ teaspoon lemon extract
2 drops yellow food coloring
Silver candies

1. Mark off a rectangle, 12x8, on each of 2 cooky sheets; grease. (If you have only 1 cooky sheet, bake half of batter at a time.)
2. Make crust: Cream butter or margarine with sugar until fluffy in small bowl; beat in egg and vanilla; gradually sift in flour and salt, blending well to make a very soft cookylike batter.
3. Spread half evenly and thinly into each rectangle as marked on cooky sheets.
4. Bake in moderate oven (375°) 10 minutes, or until golden. Cool slightly on cooky sheets on wire racks, then remove each layer very carefully with long spatula. Cool completely on wire racks. (Layers are very thin and fragile. If one should break, it won't show when put together with filling.)
5. Make filling: Combine ¼ cup sugar and gelatin in top of double boiler. (Save remaining ¼ cup sugar for Step 8.) Beat egg yolks slightly with a fork in a small bowl; stir in milk, then pour through strainer into gelatin mixture.
6. Heat over simmering water, stirring constantly, 10 minutes, or until gelatin dissolves and mixture coats a metal spoon; remove from heat.
7. Slice and blend in cream cheese, then lemon juice, until completely smooth. Chill 15 minutes, or just until thick enough to mound slightly on a spoon.
8. Beat egg whites until foamy-white and double in volume in large bowl; beat in saved ¼ cup sugar, 1 tablespoon at a time, until meringue forms soft peaks. Beat cream until stiff in medium-size bowl.
9. Beat thickened gelatin mixture until fluffy-light; gently fold into meringue, then fold in cream until no streaks of white remain.
10. Place one crust in bottom of baking pan, 13x9x2; spoon filling over crust, spreading evenly. Top with second crust; chill overnight.
11. Make frosting: Blend 10X sugar with butter or margarine, milk, vanilla, and lemon extract in small bowl, then beat until thick and smooth. Blend in food coloring to tint pale yellow.
12. Cut cheesecake crosswise into 8 even strips, then lengthwise into 6 strips to make 48 small cakes. Remove from pan; place on cooky sheet.
13. Fill cake decorator with frosting; make a flower on top of each cake; decorate with a silver candy. Keep chilled until serving time. Makes 4 dozen, or about 25 servings.

Hostess note: When cake is served directly from refrigerator, it is firm enough to eat finger style. If it must stand on the table for a while, you may like to provide small plates and forks. For serving 100, make 3 cakes.

■ DAISY TEACAKE

1 package white cake mix
1 package fluffy white frosting mix
Yellow food coloring
1 cup flaked coconut

1. Prepare cake mix, following label directions; pour into 2 greased 9-inch layer-cake pans.
2. Bake in moderate oven (350°) 30 minutes, or until centers spring back when lightly pressed with fingertip. Cool 5 minutes in pans on wire rack; loosen around edges with knife; turn out onto wire racks. Cool completely. Split each layer in half.
3. Prepare frosting mix, following label directions. Spoon about 1 cup frosting into a second bowl; tint remaining frosting pale yellow with about 6 drops yellow food coloring.
4. Place ¼ cup flaked coconut in small jar; add 3 drops yellow food coloring. Cover jar; shake until coconut is evenly tinted.
5. Put each split layer together with yellow frosting; cut a 4-inch circle from center of each cake; cut each rim in half; remove centers.
6. Frost centers with yellow frosting; sprinkle with yellow coconut; cut each into 6 wedges.
7. Frost tops of 2 half-rims with white frosting and remaining 2 half-rims with yellow frosting; sprinkle all with white coconut; cut each half-rim into 9 wedges.
8. Put wedges together on serving plates with yellow centers and alternating white- and yellow-frosted "petals." Makes 2 nine-inch cakes, or 48 servings.

Hostess note: For 100 guests, make recipe 3 times.

■ STRUDELETTES

1¼ cups sifted flour
½ cup (1 stick) butter or margarine
3 egg yolks, beaten
1 teaspoon lemon rind
1 tablespoon lemon juice
3 egg whites
½ cup sugar
1 cup ground walnuts
10X (confectioners' powdered) sugar

1. Sift flour into a medium-size bowl; cut in butter or margarine with pastry blender until mixture is crumbly. Stir in mixture of egg yolks, lemon rind and juice; blend lightly with a fork to form a stiff pastrylike dough.
2. Divide and shape into 24 small balls; place in shallow pan; chill at least 4 hours.
3. Beat egg whites until foamy-white and double in volume in medium-size bowl; beat in sugar, 1 tablespoon at a time, until mixture stands in firm peaks; fold in ground walnuts.
4. Roll out each ball of dough to a 4-inch round on a lightly floured pastry cloth or board; spread with 2 tablespoonfuls of nut mixture. Roll up, jelly-roll fashion; arrange, seam side down, on ungreased cooky sheets.
5. Bake in moderate oven (350°) 15 minutes, or until golden; cool on wire racks. Slice each diagonally into 3 pieces; sprinkle with 10X sugar. Makes 6 dozen.

Hostess note: These dainties will disappear in no time, for each is just a 1-inch–long bite of shattery rich pastry. For a tea for 100, make the recipe at least 3 times.

■ POSY PUFFS

1 stick cream-puff mix
Chocolate-cream Filling *(recipe follows)*
Butter-cream Frosting *(recipe follows)*
Silver candies

1. Prepare cream-puff mix, following label directions; drop by ½ teaspoonfuls, 1 inch apart, onto ungreased cooky sheets.
2. Bake in hot oven (425°) 15 minutes, or until golden; remove from cooky sheets; cool completely on wire racks.
3. Cut each cream puff in half crosswise; scoop out any bits of soft dough with tip of teaspoon. Fill each bottom with about 1½ teaspoonfuls CHOCOLATE-CREAM FILLING; replace tops. Decorate with rosette of BUTTER-CREAM FROSTING (use a cake-decorating set); top with a silver candy. Makes about 5 dozen cream puffs.

CHOCOLATE-CREAM FILLING—Combine 1 package vanilla-flavor pudding mix and 1¾ cups milk in medium-size saucepan; heat slowly, stirring constantly, until mixture thickens and comes to a boil; remove from heat. Stir in ½ cup semisweet-chocolate pieces and 1 tablespoon instant coffee powder; blend until chocolate is melted and mixture is creamy-smooth. Pour into medium-size bowl. Cool completely. Makes about 2 cups.

BUTTER-CREAM FROSTING—Cream 2 tablespoons butter or margarine in small bowl; gradually beat in 1 cup sifted 10X (confectioners' powdered) sugar; stir in 1 tablespoon cream and 3 drops yellow food coloring; beat until smooth. Makes about ½ cup.

Hostess note: These sweet morsels can be made up hours before teatime and kept chilled. Each package of cream-puff mix has 2 sticks, enough to make about 120 cream puffs. For 100 guests, make recipe 2 times.

■ TEA FOR A CROWD

For a party of 12, make tea as you do for the family, allowing 1 teaspoon, or 1 tea bag, for each cup. Heat pot first by filling with boiling water; empty; measure in tea; pour freshly boiling water over (¾ measuring cup for each 1 teaspoon tea); cover; brew 3 to 5 minutes. Have a second pot of hot water handy for those who prefer a weaker brew.

TEA ESSENCE

For serving a larger group, it is easier to start with TEA ESSENCE. To make: Measure 1 cup loose tea, or 30 tea bags, into a heated 6-cup pot; pour over 4 cups freshly boiling water. Cover; brew 5 minutes, then strain. It is now ready to serve in either of these ways: (1) Pour about 1 tablespoonful from serving pot into a cup and fill cup with hot water from a second pot. (2) Measure ½ cup TEA ESSENCE at a time into a heated 6-cup serving pot; fill with freshly boiling water; pour directly into cups. Recipe makes about 50 tea cupfuls, or enough for about 25 guests.

Hostess note: Instant tea makes a delicious quick brew also. Measure 1 level teaspoonful for each cup into teapot; fill with boiling water. Plan on 2 cups of tea for each guest when entertaining a group of 25 or fewer, 1½ cups for a larger group.

YOUR TEA SHOPPING LIST

	25 guests*	100 guests
Tea, loose	3 ounces	¾ pound
bags	25	8 dozen
instant	¾-ounce jar	4 jars
Cube sugar	8 ounces	2 pounds
Cream	1½ cups	6 cups
Crystallized ginger	4 ounces	1 pound
Lemons	3	1 dozen

*For 12 guests, you will need about half these amounts.

GO HAWAIIAN WITH A LUAU

■ MAUNA LOA PUNCH

2 cans (6 ounces each) frozen concentrated
    pineapple-grapefruit juice
2 bottles (about 28 ounces each) ginger ale, chilled
2 pints raspberry sherbet

1. Line a large roasting pan with ferns or tropical greens. Set a punch bowl in middle; half fill pan with cold water.
2. Spoon frozen juices into punch bowl; pour ginger ale over. Add a tray of ice cubes, then stir in sherbet until well-blended.
3. To make the bubbling "lava," drop 3 or 4 chunks of dry ice (use tongs or mitts—don't touch the dry ice) into water in pan—*not in punch.* Dry ice will steam to make an active tropical "volcano." Each small piece will dissolve in about 15 minutes so add more, as needed, to keep volcano "active." Makes about 20 punch-cup servings.

■ FRESH COCONUT CHIPS

You can buy this gourmet treat packed in cans, but it's fun to make your own. Here's how: First step is to drain all the milk from a fresh coconut. Look for the three soft spots or "eyes" at pointed end, then puncture each with a screwdriver and hammer. When all are opened, hold coconut over a bowl and drain off milk. (The milk gives a wonderful flavor plus to custard pie or baked custard. Just use as part of the milk called for in your favorite recipe.) Next, crack shell open with the hammer. The brown woody shell will fall away easily, leaving chunks of the big white nut covered with a thin wrinkly brown skin. Use your handy vegetable parer to shave off the skin. Work with little or big pieces of coconut, whichever are easier for you to handle. Discard skin. Now, using your vegetable parer or a sharp thin-blade knife, shave the moist white coconut into thin-as-thin curls. Spread in a thin layer in a shallow baking pan or jelly-roll pan. Bake in slow oven (300°), turning often so chips will dry out and toast evenly, 50 minutes, or until crispy. Sprinkle generously with salt. One medium-size coconut will make about 4 to 6 cups of chips.

■ HONOLULU RIBS

6 to 8 pounds spareribs
1 large onion, chopped (1 cup)
½ cup vinegar
2 teaspoons salt
6 whole allspice
    Honolulu Sauce *(recipe follows)*

1. Buy the loin back-rib spareribs, if possible,

for they are extra meaty. Cut into serving-size pieces of 2 or 3 ribs each.
2. Place in large kettle; cover with cold water; add onion, vinegar, salt, and allspice; cover.
3. Heat to boiling, simmer 1½ hours, or until tender. Drain. (This much can be done ahead.)
4. When ready to glaze, arrange ribs in a single layer on grill over hot coals. (Or if cooking indoors, arrange on rack of broiler pan.) Brush with HONOLULU SAUCE.
5. Grill, turning and basting often with sauce, 15 to 20 minutes, or until glazed and crispy-brown. (Or broil, turning once, about 5 minutes on each side.) Makes 8 servings.

HONOLULU SAUCE

4 tablespoons flour
2 tablespoons curry powder
2 tablespoons salad oil
2 cups canned pineapple juice
2 tablespoons lemon juice
1 small onion, grated
2 teaspoons salt
½ teaspoon ground ginger

1. Stir flour and curry powder into salad oil in small saucepan; heat slowly just until mixture bubbles, then stir in the remaining ingredients.
2. Cook, stirring constantly, until sauce thickens and boils 1 minute. Makes 2 cups.

■ SHRIMPS MANDARIN

2 pounds fresh raw shrimps
¼ cup salad oil
2 large onions, sliced thin
3 cups sliced celery
2 cans (3 or 4 ounces each) mushrooms, drained
2 pounds spinach, washed
1 can (5 ounces) water chestnuts, drained and
    sliced
1 can (about 11 ounces) mandarin-orange
    segments, drained
2 tablespoons soy sauce
2 tablespoons sugar
2 teaspoons salt

1. Wash, shell, and devein shrimps. (Turn to page 30 for easy directions.)
2. Pour salad oil into a large shallow saucepan. (Or use a Chinese *wok* cooking dish.) Fill with layers of onions, celery, mushrooms, spinach, raw shrimps, water chestnuts, and mandarin oranges.
3. Combine soy sauce, sugar, and salt in cup; sprinkle over top. Cover tightly.
4. Heat slowly until steaming, then cook 10 to 15 minutes, or just until shrimps are tender and vegetables are crisply cooked.
5. Toss to mix; serve with rice. Pass soy sauce to sprinkle over. Makes 8 servings.

■ FRIED RICE

6 slices bacon, diced
6 cups cooked rice
6 green onions, sliced thin
1½ tablespoons soy sauce
3 eggs, beaten

1. Saute bacon just until starting to crisp in large frying pan; stir in rice and onions.
2. Heat, stirring constantly, 10 minutes, or until rice is hot. Stir in soy sauce, then beaten eggs.
3. Cook, tossing lightly with a fork, 5 minutes longer, or just until eggs are cooked. Makes 8 servings.

■ ISLANDS VEGETABLE BAKE

4 large yams or sweet potatoes, pared and halved lengthwise (about 2 pounds)
¾ cup reconstituted frozen tangerine juice
1 small onion, grated
¼ cup firmly packed brown sugar
1 teaspoon salt
¼ teaspoon nutmeg
4 firm bananas, peeled and halved lengthwise
2 tablespoons butter or margarine

1. Place yams or sweet potatoes in single layer in baking pan, 13x9x2; pour over mixture of tangerine juice, onion, brown sugar, salt, and nutmeg; cover.
2. Bake in moderate oven (350°) 1 hour, or until potatoes are tender. Top each with a half banana; baste with juices in pan; dot with butter or margarine.
3. Bake, uncovered, 10 minutes longer, or until potatoes and bananas are richly glazed. Makes 8 servings.

■ FLOWER SALAD BOWL

6 bunches of Bibb lettuce
  OR: 2 medium-size heads of Boston lettuce
2 cups cherry tomatoes, halved
2 avocados, peeled and diced
3 hard-cooked eggs, shelled and chopped
Lime Dressing (recipe follows)

1. Halve the small heads of Bibb lettuce. (If using Boston, halve, then cut each into 4 wedges.) Place in a large salad bowl.
2. Arrange a ring of cherry tomatoes on top; next, place a circle of diced avocados within tomato ring; pile chopped eggs in center.
3. Just before serving, pour LIME DRESSING over; toss lightly to coat greens well. Makes 8 servings.

LIME DRESSING—Combine 4 tablespoons salad oil, 2 tablespoons lime juice, 1 teaspoon sugar, and ¼ teaspoon salt in jar with tight-fitting cover. Shake to blend, then shake again just before serving. Makes about ⅓ cup.

■ PARADISE PARFAITS

2 cups diced cantaloupe
1 cup red raspberries or sliced strawberries
3 pints strawberry ice cream
1 cup cream, whipped
4 peaches, peeled, halved, and pitted

1. Layer fruits and ice cream, dividing evenly, into stemmed glasses this way: Cantaloupe, raspberries or strawberries, ice cream. Top each with whipped cream, then with a peach half.
2. Stick a perky Oriental paper parasol or lantern into each peach half, if you wish. Makes 8 servings.

■ KONA SUNDAES

¾ cup firmly packed light brown sugar
1 tablespoon instant coffee powder
  Dash of salt
½ cup water
1 can (15 ounces) sweetened condensed milk
3 pints vanilla or coffee ice cream

1. Mix brown sugar, instant coffee, salt, and water in medium-size heavy saucepan; heat, stirring constantly, to boiling, then cook, without stirring, to 230° on a candy thermometer. (A little syrup will spin fine threads when dropped from tip of spoon.) Remove from heat.
2. Place sweetened condensed milk (not evaporated milk) in medium-size bowl; blend in hot syrup slowly; cool.
3. When ready to serve, scoop ice cream into dessert dishes, dividing evenly; spoon sauce over. Makes 8 servings.

*D*INNER—the no-will-power meal of the day—needn't say "diet" even though you are trimming down. And dessert is no exception. The refreshingly bright mold (*opposite*), handsome as a new spring bonnet, is just a teaser to all the desserts that go along with the equally satisfying main dishes, vegetables, and salads that follow in this chapter.

Included, also, are two big bonuses for you—the cook of the family. Each meal is not only nutritiously good but one the whole family *should* eat. There's no double cooking here! Trim-

Slim-down dinners the whole family can enjoy

downers stay with the portions suggested in each starred recipe. (Calorie counts go with every menu, too.) Nondieters may enjoy their fill of anything they wish.

Some of these recipes may surprise you as diet foods, but each hides a secret or two for snipping off calories without changing one whit of flavor. And remember, too, there are morale boosters aplenty in the diet-foods department of your supermarket to help spur you on toward your goal.

Apricot-raspberry Snow *(recipe on page 165)*, with ▶ its crown of golden fruit and snowy coconut, stretches dessert calories a long way. Fluffy-light berry-pink gelatin and egg whites make the handsome mold

Dinners that don't say "diet"

	MAIN DISH	GO-WITHS	DESSERT	TOTAL CALORIES
STEAK REWARD *(pictured on page 157)*	★Sliced Steak Broil with Garlic-mushroom Sauce	Riced Potatoes Broccoli with Lemon Raw Relishes	★Honey-glazed Apples	625 calories per serving
	You'll rarely hear a grumble when steak is the meat choice — and what a morale booster when you're trying to whittle down the weight. Dieter's dinner here starts		with 3 juicy slices of rare steak with sauc a whole cup each of riced potatoes an steamed broccoli, plus vegetable nibble and ends with a plump baked-apple hal	
COMPANY STYLED	★Broiled Lamb-vegetable Sticks Hot Tomato Wedges	Jellied Consomme ★Vitamin Relish	★Surprise Custard Pie	435 calories per serving
	Here's a menu for entertaining, yet it has cooking secrets to keep the calorie tally 'way down. Marinade for lamb and vegetables is low-calorie salad dressing;		seasoning for salad, zesty lemon juic Dessert's a real treat—custard pie. Coun just 15 calories for 1 cup consomme other counts are given with each recip	
GOURMET STEW SPLURGE *(pictured on page 157)*	★Beef-vegetable Ragout	Dill-pickle Sticks	★Butterfly Eclairs	430 calories per serving
	Most would-be slim Jims and Janes will agree dieting can be fun with this heaping plateful of stew. One serving measures a man-size 1⅔ cups—with broth so rich		you'll never miss the thick gravy. An if you still have room, two midget-siz eclairs—cream-filled to make you feel yo are really splurging—complete the dinne	
SALAD-DAY WINNER	★Sea-food Chef's Salad ★Tomato Dressing	★Curry-celery Soup	★Diet-light Spongecake	430 calories per serving
	Rich in "meaty" proteins and a real bargain in calories—that's sea food. And even most meat-and-potato fans don't think of it as fish. Dieter rates a generous		quarter of this crab-meat–and–scallop salad bowl, along with one full cup o curry-sparked celery soup and a husky slice of the most heavenly light spongecake	
FRIDAY FEAST	★Spaghetti with Tomato-scallop Sauce	Grated Parmesan Cheese	★Bouquet Fruit Compote	460 calories per serving
	Imagine—spaghetti topped with a tomato-rich sauce on your diet plate! It's true. And dinner includes inviting mixed fruits big enough to double as a salad-dessert.		Dieter's portion: 1¼ cups spaghetti wit ¾ cup of the high-protein, low-calorie sca lop sauce and just a sprinkling of cheese-please! But dessert—a whole saucedishf	
DE LUXE SLIM-DOWNER	★Peachy Golden Chicken	★Spring Broccoli ★Dill Onion Rings ★Water-cress Soup	★Molded Mocha Cream	409 calories per serving
	Be-svelte training's easy with this dinner of chicken baked golden-rich with a diet-fruit glaze. Allow 1 drumstick or thigh, ½ breast, and a peach half for a		diet portion. Menu mates: ⅙ of the br coli, ¼ cup nippy-sweet onion rings, a ½ cup soup for a starter. Save room dessert—it's a surprise chocolate m	

	MAIN DISH	GO-WITHS	DESSERT	TOTAL CALORIES

FAVORITE STAND-BY

| ★Patty-cake Meat Loaf | ★White Cauliflower ★Green-bean Crisps ★Mushroom-aspic Molds | ★Pineapple Sherbet in Orange Cups | 510 calories per serving |

Here's a bountiful meat-loaf meal for the whole family—and you'll like its easy-to-put-together-and-bake directions. Each whopping diet portion of meat is 1 wedge, or ⅛ of the loaf, 1 cauliflower "flower," ½ cup green beans, and a salad-aspic mold. Dessert—so worth waiting for—is ¾ cup frosty sherbet nestled in a juicy orange

DESIGNED FOR DAD

| ★Boiled-beef Platter | Potatoes and Onions Cabbage Wedges Carrot Sticks | ★Apricot-raspberry Snow *(pictured on page 153)* | 415 calories per serving |

A real easy dinner it is to fix, for everything simmers together with little watching. Meat is thrifty boneless beef chuck. And just see what each dieter may have: Two ¼-inch-thick slices lean beef, 1 each potato, onion, and cabbage wedge, 4 carrot sticks, and ¼ cup skimmed broth. Dessert: Fluffy pink gelatin with fruit and coconut

BONANZA DINNER

| ★Lobster Slices with ★Curry Dip | ★Zucchini Sticks ★Hot Spinach Salad | ★Cinnamon Pears | 205 calories per serving |

This sea-food favorite cooks sweetly tender in minutes. And with its spicy dip, no one will miss the butter. For the main course, each dieter may have two meaty lobster tails to dunk into ¼ cup dip, and ⅙ each of the zucchini and spinach—few calories for big servings. Even dessert—a plump baked pear half—has a low count

GOOD-FOR-YOU TEMPTER *(pictured on page 163)*

| ★Skillet Liver and Onions | ★Garden Potatoes and Peas Salad Relishes | ★Coconut Cup Custards | 407 calories per serving |

The whole family will polish off this gourmet meal with its sweet coconut-capped custard ending. Here the onions, topping mildly-seasoned liver, are "fried" the dieter's way. Each calorie-counted plate allows 2 slices of liver with ⅓ cup onions and 2 tablespoons sauce, 2 potatoes and ⅓ cup sauce, and relishes and dessert

FAR EAST FANCY *(pictured on page 163)*

| ★Chicken Orientale with Fluffy Rice | Soy Sauce Hot Mustard Green Tea | Gelatin Cubes ★Almond Meringues | 424 calories per serving |

Calorie trimmers won't feel sorry for themselves with this luxury dinner—right down to a serving of low-calorie gelatin cubes and a meringue cooky. Each diet helping includes a full cup of slivered white-meat chicken with pineapple and vegetables framed with ½ cup of snowy rice. Bonuses: Soy sauce and mustard don't count at all

MEAT-LOAF SPECIAL

| ★Veal-vegetable Loaf | ★Tomato Cups Steamed Spinach Green-pepper Sticks | ★Carioca Fluff | 350 calories per serving |

Who would ever guess that this generous meal was meant for waistline watchers? Each hefty serving of meat loaf counts 2 slices; salad's a whole tomato seasoned with a tart dill dressing. Spinach—a full cupful—plus raw sweet-pepper sticks go along too. Best yet—a chocolaty dessert topped with just a wisp of whipped cream

155

MAIN DISHES

■ SLICED STEAK BROIL

1 small onion, chopped (¼ cup)
1 small clove of garlic, minced
½ cup water
2 teaspoons flour
1 can (3 or 4 ounces) sliced mushrooms
1 envelope instant beef bouillon
  OR: 1 beef-bouillon cube
1 tablespoon chili sauce
  Granulated, liquid, or tablet no-calorie
    sweetener
1 flank steak (about 2 pounds)
  Instant unseasoned meat tenderizer

1. Heat onion, garlic, and water to boiling in small saucepan; cook 10 minutes, or just until liquid evaporates. Lower heat and continue cooking, stirring constantly, 3 to 5 minutes, or until onion browns lightly.
2. Stir in flour; remove from heat.
3. Drain liquid from mushrooms into 1-cup measure; add water to make 1 cup. (Save mushrooms for next step.) Stir liquid, instant bouillon or bouillon cube, and chili sauce into onion mixture. Cook, stirring constantly, until mixture thickens and boils 1 minute.
4. Stir in mushrooms and your favorite no-calorie sweetener, using the equivalent of ½ teaspoon sugar. Simmer, uncovered, 10 to 15 minutes to blend flavors.
5. Moisten steak and sprinkle with meat tenderizer, following label directions.
6. Broil, following range manufacturer's directions, 3 to 4 minutes; turn; broil 3 to 4 minutes longer for rare, 5 to 6 minutes for medium.
7. Remove steak to cutting board; carve diagonally into thin slices. Spoon hot sauce over. Makes 6 servings.

Weight-watcher's portion: 3 slices of steak plus 3 tablespoons sauce—389 calories.

■ BROILED LAMB-VEGETABLE STICKS

1½ pounds lean shoulder or leg of lamb, cubed
2 tablespoons low-calorie Italian dressing
2 tablespoons water
1 medium-size acorn squash
2 medium-size tomatoes

1. Trim any fat from lamb cubes; place cubes in shallow pan; pour mixture of salad dressing and water over. Let stand, turning meat often, 1 hour.
2. Cook squash whole in boiling water to cover in medium-size saucepan 25 minutes, or just until tender. Drain; halve; scoop out seeds and membrane. Cut each half into 4 chunks;

then brush evenly with marinade from lamb.
3. Thread lamb alternately with squash on skewers (about 4 pieces of meat and 2 of squash) ; lay skewers, not touching, on rack on broiler pan.
4. Broil, following range manufacturer's directions, turning often and brushing with marinade, 12 to 15 minutes, or until lamb is done as you like it.
5. While lamb cooks, wash and cut each tomato into 8 wedges; place in pie plate; brush with marinade. Place on broiler rack beside lamb; broil 5 minutes, or just until heated. Makes 4 servings.

Weight-watcher's portion: 1 skewerful of lamb and squash, plus 4 tomato wedges— 220 calories.

■ BEEF-VEGETABLE RAGOUT

1 small onion, chopped (¼ cup)
½ cup water (for onion)
1½ pounds lean beef round or chuck, cut into
    1-inch cubes
1 bay leaf
½ teaspoon seasoned salt
¼ teaspoon seasoned pepper
1 can condensed beef bouillon
1 cup water (for ragout)
6 small potatoes, pared
3 cups sliced celery
1 small eggplant, diced (3 cups)
  Granulated, liquid, or tablet no-calorie
    sweetener
½ small head of escarole, chopped (3 cups)
3 medium-size tomatoes, cut into wedges

1. Simmer onion in ½ cup water in kettle or Dutch oven 10 minutes, or just until water evaporates. Lower heat and continue cooking, stirring constantly, 3 to 5 minutes, or until onion browns lightly; remove and set aside.
2. Brown beef cubes, a few at a time, in same kettle. (No need to add fat.) Return all beef and onion to kettle; stir in bay leaf, seasoned salt and pepper, beef bouillon, and 1 cup water. Heat to boiling; cover; simmer 1½ to 2 hours, or just until beef is tender.
3. Arrange potatoes on top; cover; simmer 20 minutes. Add celery and eggplant; simmer 10 minutes, or until potatoes are tender.
4. Stir in your favorite no-calorie sweetener, using the equivalent of 1 teaspoon sugar. Lay escarole and tomatoes on top; cover again; simmer 5 minutes, or just until greens are wilted. Remove bay leaf.
5. Spoon a potato in the middle of each heated serving dish; surround with ragout. Garnish with dill-pickle strips, if you wish. Makes 6 servings.

Weight-watcher's portion: 1⅔ cups ragout plus 1 potato and ½ dill pickle—334 calories.

Two diet delights—lean beef and mushrooms—go together invitingly in this **Sliced Steak Broil**. Menu

Each whopping-big diet serving of **Beef-vegetable
Ragout** boasts lots of meat, a whole potato, four

mates are riced potatoes, broccoli, crisp -nibbles,
and for dessert, a rosy apple half glazed with honey

vegetables, and dill-pickle sticks. Splurgy dessert counts two eclairs filled with velvety cream

■ SEA-FOOD CHEF'S SALAD

Tomato Dressing (recipe follows)
Marinated Scallops (recipe follows)
1 can (about 6 ounces) king crab meat
1 head of Boston or leaf lettuce
10 radishes, sliced
2 medium-size carrots, scraped and cut into
  2-inch sticks
2 hard-cooked eggs, shelled and quartered
  lengthwise
1 cup (½ pound) dry cottage cheese
  Paprika

1. Prepare TOMATO DRESSING, then MARINATED SCALLOPS and let chill.
2. Drain crab meat; remove any bony tissue, but keep meat in big chunks; place in small bowl; chill.
3. When ready to put salad together, line a large salad bowl with lettuce leaves; break up remaining into bite-size pieces in bowl.
4. Arrange mounds of MARINATED SCALLOPS, crab meat, radishes, carrots, and eggs in a ring on lettuce. Fill center with cottage cheese; sprinkle with paprika. Serve with remaining TOMATO DRESSING if you wish. Makes 4 servings.

Weight-watcher's portion: ¼ of salad with 2 tablespoons dressing—215 calories.

TOMATO DRESSING

1 envelope French-dressing mix
¾ cup tomato juice
¼ cup vinegar
2 tablespoons water

Combine all ingredients in 2-cup jar with tight-fitting cover; shake well to mix; chill. Shake again just before serving. Makes about 1¼ cups. (1 tablespoon is 4 calories.)

MARINATED SCALLOPS

½ pound fresh sea scallops
  OR: 1 package (7 ounces) frozen sea scallops
2 cups water
1 slice of onion
1 slice of lemon
2 peppercorns
3 tablespoons Tomato Dressing (recipe above)

1. Wash fresh scallops under cold running water; drain. (No need to thaw frozen ones.)
2. Heat water, onion, lemon, and peppercorns to boiling in medium-size saucepan; simmer 5 minutes. Add scallops; cover; simmer 5 minutes. (If using frozen ones, it will take 7 to 10 minutes.)
3. Remove with slotted spoon; drain well; place in shallow dish. Spoon TOMATO DRESSING over; cover; chill at least 30 minutes to season and blend flavors.

■ SPAGHETTI WITH TOMATO-SCALLOP SAUCE

1 large onion, chopped (1 cup)
½ clove of garlic, minced
1 tablespoon salad oil
1 can (about 1 pound) tomatoes
1 can (6 ounces) tomato paste
½ cup water
¼ cup chopped parsley
1 tablespoon mixed Italian herbs
1½ teaspoons salt
¼ teaspoon pepper
  Granulated, liquid, or tablet no-calorie sweetener
1 pound fresh or frozen sea scallops
1 package (1 pound) thin spaghetti,
  cooked and drained
  Grated Parmesan cheese

1. Saute onion and garlic in salad oil just until soft in large saucepan. Stir in tomatoes, tomato paste, water, parsley, Italian herbs, salt, pepper, and your favorite no-calorie sweetener, using the equivalent of 1½ teaspoon sugar. Cover; simmer 1 hour.
2. Chop scallops. (If using frozen ones, thaw slightly.) Stir into sauce; cook 15 minutes longer, or until scallops are tender and flavors blended.
3. Spoon spaghetti into a heated large serving bowl; make a well in center and fill with sauce. Or pour sauce over spaghetti in kettle; toss to mix well. Pass cheese separately to sprinkle over. Makes 6 servings.

Weight-watcher's portion: 1¼ cups spaghetti plus ¾ cup sauce and 1 tablespoon Parmesan cheese—360 calories.

■ PEACHY GOLDEN CHICKEN

3 whole chicken breasts, split
3 chicken drumsticks
3 chicken thighs
1 can (about 1 pound) diet-pack cling
  peach halves
2 tablespoons lemon juice
1 teaspoon soy sauce

1. Arrange chicken pieces in single layer in shallow baking dish, 12x8x2.
2. Drain peach syrup into a cup (save halves for Step 3). Stir lemon juice and soy sauce into syrup; brush about half over chicken.
3. Bake in hot oven (400°), brushing every 15 minutes with remaining peach-syrup mixture and pan juices, 1 hour, or until chicken is tender and richly golden. Place peach halves around chicken; brush with pan juices; bake 5 minutes longer to heat peaches. Makes 6 servings.

Weight-watcher's portion: ½ chicken breast, 1 drumstick or thigh, and ½ peach—210 calories.

■ PATTY-CAKE MEAT LOAF

1½ pounds lean ground beef
1 jar (about 5 ounces) baby-pack strained carrots
½ cup tomato juice
¼ cup chopped parsley
1 small onion, chopped (¼ cup)
1½ teaspoons salt
½ teaspoon mixed Italian herbs

1. Combine ground beef, carrots, tomato juice, parsley, onion, salt, and Italian herbs in large bowl; stir lightly with a fork just until mixed. (Heavy handling tends to toughen ground beef.)
2. Form lightly into a thick 8-inch round patty; place on rack of broiler pan (so fat will drip through) or set on wire rack in shallow baking pan.
3. Bake in moderate oven (375°) 35 minutes, or until brown on top and done as you like beef. Slice patty into 6 wedges. Makes 6 servings.

Weight-watcher's portion: 1 wedge or ⅙ of meat loaf—260 calories.

■ BOILED-BEEF PLATTER

3 to 4 pounds lean boneless beef chuck roast
1 tablespoon salt
2 peppercorns
1 bay leaf
6 cups water
6 small potatoes, scrubbed
6 yellow onions, peeled
6 medium-size carrots, scraped and quartered
1 small head of cabbage (about 2 pounds)

1. Place meat in kettle or Dutch oven; add salt, peppercorns, bay leaf, and water. Cover; heat to boiling; simmer 1½ hours.
2. Remove meat; let any fat rise to top of broth; skim off. Return meat to kettle.
3. Cut off a band of skin around middle of each potato; place potatoes, onions, and carrots around meat in kettle; simmer 30 minutes longer, or until meat is tender.
4. Cut cabbage into 6 wedges; arrange on top of meat and vegetables; cover. Cook 15 minutes, or until vegetables are tender.
5. Remove cabbage with slotted spoon and place at one side of heated large serving platter; place meat in middle and remaining vegetables around it. Keep hot.
6. Skim any last traces of fat from broth; remove bay leaf. Heat broth to spoon over meat and vegetables, or chill to make soup for another meal. Makes 6 servings.

Weight-watcher's portion: 2 slices of meat (each about ¼ inch thick), 1 potato, 1 carrot (4 pieces), 1 onion, a wedge of cabbage, and ¼ cup broth—385 calories.

■ LOBSTER SLICES WITH CURRY DIP

12 small frozen South African lobster tails (4 packages, 10 ounces each)
1 lemon, sliced
1 tablespoon mixed whole spices
Curry Dip *(recipe follows)*

1. Cook lobster tails in boiling salted water with lemon and mixed whole spices, following label directions; drain.
2. When shells are cool enough to handle, cut with scissors through thick membrane on each side where it joins to hard shell; remove. Peel hard shells back with one hand, pulling lobster meat out with the other.
3. Place in a colander over boiling water; cover lightly and steam to keep hot. (Or prepare early in day, chill lobster, then reheat at serving time.) Serve with CURRY DIP. Makes 6 servings.

Weight-watcher's portion: 2 lobster tails—95 calories, plus ¼ cup dip—30 calories.

CURRY DIP

1 large onion, chopped (1 cup)
1 cup water
1 tablespoon curry powder
1 chicken-bouillon cube
¼ teaspoon salt
¼ teaspoon ground ginger
1 can (about 8 ounces) diet-pack applesauce
Granulated, liquid, or tablet no-calorie sweetener
2 teaspoons lemon juice

1. Cook onion slowly in ½ cup water in small saucepan, stirring often, 10 minutes.
2. Stir in curry powder; cook 1 minute. Add bouillon cube, salt, ginger, applesauce, and remaining ½ cup water. Sweeten to taste with your favorite no-calorie sweetener, using the equivalent of 4 teaspoons sugar.
3. Simmer, stirring often, 5 minutes, or until thick. Just before serving, stir in lemon juice. Serve warm or chilled. Makes 1½ cups.

■ SKILLET LIVER AND ONIONS

3 large onions, sliced and separated
    into rings
2 cups water (for onions)
1½ pounds sliced beef or lamb liver
1 teaspoon butter or margarine
2 tablespoons low-calorie French dressing
6 tablespoons water (for sauce)
½ teaspoon salt
¼ teaspoon pepper

1. Cook onions in 2 cups water, stirring often, in large frying pan 15 to 20 minutes, or just until water evaporates and onions brown lightly. Remove from pan.
2. While onions cook, snip out veiny parts and skin from liver. (Scissors do a quick job.) Cut into 12 even-size slices. Brown, 1 minute on each side, in butter or margarine in same frying pan.
3. Return onions to pan. Mix French dressing with 6 tablespoons water, salt, and pepper in a cup; pour over.
4. Cover pan; heat quickly to boiling; simmer 3 minutes, or just until liver loses its pink color. Makes 6 servings.

Weight-watcher's portion: 2 slices liver plus ⅓ cup onions and about 2 tablespoons sauce —183 calories.

■ CHICKEN ORIENTALE

3 whole chicken breasts (about 2½ pounds)
3 tablespoons soy sauce
1 teaspoon salad oil or peanut oil
1 can (1 pint, 2 ounces) unsweetened
    pineapple juice
4 tablespoons cornstarch
1 can (8 ounces) diet-pack pineapple chunks
2 cans (3 or 4 ounces each) sliced
    mushrooms
½ teaspoon salt
1 package (10 ounces) frozen peas, thawed
6 cups shredded Chinese cabbage (about
    1 head)
3 cups cooked hot rice

1. Remove skin and bones from chicken breasts; slice meat into long thin strips.
2. Place soy sauce in pie plate; dip chicken strips into sauce; brown quickly in salad oil or peanut oil in large frying pan.
3. Stir just enough unsweetened pineapple juice into cornstarch in cup to make a smooth paste; save for Step 5.
4. Stir remaining pineapple juice, and pineapple chunks and mushrooms with liquid into chicken in frying pan; heat to boiling.
5. Stir in cornstarch mixture and salt; cook, stirring constantly, until sauce thickens and boils 3 minutes. Cover; simmer about 15 minutes.
6. Stir in peas; arrange cabbage on top. Cover;

cook 8 minutes, or until peas and cabbage are tender. Serve over cooked hot rice. Makes 6 servings.

Weight-watcher's portion: 1 cup chicken mixture and ½ cup rice—398 calories.

■ VEAL-VEGETABLE LOAF

1 pound ground lean veal shoulder meat
1 cup (½ pound) cream-style cottage cheese
3 medium-size carrots, scraped and shredded
    (about 1 cup)
1 small onion, chopped (¼ cup)
1 egg
1 teaspoon salt
½ teaspoon basil
¼ teaspoon pepper

1. Mix all ingredients lightly in large bowl. Shape into a loaf in middle of an ungreased shallow baking pan.
2. Bake in moderate oven (350°) 50 minutes, or until top browns lightly. Cut into 12 slices with a sharp knife. Makes 6 servings.

Weight-watcher's portion: 2 slices—178 calories.

GO-WITHS

■ VITAMIN RELISH

3 cups finely chopped cabbage
1 medium-size cucumber, pared and chopped
½ cup chopped green pepper
2 pimientos, chopped
1 tablespoon lemon juice
1 tablespoon water
1 teaspoon salt
    Granulated, liquid, or tablet no-calorie
    sweetener

1. Combine cabbage, cucumber, green pepper, and pimientos in medium-size bowl.
2. Mix lemon juice, water, salt, and your favorite no-calorie sweetener, using the equivalent of 3 teaspoons sugar, in cup. Pour over vegetables; toss to mix. Cover; chill at least a half hour to season and blend flavors. Makes 4 servings.

Weight-watcher's portion: 1 full cup—25 calories.

■ SPRING BROCCOLI

1 bunch fresh broccoli (about 2 pounds)
2 beef-bouillon cubes
1½ cups boiling water
30 thin pretzel sticks, broken

1. Trim and discard outer leaves and tough

ends from broccoli; split large stalks lengthwise.

2. Dissolve bouillon cubes in water in medium-
size frying pan; arrange broccoli in pan;
cover.
3. Cook 15 minutes, or just until crisply tender.
Lift out stalks with slotted spoon into
heated serving dish; spoon a little of remaining juices in pan over, if you wish.
Sprinkle pretzels over top just before serving so they'll stay snappy-crisp. Makes 6
servings.

Weight-watcher's portion: ⅙ serving from
dish—35 calories.

■ DILL ONION RINGS

1 large Bermuda onion
½ cup white vinegar
¼ cup water
2 teaspoons salt
½ teaspoon dill weed
Granulated or liquid no-calorie sweetener

1. Peel and cut onion into thin crosswise
slices; separate into rings; place in small
bowl.
2. Combine vinegar, water, salt, dill weed, and
your favorite no-calorie sweetener, using the
equivalent of 24 teaspoons (½ cup) sugar,
in small saucepan. Heat to boiling; pour over
onion rings.
3. Cover tightly; chill at least one hour to
blend flavors. Makes 2 cups.

Weight-watcher's portion: ¼ cupful—15
calories.

■ WATER-CRESS SOUP

1 bunch water cress
1 tablespoon flour
3 cups skim milk
1 teaspoon instant minced onion
1 teaspoon salt

1. Wash water cress; save 6 sprigs for garnish.
Chop remaining stems and leaves. (You
should have about 1¾ cups.)
2. Smooth flour and 1 to 2 tablespoons skim
milk to a paste in medium-size saucepan;
slowly stir in remaining milk; add onion and
salt. Cook, stirring constantly, until mixture
thickens slightly and boils 1 minute.
3. Remove from heat; stir in water cress.
Serve at once or keep hot over very low
heat. Do not let it boil. (If you prefer the
soup pureed, twirl it in an electric blender.)
4. Ladle into heated cups; garnish each with
a sprig of water cress. Makes 6 servings.

Weight-watcher's portion: ½ cupful—50
calories.

■ CURRY-CELERY SOUP

½ cup finely diced celery
2 tablespoons butter or margarine
2 tablespoons flour
1 teaspoon curry powder
1 teaspoon salt
¼ teaspoon pepper
3 cups water
1 cup skim milk

1. Saute celery lightly in butter or margarine
in medium-size saucepan. Stir in flour, curry
powder, salt, and pepper; cook, stirring all
the time, just until mixture bubbles.
2. Stir in water and milk slowly; continue
cooking and stirring until mixture thickens
slightly and starts to boil.
3. Cover; simmer 10 minutes to blend flavors.
Ladle into heated soup bowls. Makes 4
servings.

Weight-watcher's portion: 1 full cup—90
calories.

■ WHITE CAULIFLOWER

1 firm white cauliflower (about 2 pounds)
1 cup water
1 tablespoon lemon juice
1 teaspoon salt
Paprika

1. Cut off thick green leafy stems from cauliflower. (Save to trim, dice, and cook for
another meal.) Wash head and separate into
6 large flowerets.
2. Heat water, lemon juice, and salt to boiling
in medium-size saucepan. Add cauliflower;
cover; cook 15 minutes, or just until crisply
tender. Drain well. (To keep cauliflower
snowy-white, do not peek during cooking.)
3. Spoon into heated serving bowl; sprinkle
lightly with paprika. Makes 6 servings.

Weight-watcher's portion: 1 caulisloweret—
30 calories.

■ GREEN-BEAN CRISPS

1 pound green beans
1 tablespoon salad oil
1 teaspoon Worcestershire sauce
¼ teaspoon salt
⅓ cup water

1. Wash, tip, and split green beans lengthwise.
2. Heat salad oil in large frying pan; add beans all at once. Cook, stirring constantly, 3 to 4 minutes, or just until shiny-moist.
3. Stir Worcestershire sauce and salt into water in cup; pour over beans. Cover; cook 15 minutes, or just until crisply tender. Makes 6 servings.

Weight-watcher's portion: ½ cupful—35 calories.

■ MUSHROOM-ASPIC MOLDS

1 can (3 or 4 ounces) sliced mushrooms
1 envelope unflavored gelatin
1½ cups tomato juice
½ teaspoon celery salt
½ teaspoon basil

1. Pour mushrooms and liquid into medium-size bowl; sprinkle gelatin over; let soften.
2. Simmer tomato juice, celery salt, and basil 5 minutes in small saucepan; pour over mushroom mixture in bowl; stir until gelatin dissolves.
3. Chill until mixture starts to thicken; stir; then spoon into 6 small molds or custard cups, dividing evenly. Chill until firm.
4. Unmold onto serving plates; serve plain or garnish with water cress. Makes 6 servings.

Weight-watcher's portion: 1 mold or custard cup—25 calories.

■ TOMATO CUPS

2 cans (1 pound each) peeled whole tomatoes
2 tablespoons vinegar
Granulated, liquid, or tablet no-calorie sweetener
Salt and pepper
½ teaspoon dill weed

1. Empty tomatoes carefully into a shallow pan. (There will be about 6 big ones.) Lift out, one at a time, with two spoons to keep from mashing; place in individual serving bowls. (Serve juice as a beverage for another meal.)
2. Combine vinegar and your favorite no-calorie sweetener, using the equivalent of 1½ teaspoons sugar, in a cup. Spoon over tomatoes; sprinkle with salt and pepper, then with dill weed. Chill. Makes 6 servings.

Weight-watcher's portion: 1 tomato—30 calories.

■ ZUCCHINI STICKS

4 medium-size zucchini (about 1 pound)
¼ cup water
1 teaspoon celery salt

1. Wash zucchini; trim ends and quarter each lengthwise, then cut into 3-inch sticks. Place in medium-size frying pan; add water and celery salt; cover pan.
2. Cook, stirring once or twice, 20 minutes, or until crisply tender. Makes 6 servings.

Weight-watcher's portion: ⅙ serving from pan—10 calories.

■ HOT SPINACH SALAD

1 pound fresh spinach
2 tablespoons lemon juice
1 teaspoon salad oil
¼ teaspoon seasoned salt
¼ teaspoon Worcestershire sauce
Granulated, liquid, or tablet no-calorie sweetener

1. Cut out any large ribs and all stems from spinach; wash leaves well; drain.
2. Steam, covered, in a large saucepan, without adding any water, 2 to 3 minutes, or just until wilted. Drain any liquid from pan.
3. Mix lemon juice, salad oil, seasoned salt, Worcestershire sauce, and your favorite no-calorie sweetener, using the equivalent of 1 teaspoon sugar, in cup. Pour over spinach; toss to coat leaves well. Spoon into heated serving bowl. Makes 6 servings.

Weight-watcher's portion: ⅙ serving from bowl—20 calories.

■ GARDEN POTATOES AND PEAS

12 small new potatoes (1½ pounds)
1 package (10 ounces) frozen green peas
1 tablespoon flour
½ teaspoon salt
⅛ teaspoon pepper
Dash of nutmeg
1 cup skim milk

1. Scrub potatoes well; cut off a band of skin around middle of each. Cook in boiling salted water in medium-size saucepan, 15 minutes, or until tender. Drain well; keep hot.
2. Cook peas, following label directions. (No need to drain.)
3. Sprinkle flour, salt, pepper, and nutmeg over peas; stir in milk until well-mixed. Cook, stirring constantly, until mixture thickens slightly and boils 1 minute.
4. Spoon potatoes into heated serving dish; pour creamed peas over. Makes 6 servings.

Weight-watcher's portion: 2 potatoes plus ⅓ cup creamed peas—138 calories.

Showy yet hearty—that's **Chicken Orientale** (recipe on page 160) framed with fluffy rice. Soy sauce and mustard to dash on as you please are calorie-free. Top-off: Cubes of gelatin and a meringue cooky

Nippy French-dressing sauce seasons this diet-smart **Skillet Liver and Onions** (recipe on page 160) with a chef's flair. Creamed vegetables, green salad bouquet, and custard drifted with coconut finish menu

■ HONEY-GLAZED APPLES

3 large baking apples
½ cup water
¼ cup honey
½ teaspoon grated lemon rind
Few drops red food coloring

1. Pare, halve, and core apples; place, cut side down, in shallow baking dish.
2. Mix water, honey, lemon rind, and food coloring in 1-cup measure; pour over apples; cover.
3. Bake in hot oven (400°), basting once or twice with syrup in dish, 30 minutes. Uncover; baste apples again. Bake 15 minutes longer, or until tender but still firm enough to hold their shape.
4. Let apples cool in baking dish, basting once or twice to make a rich glaze. Garnish with a sprig of mint, if you like. Serve warm. Makes 6 servings.

Weight-watcher's portion: ½ glazed apple—98 calories.

■ SURPRISE CUSTARD PIE

Margarine Pastry *(recipe follows)*
4 eggs
¼ teaspoon salt
⅛ teaspoon nutmeg
1 teaspoon grated lemon rind
3 cups skim milk
Granulated or liquid no-calorie sweetener
1 teaspoon vanilla

1. Make MARGARINE PASTRY. Roll out to a 12-inch round between two sheets of waxed paper (no flour needed). Fit into a 9-inch pie plate; trim overhang to ½ inch; turn under and flute. Chill while preparing filling.
2. Beat eggs slightly with salt, nutmeg, and lemon rind in medium-size bowl; stir in milk

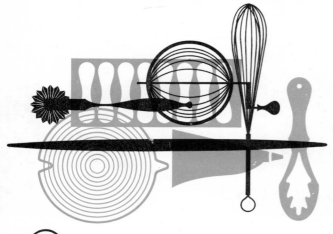

and your favorite no-calorie sweetener, using the equivalent of 16 teaspoons (⅓ cup) sugar, and vanilla.
3. Set pie plate on a cooky sheet; place on rack in oven; strain custard mixture into shell.
4. Bake in hot oven (450°) 10 minutes; reduce heat to slow (300°); bake 45 minutes longer or until center is almost set but still soft. (Do not overbake, for custard will set as it cools.) Cool pie completely on wire rack. Makes 1 nine-inch pie or 8 wedges.

MARGARINE PASTRY—Sift ½ cup sifted flour and ½ teaspoon salt into medium-size bowl; cut in 4 tablespoons (½ stick) margarine with pastry blender until mixture is crumbly. Blend in another ½ cup sifted flour until well-mixed and crumbly. Sprinkle about 2½ tablespoons *ice water* over, ⅓ at a time; mix quickly and lightly with pastry blender until dough clings together in a ball and leaves side of bowl clean. Makes 1 nine-inch shell.

Weight-watcher's portion: 1 wedge or ⅛ of pie—175 calories.

■ BUTTERFLY ECLAIRS

½ cup water
4 tablespoons (½ stick) butter or margarine
½ cup sifted flour
⅛ teaspoon salt
2 eggs
2 envelopes low-calorie vanilla-flavor pudding mix (3 to a package)
2 cups skim milk

1. Heat water and butter or margarine to boiling in medium-size saucepan. Stir in flour and salt all at once with a wooden spoon; continue stirring vigorously about 2 minutes, or until batter forms a thick smooth ball that follows spoon around pan.
2. Remove from heat; cool slightly; beat in eggs, 1 at a time, until mixture is thick and shiny-smooth.
3. Shape batter, 1 tablespoonful at a time, into a thin strip, about 1 inch apart, on ungreased cooky sheets.
4. Bake in hot oven (400°) 30 minutes, or until puffed and lightly golden. Remove at once from cooky sheets; cool completely.
5. Prepare vanilla-pudding mix with skim milk, following label directions; chill.
6. Cut a slice across top of each eclair and lift off. Scoop out any bits of soft dough from bottoms with tip of teaspoon. Fill each shell with 1 rounded tablespoon pudding. Cut each top in half crosswise; push pieces into pudding in shell, butterfly style. Garnish each with half a fresh strawberry, if you like. Makes 18 eclairs.

Weight-watcher's portion: 2 eclairs, each with a halved strawberry—96 calories.

■ DIET-LIGHT SPONGECAKE

1⅓ cups sifted cake flour
1½ teaspoons baking powder
¼ teaspoon salt
3 eggs, separated
1 cup granulated sugar
½ teaspoon vanilla
½ teaspoon lemon extract
⅓ cup boiling water
1 tablespoon 10X (confectioners' powdered) sugar

1. Measure cake flour, baking powder, and salt into sifter.
2. Beat egg whites until foamy-white and double in volume in large bowl; sprinkle in ½ cup sugar, 1 tablespoon at a time, beating well after each addition, until meringue forms soft peaks. (Save remaining ½ cup sugar for next step.)
3. Beat egg yolks with vanilla and lemon extract in medium-size bowl; beat in saved ½ cup sugar, 1 tablespoon at a time, until creamy-thick. Stir in boiling water; beat vigorously 3 minutes, or until mixture forms soft peaks.
4. Fold egg-yolk mixture into egg-white mixture until no streaks of yellow or white remain. Sift dry ingredients, a quarter at a time, over top; gently fold in until blended. Pour into an ungreased 9-inch tube pan.
5. Bake in slow oven (325°) 55 minutes, or until top springs back when lightly pressed with fingertip.
6. Turn pan upside down and set on bottle to cool completely. Loosen cake around edge and tube with knife; turn out, then turn right side up. Sprinkle top with 10X sugar. Makes 1 nine-inch tube cake or 12 wedges.

Weight-watcher's portion: 1 wedge of cake —125 calories.

■ MOLDED MOCHA CREAM

1 envelope unflavored gelatin
4 teaspoons instant coffee powder
½ cup water
2½ cups chocolate-flavor dietary drink for weight control
1 teaspoon vanilla
Liquid no-calorie sweetener

1. Combine gelatin and coffee in water in small saucepan; heat slowly, stirring constantly, just until gelatin dissolves. Stir into dietary drink, vanilla, and no-calorie sweetener, using the equivalent of 2 teaspoons sugar, in medium-size bowl.
2. Pour into 6 small molds or custard cups, dividing evenly. Chill until firm. Unmold on dessert plates. Makes 6 servings.

Weight-watcher's portion: 1 mold or custard cup—99 calories.

■ BOUQUET FRUIT COMPOTE

2 grapefruits, pared and sectioned
1 can (about 1 pound) diet-pack fruits for salad
1 can (8 ounces) diet-pack prunes

Combine fruits and juices in medium-size bowl; spoon into 6 dessert dishes, dividing evenly. Garnish with a sprig of mint or water cress, if you wish. Makes 6 servings.

Weight-watcher's portion: 1 dessert dish—100 calories.

■ PINEAPPLE SHERBET IN ORANGE CUPS

2 cups buttermilk
1 can (6 ounces) frozen concentrated pineapple juice, thawed
Granulated or liquid no-calorie sweetener
6 small oranges, pared
6 whole strawberries, washed and hulled

1. Combine buttermilk and pineapple juice in medium-size bowl; sweeten with your favorite no-calorie sweetener, using the equivalent of 48 teaspoons (1 cup) sugar; beat until well-blended.
2. Pour into ice-cube tray, or pan, 8x8x2; freeze until firm almost to middle.
3. Spoon into chilled medium-size bowl; beat until fluffy-smooth. Return to tray; freeze 2 to 3 hours longer, or until firm.
4. Separate sections of each orange slightly to form a cup; place in dessert dishes. Scoop sherbet into center; garnish each with a fresh strawberry. Makes 6 servings.

Weight-watcher's portion: ¾ cup sherbet— 100 calories; 1 orange—60 calories.

■ APRICOT-RASPBERRY SNOW

2 envelopes low-calorie raspberry-flavor gelatin (3 to a package)
1½ cups hot water
2 egg whites
6 diet-pack apricot halves
2 tablespoons flaked coconut

1. Dissolve gelatin in hot water in large bowl; chill about 1 hour, or until as thick as unbeaten egg white.
2. Add unbeaten egg whites; beat with electric mixer at high speed, or vigorously with a rotary beater, until mixture starts to hold its shape. Pour into an 8-cup mold; chill until firm.
3. Unmold onto serving plate; decorate with a crown of apricot halves; sprinkle coconut in center. Makes 6 servings.

Weight-watcher's portion: ⅙ of mold plus ½ apricot and 1 teaspoon coconut—30 calories.

■ CINNAMON PEARS

4 medium-size firm ripe pears
½ cup water
Granulated, liquid, or tablet no-calorie sweetener
1 two-inch stick of cinnamon

1. Halve, core, and pare pears; place, cut side down, in large frying pan.
2. Sweeten water with your favorite no-calorie sweetener, using the equivalent of 12 teaspoons (¼ cup) sugar. Pour over pears; add cinnamon stick; cover pan.
3. Heat to boiling; simmer 10 minutes, or just until pears are tender.
4. Spoon into serving dish; pour any sauce from pan over. Makes 8 servings.

Weight-watcher's portion: ½ pear with sauce—50 calories.

■ COCONUT CUP CUSTARDS

3 eggs
½ teaspoon grated lemon rind
⅛ teaspoon salt
2¼ cups skim milk
½ teaspoon vanilla
Granulated, liquid, or tablet no-calorie sweetener
2 tablespoons flaked coconut

1. Beat eggs slightly with lemon rind and salt in medium-size bowl. Stir in milk, vanilla, and your favorite no-calorie sweetener, using the equivalent of 12 teaspoons (¼ cup) sugar. Strain into 6 ungreased 5-ounce custard cups, using about ½ cup for each.
2. Set cups in shallow pan; place on oven shelf; pour boiling water into pan to depth of 1 inch.
3. Bake in slow oven (325°) 40 minutes, or until centers are almost set but still soft. (Custard will set as it cools.) Remove at once from pan of water. Serve warm or chilled, in cups, or unmold by first loosening custards around edges with a thin-blade knife, then inverting into dessert dishes. Sprinkle with coconut. Makes 6 servings.

Weight-watcher's portion: 1 custard plus 1 teaspoon coconut—81 calories.

■ ALMOND MERINGUES

3 egg whites
¼ teaspoon cream of tartar
Liquid no-calorie sweetener
3 cups oven-popped rice cereal
¼ cup blanched almonds, chopped

1. Beat egg whites, cream of tartar, and no-calorie sweetener, using the equivalent of 16 teaspoons (⅓ cup) sugar, until meringue forms soft peaks in medium-size bowl. Fold in cereal and almonds.
2. Drop by rounded teaspoonfuls onto lightly greased cooky sheets.
3. Bake in moderate oven (350°) 15 minutes, or until lightly browned. Remove at once from cooky sheets; cool on wire racks. Makes 3 dozen.

Weight-watcher's portion: 1 meringue—16 calories.

■ CARIOCA FLUFF

1 envelope unflavored gelatin
2 cups skim milk
1 square unsweetened chocolate
⅛ teaspoon cinnamon
Granulated, liquid, or tablet no-calorie sweetener
¼ teaspoon vanilla
3 tablespoons cream, whipped

1. Soften gelatin in milk in top of double boiler; stir in chocolate and cinnamon. Heat over boiling water, stirring often, until chocolate melts and gelatin dissolves; remove from heat.
2. Sweeten with your favorite no-calorie sweetener, using the equivalent of 3 teaspoons sugar; stir in vanilla. Chill 1 hour, or until as thick as unbeaten egg white.
3. Set top of double boiler in a pan of ice and water; beat mixture until fluffy-light and double in volume.
4. Spoon into 6 small molds or custard cups, dividing evenly. Chill until firm.
5. Unmold onto dessert plates, or serve in cups. Garnish each with a dollop of whipped cream, if you like. Makes 6 servings.

Weight-watcher's portion: 1 mold plus 1 tablespoon unsweetened whipped cream—88 calories. Plain, with no whipped cream—61 calories.

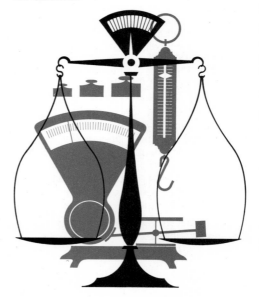

More diet desserts

Enjoy these sweets with a clear conscience. Calorie count for each portion is here, too.

■ CAFE-AU-LAIT FROSTED

½ cup instant nonfat dry milk
2 teaspoons instant coffee powder
1 cup crushed ice
½ cup water
½ teaspoon vanilla
Granulated, liquid, or tablet no-calorie sweetener

1. Combine nonfat dry milk, coffee, ice, water, and vanilla in electric-blender container. Sweeten with your favorite no-calorie sweetener, using the equivalent of 4 teaspoons sugar.
2. Cover; beat at high speed 2 minutes, or until frothy-light. Pour into 2 tall glasses. Makes 2 servings.

Weight-watcher's portion: 1 glassful—73 calories.

■ PLUM-GOOD WHIP

1 can (1 pound) diet-pack purple plums
2 egg whites
¼ teaspoon cream of tartar
Dash of salt
1 tablespoon lemon juice
Granulated or liquid no-calorie sweetener
Red food coloring

1. Drain plum juice from can and save for dessert sauce for another meal. Pit plums and cut into small pieces.
2. Beat egg whites with cream of tartar and salt until they stand in firm peaks in medium-size bowl. Gradually beat in cut-up plums until mixture is thick, then beat in lemon juice.
3. Sweeten to taste with your favorite no-calorie sweetener; tint delicate pink with a few drops red food coloring.
4. Spoon into 6 dessert dishes, dividing evenly. Makes 6 servings.

Weight-watcher's portion: 1 serving—46 calories.

■ SUNSHINE FRUIT CUP

4 oranges
2 grapefruits
Granulated or liquid no-calorie sweetener
12 seedless grapes
Crystallized ginger

1. Pare and section oranges and grapefruits into a medium-size bowl.

2. Squeeze juice from membrane into a cup; sweeten to taste with your favorite no-calorie sweetener.
3. Spoon fruits into 6 dessert dishes; pour sweetened juices over, dividing evenly. Garnish each with a kebab of 2 grapes and 1 small piece crystallized ginger threaded onto a wooden pick. Makes 6 servings.

Weight-watcher's portion: 1 serving—96 calories.

■ SURPRISE CHEESECAKE

2 eggs
1 cup water
¼ teaspoon salt
Granulated or liquid no-calorie sweetener
2 envelopes unflavored gelatin
⅓ cup instant nonfat dry milk
1 teaspoon grated lemon rind
3 tablespoons lemon juice
1 teaspoon vanilla
3 cups (1½ pounds) cream-style cottage cheese
1 cup evaporated milk, well-chilled
3 tablespoons graham-cracker crumbs (2 crackers)

1. Separate eggs, putting whites in small bowl, yolks in second small bowl. Beat egg yolks slightly; beat in water and salt; sweeten with your favorite no-calorie sweetener, using the equivalent of 48 teaspoons (1 cup) sugar.
2. Mix gelatin and nonfat dry milk powder in top of double boiler; stir in egg-yolk mixture.
3. Cook, stirring constantly, over simmering water, about 5 minutes, or until gelatin dissolves and mixture coats a metal spoon. Strain into large bowl; stir in lemon rind, 2 tablespoons lemon juice, and vanilla. (Save remaining lemon juice for Step 5.) Chill 30 minutes, or until mixture is as thick as unbeaten egg white.
4. Press cottage cheese through sieve; stir into gelatin mixture until blended.
5. Beat egg whites until they stand in firm peaks. Beat *chilled* evaporated milk with saved 1 tablespoon lemon juice until stiff in small bowl.
6. Fold beaten egg whites, then whipped milk into cheese mixture; pour into 8-cup mold. Chill at least 4 hours, or until set.
7. Run a sharp-tip, thin-blade knife around top of mold, then dip mold *very quickly* in and out of a pan of hot water. Cover mold with serving plate; turn upside down, then gently lift off mold. Sprinkle top with graham-cracker crumbs. Slice into 10 wedges. Makes 10 servings.

Weight-watcher's portion: 1 wedge—130 calories.

■ RASPBERRY-BANANA "CREAM"

½ cup instant nonfat dry milk
2 cups water
1 package raspberry-flavor rennet custard
½ small banana

1. Dissolve nonfat dry milk in water in small saucepan; heat, stirring constantly, until lukewarm. Stir in rennet custard, following label directions.
2. Pour into 4 sherbet glasses, dividing evenly. Let set for 10 minutes, then chill.
3. Just before serving, top each with 3 thin slices of banana. Makes 4 servings.

Weight-watcher's portion: 1 serving—97 calories.

■ FLUFFY LEMON TAPIOCA PUDDING

1 egg
2¾ cups skim milk
3 tablespoons quick-cooking tapioca
⅛ teaspoon salt
½ teaspoon vanilla
  Grated rind of ½ lemon
  Granulated, liquid, or tablet no-calorie sweetener

1. Beat egg with milk in medium-size saucepan; stir in tapioca and salt. Let stand about 5 minutes.
2. Cook, stirring constantly, 5 to 8 minutes, or until mixture comes to a full rolling boil. Remove from heat.
3. Stir in vanilla, lemon rind, and your favorite no-calorie sweetener, using the equivalent of 8 teaspoons sugar; cool.
4. Spoon into 6 sherbet glasses, dividing evenly. Serve warm or chilled. Makes 6 servings.

Weight-watcher's portion: 1 sherbet glassful—72 calories.

■ BANANA FROSTY

1 ripe banana
½ cup cold water
⅓ cup instant nonfat dry milk
¼ teaspoon vanilla
½ cup crushed ice
  Granulated, liquid, or tablet no-calorie sweetener

1. Slice banana into electric-blender container. Add water, instant nonfat dry milk, vanilla, crushed ice, and your favorite no-calorie sweetener, using the equivalent of 2 teaspoons sugar.
2. Cover; beat at high speed 2 minutes, or until frothy-thick. Pour into 2 tall glasses. Garnish with a sprig of fresh mint, if you like. Makes 2 servings.

Weight-watcher's portion: 1 glassful—91 calories.

■ APRICOT FLUFF

1 egg
⅛ teaspoon salt
⅛ teaspoon cream of tartar
2 tablespoons sugar
½ teaspoon lemon juice
1 jar (8 ounces) junior-pack apples-and-apricots
  Red food coloring
  Yellow food coloring
  Lemon-custard Sauce *(recipe follows)*

1. Beat egg white, salt, and cream of tartar until foamy-white and double in volume in small bowl; beat in sugar, 1 tablespoon at a time, until meringue forms soft peaks. (Save egg yolk for making sauce.)
2. Fold in lemon juice and fruit. Tint mixture light apricot color with 1 drop each of red and yellow food colorings. Spoon into 4 dessert dishes, dividing evenly; top with LEMON-CUSTARD SAUCE. Serve at once, for this dessert loses its fluffiness on standing. Makes 4 servings.

Weight-watcher's portion: 1 dessert-dish serving with 1 generous tablespoon sauce—106 calories.

LEMON-CUSTARD SAUCE

1 egg yolk
1 tablespoon sugar
1 tablespoon lemon juice
1 tablespoon milk

Beat egg yolk and sugar until thick in small bowl. Blend in lemon juice and milk.

■ HARLEQUIN PARFAIT

2 envelopes low-calorie lime-flavor gelatin
  (3 to a package)
1 envelope low-calorie raspberry-flavor gelatin
  (3 to a package)
3 cups hot water

1. Place lime-flavor and raspberry-flavor gelatins in separate small bowls. Stir 2 cups hot water into lime gelatin and 1 cup hot water into raspberry gelatin, stirring each constantly, until gelatin dissolves.
2. Pour 1 cup lime-flavor gelatin into 6 parfait glasses, dividing evenly; chill until set. Keep remaining gelatins at room temperature for layering into glasses.
3. When gelatin in parfait glasses is set, place bowl of raspberry gelatin in a larger bowl or pan partly filled with ice cubes to speed setting. Beat until mixture forms soft peaks; spoon over lime-gelatin layer in glasses, dividing evenly; chill until set.
4. Top with remaining 1 cup lime gelatin; chill until serving time. Makes 6 servings.

Weight-watcher's portion: 1 serving—12 calories.

■ FRUIT SPONGE ROLL

½ cup sifted cake flour
¾ teaspoon baking powder
¼ teaspoon salt
3 eggs
½ cup sugar
1 teaspoon vanilla
¼ teaspoon almond extract
2 tablespoons 10X (confectioners' powdered) sugar
1 jar (8 ounces) diet-pack cherry jelly

1. Grease baking pan, 15x10x1; line with waxed paper cut ½ inch smaller than pan; grease paper.
2. Measure flour, baking powder, and salt into sifter.
3. Beat eggs until foamy in medium-size bowl; gradually beat in sugar until mixture is thick. Stir in vanilla and almond extract.
4. Sift dry ingredients over and fold in until no streaks of flour remain. Spread batter evenly into prepared pan.
5. Bake in hot oven (400°) 8 minutes, or until center springs back when lightly pressed with fingertip.
6. Cut around cake about ½ inch in from edge of pan with sharp knife; invert pan onto clean towel dusted with 1 tablespoon 10X sugar; peel off waxed paper. (Save remaining 1 tablespoon 10X sugar for topping.) Starting at one end, roll up cake; wrap in towel; cool completely on wire rack.
7. Unroll cake carefully; spread evenly with jelly; reroll; dust top with saved tablespoon 10X sugar.
8. To serve, cut crosswise into 10 slices. Makes 10 servings.

Weight-watcher's portion: 1 jelly-filled slice —95 calories.

■ COFFEE WHIP

1 envelope unflavored gelatin
½ cup cold water
1½ cups hot strong brewed coffee
Granulated, liquid, or tablet no-calorie sweetener
½ teaspoon vanilla
Dash of salt

1. Soften gelatin in cold water in medium-size bowl; stir in coffee until gelatin dissolves.
2. Stir in your favorite no-calorie sweetener, using the equivalent of 12 teaspoons sugar, vanilla, and salt.
3. Chill until as thick as unbeaten egg white, then beat until fluffy-light and about double in volume.
4. Spoon into 6 sherbet glasses, dividing evenly. Makes 6 servings.

Weight-watcher's portion: 1 sherbet glassful —6 calories.

Snacktime morale boosters

When you're thirsty

• Enjoy a mug of hot beef or chicken bouillon made with cubes, paste, or the instant kind packed in tiny envelopes or jars. Calories—practically zero. Rich canned condensed beef broth, diluted with an equal part water or poured as is over ice, is a low 10 calories per cup.
• Have a glass of skim milk or buttermilk for an afternoon or bedtime treat. Calories—just 85. Add 5 thin pretzel sticks for just 5 calories.
• Check the many no-calorie carbonated beverages in your supermarket. True to their name, their count is zero.
• Hail to tea and coffee. Plain, with no sugar or cream, they are calorie-free. Hot, they stimulate; iced, they refresh. Add fresh lemon or lime juice with a clear conscience.
• Treat yourself to tomato juice as a midmorning pickup. Count 25 calories for half a cup. Add 1 envelope of unflavored gelatin for extra protein goodness and a plus of 35 calories. (Sprinkle gelatin into juice to soften, then stir in and sip cold. Or, heat until gelatin dissolves.) Nibble a crisp rye wafer—it's just 25 calories.

Something to munch

• Keep any of these vegetable snacks fixed and handy in your refrigerator: Sliced raw cauliflowerets; celery, cucumber, carrot, or green-pepper sticks; water cress; radishes; lettuce wedges. All you want at one time won't add up to more than 25 calories.
• Slice half an unpared apple thin—35 calories. Spread with 2 tablespoons pot cheese—25 more.
• Open and drain a can of mushroom caps or slices, or slice unpeeled fresh mushrooms. Dip into any of these no-calorie seasoners: Seasoned salt, lightly salted lemon juice, chopped parsley or dill, chopped water cress sprinkled with paprika. Calories—about 10 in a small can.
• Remember the diet wafers and fresh and canned diet foods for weight control, among which are soups, and chocolate, vanilla, coffee, and fruit-flavor drinks.

Fruit rewards

• Dip ½ cup fresh sweet strawberries into ¼ cup creamy yogurt. Count just 25 calories for the berries, and 30 for the yogurt.
• Keep low-calorie diet-pack fruits—peaches, apricots, pears, fruit cocktail—chilled in the refrigerator. Calories—45 for ½ cup.
• Combine diced cantaloupe and honeydew melon, then flavor with a squeeze of fresh lime and chopped fresh mint for a fruit refresher. Count 25 calories for ½ cup.

Index to starred (★) recipes